D0154333

Contemporary
Chinese Stories

Contemporary
Chinese Stories

Translated by
CHI-CHEN WANG

GREENWOOD PRESS, PUBLISHERS
NEW YORK

To Katharine Seelye Wallace

1891-1938

Preface

When an American teacher in a missionary school in Shanghai asked some of her students what they thought of *Ah Q & Others,* they all "tabooed it, seemed rather embarrassed that I had read it, and showed plainly that they wished that I had not read this 'other side of China's life.'" (*The Chinese Recorder,* November, 1941.)

Here are more stories of contemporary China that will probably embarrass most Chinese of the "better sort," for a good many of these stories are, like those of Lusin, preoccupied with the "other side of China's life." They are offered here not in a spirit of "debunking" but in the belief that the only way to banish darkness is to turn on it the searchlight of truth and that there is no better justification for our faith in China's future than that its most influential writers today have elected to man the searchlight batteries rather than play gigolo to faded old hags under the deceptive moon. Moreover, it is inevitable that any truly representative anthology of contemporary Chinese stories should reflect so much of the other side of China's life, for modern Chinese fiction began as part of a general movement for reform toward the end of the last century, when such intellectual leaders as Yen Fu and Liang Ch'i-ch'ao saw in fiction a powerful weapon for political agitation and decided to adopt it as a means for "arousing people's hearts."

If it had not been for this spirit of change and reform that has dominated China during the past decades, if China had remained a nation of smug Ah Q's instead of awakening to its own weaknesses and trying to do something about them, China would probably have capitulated to Japanese aggression long before this, taking comfort in the delusion that in the end it would be able to "absorb" its Japanese conquerors through its "superior" civilization as it has absorbed the Mongols and Manchus in the past. Surely it is sense-less to sacrifice millions of lives and bring misery to untold millions more as China has been doing, when she could have let the enemy in and then proceeded to annihilate them with her magic power of assimilation!

This anthology covers the period from 1918, when the Literary Revolution began in earnest, to 1937, when the present Sino-Japanese war broke out. With the exception of "Yuchun" and the two stories by Lusin, practically everything included here was written during the second ten years of this period, for the simple reason that most of the earlier products have, as stories, little intrinsic value to recommend them. I have not attempted to include anything later than 1937 because there is no adequate collection of such material available in this country from which a fair selection can be made.

I have tried to make this collection as representative as possible and have for that reason included a transitional piece more because of its faults than its virtues. On the whole, however, I have taken into consideration (1) the technical excellence of the stories as such; (2) the position occupied by the author by general consensus; (3) the light the story throws on Chinese life and problems. I have also taken into account the availability of the authors in English translation. If the best of Lusin had not already been published in an independent volume, I would have given him much more space than I have, and I would have included at least one story each from the works of Kuo Mo-jo, Yü Ta-fu, Miss "Ting Ling" and Miss "Ping Hsin" if they had not already been represented in the an-thologies listed in the Bibliographical Note. In the arrangement of the stories I have placed first those which have been most influenced by Western technique.

In some of the stories I have found it necessary to introduce a number of Chinese words and honorifics in order to make the dialogues faithful to Chinese conventions. The meanings of these words and terms are in most cases self-evident, but for those curious to know their exact meanings, a glossary has been provided. I have followed consistently the Wade system of transliteration only in the case of actual names. With names of characters and Chinese words, I have generally followed the same system but have omitted all aspirates and diacritical marks except when these are essential.

C. C. W.

COLUMBIA UNIVERSITY
JULY, 1943

Contents

The Road

By Chang T'ien-yi

"Don't move! We'll open fire the moment anyone makes a move."

There were eight or nine of them facing us with sub-machine guns.

What their mothers' —— was up?

We looked at one another and then at the men with the guns. They kept their guns pointed at us without the slightest movement. Their faces were pale.

What could they be up to? Had they gone mad? For they were our own men. There was Lao Kan, leader of the First Troop, with Tu Erh-yeh beside him. Farther on was Liu Tai-pao, leader of the Seventh Troop. Then there was . . . They were all of our own side and yet they now pointed their guns at us.

"Don't move!" Lao Kan shouted again. "The commander will speak to us."

So that was it. Then why didn't he come out and speak? What was the idea of turning the machine guns on us?

Hsiao Lao-san tugged at the corner of my coat and asked in a low voice:

"What's wrong?"

"Don't know."

Iron Ox in front of us mumbled:

"What's got into them . . ."

Lao Yü, leader of our own Troop, and the leaders of the Third and Fourth Troops had just come back from exercising their horses. They stopped and stared at Lao Kan's mob and bit their lips. They didn't seem to know what was up either.

None of us moved or made any protest. Lao Kan and his men

were between us and our gun stacks. If we tried to make a run for our guns, they were sure to open up. *Guk, guk, guk, guk.* . .

Chang Ta-yeh finally come out of the hut. He was a little man but you couldn't judge him by his size, for he was a very clever man. He was our commander, the man who had been leading us in blowing up the Japanese railways and ambushing their armored cars. The Japanese were afraid of him, and he hated them because they had done him out of everything.

He first looked at the troop leaders and then at us, and then said: "Men, we have gotten ourselves into an untenable position." I don't know whether it was the cold or what but his voice shook. "We are surrounded on all four sides by the Japanese. Men, you have been with me . . ."

The wind blew the rest of his words away.

"How did it happen that we got into this?" Iron Ox spat.

"We should have made contact with our forces at the Cockscomb Ridge." That was a student who spoke. There were all sorts of people in our outfit: it started with Chang Ta-yeh's own militia of five hundred men, but later students, bandits, soldiers, and peasants joined up.

"Who wouldn't have known that the Japanese would be around this railway district," another student complained.

"Chang Ta-yeh is bound to have a trick that he can pull," Hsiao Lao-san said.

"Tricks? I suppose we'll be marching into Changchun tomorrow, with him at the head!"

"Don't talk!" Lao Kan shouted.

"What's gotten into Lao Kan and those fellows?"

"We'll fix him first when anything happens, his mother's ——"

"Men! we are now entirely isolated," Chang Ta-yeh went on in his shaky voice, eyeing Lao Yü suspiciously. "The Japanese are in the mountains all around us. Men, do we want to die or live?"

Of course we did not want to die; that's why we had joined the Volunteers.

"We want to live!"

"We want to live!"

The shouts echoed all over the hills.

Chang Ta-yeh raised his hand for silence.

"Yes, it is because we wanted to live . . ." Chang Ta-yeh stared wildly.

"We'll fight to the last!" someone in the Third Troop shouted.

"Of course we'll fight, but do we have to be forced with machine guns?"

"We're not fools . . ."

"Don't interrupt." Chang Ta-yeh was angry and his cheeks became red.

The murmuring gradually died down. Chang Ta-yeh swept us with his eyes and went on rapidly:

"Right, we want to live; but we have entered the road of death. The Japanese troops are three or four times our number and they have big guns. We must think of a way out and there is only one way if we want to live . . ."

"Fight to the last!"

"Don't interrupt! I'll have you shot if you do." Chang Ta-yeh's voice became shrill.

Every one shut up. The only sound you could hear was the wind through the pine trees.

No one was allowed to speak except Chang Ta-yeh.

"Men, we have been together for several months now. We have gone through a great deal together. We have been like brothers, and like brothers we should share our hardships and our good fortunes. So far there has been nothing but hardships for all of us. I can't feel right unless I can bring some good fortune to you . . ."

A fine time to talk about good fortune when death was just around the corner! We looked at one another and wondered what the man was driving at.

"Men, there is only one way out for us. If we don't take it, it's death for us all; but if we do, we'll all have something to be thankful for . . ."

Everything was still. The men stopped breathing. Even the pine trees became still. All waited for Chang Ta-yeh to say what this way out was.

Chang Ta-yeh looked at us and opened his mouth once or twice but nothing came out of it. What was it that it was so difficult to say?

Lao Kan and Liu Tai-pao gave Chang Ta-yeh a look.

Suddenly Chang Ta-yeh opened his mouth again and got it out with a tremendous effort. He didn't speak so loud, but what he said shook every one around like an earthquake.

"There is only one way, only one. We must surrender . . ."

"What? Surrender? . . ."

"Surrender to the Japanese?"

"Has he gone crazy?"

A thousand heads swayed like wheat in the wind.

How could Chang Ta-yeh say such a thing? But it was Chang Ta-yeh all right who said this, the man who had been leading us in blowing up bridges and railways.

"We'll fix any one who tells us to surrender to the Japanese!"

Chang Ta-yeh looked like one possessed. He leaned forward and fixed his eyes on us, his hand clenched. He looked as if he wanted to eat us up. His face was pale and his legs shook. He roared to the men with the guns:

"Watch out for them! Don't let them move!"

Mother's ——, what a fix we were in!

I shivered all over, my hands wet with sweat. I looked at the men around me. They were all biting their lips until they were white.

Lao Yü and the troop leaders with him stood petrified, their eyes glued on Chang Ta-yeh.

Chang Ta-yeh was a terrible sight. He shouted in a shrill voice:

"Men, it's not that I, Yuan Chang-jung, don't want to do the right thing. But at a time like this I have only one thing to say to you: Do you agree to what I say or don't you? . . . If you do, you are my brothers and we'll enjoy our good fortune together. If you don't, it's mutiny and I'll have you mowed down. Attention! Open fire the moment any one makes a move! . . ."

Lao Kan and his crowd kept us covered, swinging their guns from side to side. Tu Erh-yeh kept Lao Yü's group covered with his.

We couldn't make the slightest move, damn them!

"The Japanese troops are in the hills on all sides," Chang Ta-yeh panted. "We can't go on fighting like this forever. If we surrender, we'll receive good treatment . . . They have promised to give us 200,000 dollars with promotion for everyone . . . I may have handled you a bit rough, but I, Yuan Chang-jung, have always treated you, my brothers, right and you can depend on it that I am doing this for your own good. I want to share this good fortune with you . . ."

Everything became as plain as could be, like a puzzle box that had been pulled apart. Let me tell you: it was all a trick. Why didn't he listen to Lao Liu, leader of the Fifth Troop, instead of leading us into this trap? Why didn't he try to make contact with our forces at Cockscomb Ridge? It was all a trick. But how come that a man like Chang Ta-yeh should want to sell out to the Japanese? Wasn't his village wiped out by the Japanese? Hadn't he led us against the Japanese all these months?

There was a general murmur of incredulity and indignation and protest but no one dared to make a move, with Chang Ta-yeh shouting repeatedly to Lao Kan to open fire the moment any one made the slightest movement.

Suddenly Lao Liu put his hand on his pistol and raised the other toward us:

"Men, we must fight to the end and . . ." He pulled out his pistol.

But—*guk, guk, guk, guk, guk, guk!* Lao Liu fell to the dust. Tu Erh-yeh's gun was still smoking.

"*Ma-pa-tzu!* shooting down one of our own men!"

"Rush for the guns!"

"We'll be shot down anyway!"

The men in front rushed forward.

Guk, guk, guk, guk, guk, guk, guk! All those who rushed forward fell to the ground, including Iron Ox.

We couldn't make a move. Mother's ——, mother's —— mother's
——! I——their entire families, the whole nest of them! We must
fix them . . . Yet we couldn't make a move.

"Look out! Anyone who makes another move will get it like
them," Liu Tai-pao shouted.

Lao Yü suddenly stepped forward. Tu Erh-yeh's machine gun
followed him. But Lao Yü had his hands raised high. He said to
Tu Erh-yeh:

"You must strip us of our guns. Here, take mine first. I want to
obey orders."

Tu Erh-yeh covered the troop leaders with his gun while Liu
Tai-pao disarmed them, with their men helplessly looking on.

Then Lao Yü said in a loud voice:

"I have confidential information for the commander."

"Have you got his pistol?" Chang Ta-yeh asked.

"We have."

"Come on over."

All eyes turned on Lao Yü and followed him as he approached
Chang Ta-yeh. The muzzle of Tu Erh-yeh's gun was also turned
on him and followed his movement.

Then all of a sudden Lao Yü grabbed Chang Ta-yeh and threw
him on the ground. He pinned him down with his knees, and
seized Chang Ta-yeh's throat with his right hand and held down
Chang Ta-yeh's hands with the other.

The machine guns were trained on Lao Yü but no one dared
to open fire.

"Fire if you dare!" Lao Yü growled. "I'll choke the son-of-a-
dog Yuan Chang-jung the moment you make a move."

We all came back to life.

"Choke him to death, Lao Yü, choke him to death!"

"Fix the son-of-a-dog for good!"

"Trying to sell us out to the Japanese!"

"Rush them, men!"

"Let's fix the sons of turtles!"

We rushed forward to grab for the machine guns. The eight or
nine of them were completely taken aback.

Guk, guk, guk, guk, guk, guk, guk . . .

But the muzzles were pointed in the air and no one was hit.

We ran to our gun stacks. It was now our turn. We got our guns back. We made short work of Lao Kan's crowd.

"Let's finish off Chang Ta-yeh!"

"Skin him alive!"

"Wait a moment, wait a moment!" Lao Yü shouted. He had now taken his hand off Chang Ta-yeh's throat. "You whose name is Yuan, confess, confess!"

"I'll do what you say . . ." Chang Ta-yeh panted hoarsely.

"No one wants you to do anything. Just tell us what it is all about. Wasn't it by agreement that you brought us into this trap?"

"Yes, it was by agreement."

"With whom?—The Japanese?"

"Yes, with them. They sent twenty thousand dollars first . . ."

"In silver?"

"Yes, in silver. They are waiting in the hills around us . . ."

"What else?"

"That's all . . ."

"Men," Lao Yü again shouted, "what are we to do?"

"Fix him for good!"

"Give him the black jujube!"

Everyone shouted and laughed.

"Let me off," Chang Ta-yeh whined. "We have been like . . ."

Pop, pop, pop! The bullets made big holes in Chang Ta-yeh's head. One of them came out through one eye and carried away the eyeball with it.

Lao Yü jumped up.

"Men, do we want to live or do we want to die?"

"We want to live! We want to live!" The valley again echoed with the shout.

"We are surrounded, men," the leader of the Fourth Troop said. "We must rush them!"

We all raised our guns and shouted: "Rush them! rush them!"

"Let me make a suggestion!" Lao Yü motioned for silence. "We came into the valley from the east. Let us fight our way out the same way and make for Cockscomb Ridge."

We got ready for the rush in no time. Our hearts pounded but we were very happy. We wanted to live and there was only one way out. We must fight our way out, no matter how much the Japanese outnumbered us and were better equipped.

We marched toward the mouth of the valley like a water snake.

"The Japanese!"

"Rush them, their mothers' ——!"

"Kill them!"

Hand grenades flew through the air and rifles, sub-machine guns and big swords all went to work.

Guk, guk, guk, guk, guk, guk, guk, guk . . . pop pop! pop! pop pop pop!

Almost half of our men fell but we fought our way out of the valley, with the sub-machine guns covering our retreat.

But mother's ——! Lao Yü had dropped off his horse.

"Go on, men, go on . . . Don't mind me, don't . . ."

And so we lost Lao Yü!

Tears are funny things. Nothing can stop them when they start to flow.

Go up to Heaven, Lao Yü, and rest in peace. We shall fight to the end until victory is won.

We managed to reach Cockscomb Ridge.

The Inside Story

By Chang T'ien-yi

"*Hey, hey,* listen to me, listen to me!"

Lao Ming motioned for silence, leaving the toothpick in his mouth.

Sixteen eyes turned towards him. Everyone had eaten and drunk to his full, his face red.

"You all say that a man's rise is entirely due to destiny?" Lao Ming took the toothpick out of his mouth. "I admit that luck has something to do with it, but it counts for only three parts. That's what I say. As for the rest you have to have some ability and not be afraid of hard work. But what counts most is—is to have an able helper at your side. If you are entirely alone and have no one to help you, you'll never climb to the top."

"What would you call an able helper?" a man with a close shaven head asked, his eyes brightening.

"For instance," Lao Ming went on, gesticulating with his toothpick, "take Kuang Lao-wu. He has now got to the top and I have benefited by it. He wasn't much when he was commandant of the militia, but things came his way after his troop was incorporated into the regular army. What I mean is that he entered his lucky period when he entered the regular army. This is what I mean by three parts luck. The other three parts is his ability. But the most important secret of his success was that he had a good helper. Yes, that counted for at least four parts."

"I see what you mean, I see what you mean!" interpolated a man across the table knowingly. "Kuang Lao-wu was very successful in suppressing the bandits and caught Lo Chen-ting. Wasn't it because of these achievements that he was incorporated into the regular army?"

"Hm, that's not the entire story." Lao Ming stopped and glanced around him for effect.

"What was the inside story then?" someone asked, unable to bear the suspense.

Everyone sat up straight and waited eagerly for Lao Ming to begin. They might learn something from his recital and put what they learned to practice so that they too could in three or four years' time get to where Kuang Lao-wu was and smoke all the fine Yunnan opium they wanted to and fill their arms with bought women.

"What I say is this," Lao Ming said, picking his teeth. "If it had not been for this particular person's help, Kuang Lao-wu would never have got to where he is today. This particular person . . ."

"Is it you?"

"No, I wasn't quite so useful to him."

"Who is it?"

"It is something I shouldn't tell," Lao Ming said after a while. "However, we are among friends and it will do no harm. Moreover, it happened many years ago and it will matter little to tell you about it now. But you must not tell anyone else."

Lao Ming cleared his throat and threw away his toothpick.

"The man who was so useful to Kuang Lao-wu was, was—does any of you know Tiao Chin-sheng?"

No one did.

"Aye, that's *him*," Lao Ming said with emphasis and looked at the faces around him.

"Was he the man who . . ."

"Let me tell it, let me tell it."

Lao Ming took up another toothpick, but did not handicap his story by putting it in his mouth.

Tiao Chin-sheng was a short fellow, with a yellow waxen face. But don't judge him by appearances, for he was a very clever and capable man. He was always so eager to climb up in the world, but he never got very far. He never spared himself when he went into anything. When General Wu was fighting against the Northern Expeditionary Army, Tiao Chin-sheng went in for Southern spies heart and soul. He caught many of them, all young fellows around twenty. He used to say to me, patting me on the shoulder:

"Lao Ming, I shall soon become an official. Even the General knows the name of Tiao Chin-sheng and is pleased with how well I am doing."

But as soon as forces of the Northern Expeditionary Army occupied the city, Tiao Chin-sheng began to go around with a lot of young fellows and to organize all kinds of societies and unions. He ran around everywhere, streaming with sweat.

"Revolution is the thing nowadays. Just wait and see: pretty soon everyone will be calling me Commissar Tiao."

But he never got to be a commissar. Pretty soon they began to arrest counterrevolutionaries, and Tiao Chin-sheng made himself useful to the authorities by tipping them off on the young fellows that he had worked with only a short while back.

"Of course the counterrevolution must be suppressed; I can't let my private friendships interfere with my duty. A man's got to do the best he can to get ahead. Am I not right, Lao Ming?"

He was right. Who doesn't want to get ahead? But he never got anywhere. Fate was against him. And so he hung around Kuang Lao-wu and did what odd jobs came along. Sometimes he would get impatient and say to Kuang Lao-wu:

"Wu-yeh, don't forget to help me along, will you?"

"Don't be impatient," Kuang Lao-wu invariably answered. "I know you've done a great many things to your credit. I've been trying to get incorporated into the regular army. I've talked the matter over with Colonel Tsen and he told me that as soon as I have suppressed the bandits he would . . ."

Kuang Lao-wu wasn't just talking. He did get connected up with the Colonel. This was his thirty percent luck. Colonel Tsen was green in the army business, never handled a gun in his life. He was a man of means and had studied in some new-style school. Somehow he got it into his head to try soldiering. So he got himself a commission, paid out of his own pocket for seven or eight hundred rifles of Hanyang Arsenal make, and managed to build up a skeleton regiment.

The Colonel, of course, liked nothing better than to enlarge his regiment, but he couldn't just go around incorporating militia units. He had to have some excuse. If Kuang Lao-wu distinguished himself in bandit suppression, Colonel Tsen would be able to go to Division headquarters with his recommendation, and once Division headquarters gave its permission, no one would dare to voice any opposition.

Yes, everything was just right for Kuang Lao-wu. He had only to catch some bandits.

And there were bandits to be caught—Lo Chen-ting's gang.

Though I was then in Kuang Lao-wu's troop, I did not know much about the bandits. To tell the truth, no one did. Even Kuang Lao-wu himself did not know how it came about that they were here one day and gone the next. They were very difficult to keep up with, and they were a pretty tough lot. They shot Lu Ta-yeh's son only one day after they had kidnapped him. There were not many of them, only about a hundred at the most. I was told . . .

One thing was certain: Lu Ta-yeh was out for vengeance, and a five-thousand-dollar reward was posted by the chamber of commerce. That is, five thousand milled-edges would tinkle in your pocket if you caught Lo Chen-ting, the bandit chief.

Yes, five thousand dollars. It was a lot of money.

Kuang Lao-wu jumped up from his opium couch and said:

"We must get the bandits: Tiao Chin-sheng, don't make any more pellets; I have smoked enough. Come, let us tend to serious business."

The brothers in the troop were taken aback.

"What! Get the bandits?"

"Mother's ——, he talks as if he really means business. Never a smile on his face!"

I myself also felt that Kuang Lao-wu sort of forgot himself.

"Don't be so impatient, Wu-yeh," I said. "Have another pipe and let us talk the matter over."

"I was thinking for all of us," he said a little sheepishly. "For if we get the bandits, we'll be incorporated in Colonel Tsen's regiment and we'll all . . ."

"I only want to be a lieutenant," Tiao Chin-sheng said, sighing.

"There is the five thousand milled-edges. It will buy a hundred guns. We'll make a whole battalion."

There it was, five thousand dollars waiting to be claimed. What were we going to do about it? Suddenly I got a bright idea—however, I'll tell that when the time comes. I only suggested then that we should first find out where the bandits were at the moment.

Thereupon Tiao Chin-sheng beat his breast and volunteered.

"I'll go for a reconnaissance," he said. He was always trying to show off his knowledge of military terms since he'd got a hankering to be a lieutenant. "I am a stranger around here; they'll not recognize me."

Tiao Chin-sheng was gone for a whole day and then came back with the good news. Where do you think the bandits were? Well, Kuang Lao-wu was in luck. They were not anywhere near our territory. They got only as far as Chouchiatien and then veered off, probably because they knew there wasn't much to be squeezed out where we were.

As you know, this was our chance to get after the bandits. That is the way with militia troops.

And so we marched as far as Chouchiatien, "encountering no opposition," as the saying goes. We had, of course, to fire some shots, and so we did. The men did not, however, fire from their shoulders. The guns had a terrific kick and often knocked the men flat on the ground. It was safer to stand the guns on the ground and fire into the air that way.

No one was killed, but we found later that one of the stray shots struck a peasant in the shoulder.

Then we marched back to barracks.

Kuang Lao-wu was dissatisfied, for we had not yet captured Lo Chen-ting and as long as we didn't capture him the reward money was out of our reach. It was here that I told them that I had an idea that would enable us to claim the five thousand.

"How?" Tiao Chin-sheng immediately raised his waxen face.

"We have only to say that we have already captured Lo Chen-ting."

"What!" Kuang Lao-wu exclaimed. He never thought of this trick. "But what if they wanted to examine Lo Chen-ting?"

I said, "Why couldn't we fake him?" But it was necessary to have some stranger to fake the part so that no one would recognize him.

That meant, of course, Tiao Chin-sheng.

"I'll do it!" Tiao said, beating his breast. "Wu-yeh has been good to me and I want to repay him in some way. Moreover, I'll gain by it too. But, but, Lao Ming, are you sure that there is no danger involved?"

"What danger could there be? As soon as we get the five thousand we'll be incorporated and you'll become a lieutenant."

Kuang Lao-wu was excited with the idea. He patted Tiao Chin-sheng on the head and said, "You can depend on me. You have been very useful, caught so many counterrevolutionaries. I wouldn't let you down."

I explained to them how there was absolutely nothing to be afraid of. If the district yamen should ask us to surrender Lo Chen-ting to them, we'd say that Colonel Tsen wanted to handle the case. They wouldn't dare to dispute with the Colonel over jurisdiction.

And so we had Tiao Chin-sheng tied up. We all clapped our hands and laughed. Tiao himself also grinned until his gums showed.

Everyone was pleased. I had everything figured out. If the district yamen wanted the prisoner, we'd say that the Colonel wanted to try the case himself. If the Colonel wanted the prisoner we'd say that it was not safe to send him because we might be ambushed along the way.

As I said before, the Colonel was green in the business. He had no idea how many men Lo Chen-ting had, and was scared by what we said might happen. So he sent one of his staff officers by the name of Wen to us to try the prisoner. Wen brought with him a clerk and seven or eight guards with Lugers. He was the only man in the regiment who knew anything about procedure. He was a tall man and wore glasses.

Tiao Chin-sheng was a little scared.

"Lao Ming, what am I to say?"

"Say anything you like."

"Hm . . ."

Kuang Lao-wu again patted him on the head and said: "Try to impress him with your importance, don't forget."

"All right."

I remember well what was said at the examination. The clerk wrote down all the questions and answers. The staff officer first asked him if he was Lo Chen-ting. He answered yes.

"How many bandits are there under you?"

"About thirty-eight thousand."

The staff officer appeared astonished: "What! How many guns?"

"About fifty thousand rifles, ten thousand machine guns, and five thousand cannons."

"How long have you been a bandit?"

"Over sixty years."

"What!" The staff officer looked at him for a while to size him up. "How many men have you murdered?"

"Let me see, I should say at least two hundred million."

"So you have killed more men than Chang Hsien-chung did, eh?"

"I don't know who he is."

"How did you happen to be apprehended?"

"What?"

"How did you get arrested?"

"Oh, that! That's a long story, mother's ——!"

We waited for him to go on. He looked at Kuang Lao-wu and then at myself and then went on.

"It was like this. I came to Chouchiatien with my thirty-eight thousand men and ran directly into Captain Kuang with four of his men. We charged in force, and fired away with everything we had. Somehow or other we got surrounded. Most of my thirty-

eight thousand fell and I found myself pinned down. Mother's ——!
that's how it happened."

The clerk wrote all that stuff down. The staff officer read the
thing over and had Tiao Chin-sheng sign it.

Kuang Lao-wu. jumped up and down with joy after the staff
officer left. He patted Tiao on the back of his head and said to
him:

"That's the stuff! You did very well indeed . . . Come and let's
have some wine."

Tiao Chin-sheng was beside himself with joy. He was sure now
that he would get his lieutenancy. He gulped down kaoliang one
cup after the other.

"The five thousand milled-edges is as good as yours, Wu-yeh, and
I'll . . ."

"That's right, that's right. We have been indispensable to each
other. Without me you won't get to be a lieutenant and without
you I won't be able to get the five thousand to expand . . ."

We went on talking and drinking and laughing until evening.

But that evening the staff officer returned with an order from
the Colonel and read it to Kuang Lao-wu. The prisoner was to be
executed right away upon receipt of the order. Tiao Chin-sheng
was singing "At the first watch the moon rose from the East"
when the Colonel's men went to get him. He knew nothing about
the order for his execution, of course.

"What's the idea?" he protested, but a shot rang out before he
had finished the sentence and the bullet went through the back
of his head and came out between his eyes and made a hole as big
as a wine cup . . .

Now don't interrupt. Yes, that's what I mean. That's how Tiao
Chin-sheng died. The Colonel did not want to take any chances
of having the bandit chief rescued by his men and so ordered his
immediate execution.

Of course, Tiao Chin-sheng would not have died if we had told
the truth, but then Kuang Lao-wu and I would have to face
charges, to say nothing about letting the five thousand milled-
edges slip through our fingers. As Kuang Lao-wu said, "If it hadn't

been Tiao Chin-sheng it would have been some one else. You can always find some one to do what has to be done."

And so Kuang Lao-wu got the five thousand and got incorporated into the regular army.

"Didn't any one ever. find out?" asked the man with the close-shaven head.

Lao Ming shook his head.

"So that was how Kuang Lao-wu got to where he is today, eh?"

"Yes," Lao Ming said. "That's what I mean by the importance of having help. Kuang Lao-wu had luck and ability, but he wouldn't be where he is today, smoking fine Yunnan opium and enjoying his women, if it hadn't been for Tiao Chin-sheng. Yes, I insist that success consists of three parts each of luck and ability and four parts—having such a person as Tiao Chin-sheng come along at the right time."

A Country Boy Withdraws from School[1]

By Lao Hsiang

A boy in the country gets to be at least half as useful as a grown-up by the time he is eight or nine years old. He can weed in the spring or tie up harvest bundles in summer; he is able to pass bricks when a house is built or open and shut the furrows to the irrigation ditches. That being the case, who'd want to send him to school? But an official proclamation has been issued in the city to the effect that unless a boy over six years of age is sent to school, some adult in the family will have to go to jail. This was how it happened that the Country Boy of our story went to school.

On his first day at school the Boy came back with eight books. His grandparents and his father and mother all gathered around him and marveled at the pictures in the books. Said Grandfather: "The *Four Books* and the *Five Classics* never had any pictures like these."

"The people in the pictures are not Chinese!" Father suddenly exclaimed. "Look carefully and you'll see that none of them wear the kind of clothes we do. See, these are leather shoes, this is a foreign costume, this is what is called a dog stick. They remind me of the old missionary that preaches at the cross street in the city."

"This woman at the spinning wheel is also a foreigner," Grandmother said. "We use the right hand to spin but she uses her left."

"If that makes her a foreigner, then this driver is not Chinese either. Look, have you ever seen a Chinese driver standing on this side of the cart?" commented Grandfather.

[1] For another translation see Lin Yutang, *A Nun of Taishan and Other Translations,* where it appears under the title "Ah Chuan Goes to School."

"The teacher says that the books cost a dollar and twenty cents," the Boy suddenly said, taking courage in their absorption in the books. The statement stunned everyone like a sudden clap of thunder.

Grandmother was the first to speak: "They certainly have nerve to make us pay for the books after we give up the boy for them! He's gone to school hardly a day and it's cost us over a dollar already. Who can afford such schools? We can't save that much money if we go without light for half a year, and we'll have to sell at least eight bushels of corn to raise that much money."

"I should think one book ought to be enough to start with. They can get another after they have finished that," Grandfather said.

"Moreover, why should it cost so much when there are only three or four characters on a page?" Grandmother continued. "The almanac has both large and small characters and is closely printed and it cost only five coppers. How could these be worth more than a dollar?"

The books which they had marveled at a few minutes ago had suddenly become a cause for depression. The family discussed the matter at supper and all through the rest of the evening and finally decided that they would accept this calamity and pay the amount required since it was the first time. In order to make up the sum, the Boy's mother had to contribute the proceeds from two pairs of earrings that she had recently sold. His father gave him a solemn lecture, saying, "You are now nine, no longer so young. We're sparing you from work and sending you to school, though we can't afford it in our circumstances. You'll be very ungrateful if you don't study hard and learn something."

The Boy took his father's instruction to heart and set out for school the next day at dawn. When he got there, however, the porter said to him in a low voice: "Classes don't start till nine. It's now only five-thirty. You are too early. The teacher is asleep and the class room isn't unlocked. You had better go home now." The Boy looked around the yard and found that he was indeed the only student there; he listened outside the teacher's window and heard him snoring; he walked around the lecture room and found no open door. There was nothing for him to do but run back home. Grandfather was sweeping the yard when he suddenly caught sight of the Boy. He threw down his broom and said, "What is the use of trying to make a scholar of a boy whom Heaven has intended for the hoe? Look at him, it's only the second day and he is playing truant already!" The Boy was just about to explain when his mother gave him two resounding slaps and made him tend the fire for breakfast. Needless to say, the price of the books that they had to buy had a great deal to do with their tempers.

When the Boy went to school again after breakfast, the teacher was already on the platform and was holding forth on the subject of being late to school. To illustrate his point he told a story about a little fairy that waited by the wayside with a bag of gold to reward the earliest boy. Our Boy was enchanted with the story and the words "fairy" and "gold" but he could not figure out just what was meant by "earliest."

In the afternoon our young hero came back from school at three-thirty, just as his father was going back to work after his midday nap. Luckily his father happened to see the other boys also coming home from school and the teacher taking a stroll with his "dog stick" and concluded that his son was not playing truant. He kept wondering, however, about the strange ways of these foreign schools.

The first six days of school was taken up with the first lesson in the Reader, with the text "This is mama." It couldn't be said that the Boy was not diligent. He reviewed his lesson every day after school, reading over and over again "This is mama" until dusk. With his left hand holding the book open and his right following the characters he read on faithfully and conscientiously, as if afraid that the characters would fly away if he did not fix his entire attention on them.

But every time he read "This is mama" his mother's heart would jump. On the sixth day of school, she could stand it no longer. She snatched the book from him and said, "Let me see who your mama is!" Thinking that his mother was really eager to learn, the Boy pointed to the accompanying picture and said, "This is mama, the lady with leather shoes, bobbed hair, and long dress." One glance at the picture and Mother burst out crying. Grandfather, Grandmother, and Father were frightened, thinking that she might have become possessed by some evil spirits. At first she only cried and would not say anything when they asked her what the matter was, but when they persisted, she said, "Where did the boy get that vampirelike mama?"

When they found the cause of her distress, Father said, "We'll have the boy ask his teacher whose mama this really is. Maybe it is the teacher's mama."

The next morning before dawn Mother woke up her son and made him go to school and ask the teacher for a solution of the problem that had bothered her all night. Arriving at school the Boy found that it was Sunday and that there would be no school. Moreover, the teacher had drunk more wine than was good for him the night before and was still sound asleep .The Boy told Mother the circumstances, which made her curse the institution of Sunday.

At general assembly on Monday the teacher said gently to his charges: "One who wants to learn must not be afraid to ask questions. Anyone who has any question should raise it at once, to his teacher at school or to his parents at home." Thereupon our hero stood up and asked: "The Reader says 'This is mama.' Whose mama is she really?" The teacher answered even more gently than before. "It is the mama of anyone who happens to read the book. Do you understand now?"

"No," the Boy said. This embarrassed the teacher a little but he said patiently: "Why don't you understand?"

"Baldy is also reading this, but his mama is not like this lady," the Boy said.

"Baldy's mother is lame in one arm and has only one eye," Hsiao Lin said.

"And you have no mama at all. She died a long time ago," Baldy said in self-defense.

"Don't talk among yourselves!" the teacher said, knocking on the blackboard with his ferrule. "We are going to have the second lesson today: 'This is papa.' Look, everyone. This is papa, the man with spectacles and parted hair."

After school Mother was still worried about who the picture woman was but when she heard her son reiterating "This is papa," she did not dare to pursue the question, being afraid that her husband might want to know when she'd found a new papa for their son. She was puzzled more than ever and wondered why the book insisted on presenting people with papas and mamas when they had them already.

A few days later the Boy learned two new sentences: "The ox tends the fire; the horse eats noodles." He read the text over thousands of times but he could not get over the feeling that there was something queer about the assertions. They had an ox and a horse and he had himself taken them out to graze in the hills but he had never once seen a horse eat noodles and he was sure that their ox could not tend the fire. But could the book be wrong? Since he could not answer these questions, he obeyed his teacher's injunction of the week before and asked his father about it. Father said: "I once went to a foreign circus in the city and saw a horse that could ring a bell and fire a gun. Perhaps the book is talking about such horses and oxen."

Grandmother, however, did not agree with Father's explanation. She said: "The ox must be the Ox-Head Devil King and the horse must also be a demon. Don't you see that they all wear human clothing? They haven't changed their heads for human heads yet, but that alone will take five hundred years." The old lady then went on to tell stories about demons that could command the wind and summon rain; the result was that the Boy dreamed that night of being seized by a winged wolf demon and woke up crying.

The following day the Boy asked his teacher: "Is this ox that can tend the fire a foreign ox?"

The teacher laughed and said: "You are too literal! The book has only made those things up. It is not true that oxen can really tend the fire or that horses really eat noodles."

The explanation cleared up at one stroke many things in the book that had puzzled the Boy. He had read about such things as "bread," "milk," "park," "ball," and the like which he had never seen and which had made him wonder. It dawned upon him that the book dealt only with make-believe things.

One day the Boy and his schoolmates decided that they would play "tea party" as they had read about it in their Reader. They agreed that each would contribute twenty cents so that they could send to the city for oranges, apples, chocolate, and things. Our Boy knew, of course, that he would be only inviting a beating to ask money for buying sweetmeats. Grandmother always mumbled that school would bankrupt them yet whenever he had to buy a sheet of writing paper. But he could not resist the glowing picture that his book gave of the "tea party" and decided to help himself to the money that his mother had just got from selling more of her jewels and which she had set aside for buying cabbage seedlings.

Grandfather had been suffering for a long time from a chronic cough, and someone had told him that orange peels would give him relief. He kept on asking what orange peels were like and where they could be gotten. Thinking that this was a chance for him to ingratiate himself into his grandfather's favors, the Boy said, "We are getting some oranges."

"You are getting some oranges?" Grandfather asked. "What are you getting oranges for?"

"We want to hold a tea party," the Boy said.

"What is a tea party?"

"It means to get together and eat things and drink tea," the Boy said. "It is in the book."

"What kind of book is this that is either making animals talk or teaching people to eat and play? No wonder the boys have become lazy and choosy about their food since they went to school!" Grandmother said.

"And it is always about foreign food. There doesn't seem to be any corn wowotou or bean curd with onions in it," Grandfather said.

"Remember, son, to bring back some orange peels for your grandfather's cough," said Mother.

"Where did you get the money to buy oranges?" asked Father.

"The teacher . . ." but before the Boy had finished making up his story, Baldy, who lived to the east, suddenly began to cry. Then they heard his father shout: "We can't even afford salt, and yet you want to buy candy. . . ."

This was followed by the voice of Hsiao Lin's uncle, who lived to their west: "I let you buy books with my hard-earned money because it is for your good, but I haven't any money for you to buy sweetmeats. You can ask whoever wants you to hold tea parties for it."

The truth came out. The Boy's father aimed a kick at him, but fortunately the table intervened. He only upset the table and broke a few rice bowls. Grandfather was of the opinion that it might be better to take the Boy out of school, but Grandmother did not want her son to go to jail. After long arguments it was decided that they would let the Boy try school for a few more days.

After this humiliation, our young scholar vowed to study harder and to recover his lost prestige in the family. Everyday after school he read without stopping until it was dark. He did not realize that the source of his troubles lay in the textbook itself.

For Grandmother had been feeling that her son was no longer as close to her as before his marriage and that her position in the family had been gradually slipping. Now as she listened to the Boy reading aloud his latest lessons she heard him say, "In my family I have a papa, a mama, a didi and a meimei," but nothing about Grandfather and Grandmother; she became very indignant and shouted: "So this house is now all yours and I have no longer a share in it!" She was mad with fury. She picked up a brick and broke their iron pot into pieces.

"Don't be angry any more!" the Boy's father said. "We won't let him read this kind of book any longer. I would rather go to jail."

And so the next day Father discharged a day laborer and the teacher marked the Boy's absence in the record book at school.

Black Li and White Li

By Lao She

Love is not the central theme in this story of the two brothers, but it forms a convenient point of departure.

Black Li was the elder brother, White Li the younger, with a difference of five years between them. Both of them had been my schoolmates, though Black Li and I graduated shortly after White Li entered the middle school. Black Li was a good friend of mine and as I was a frequent visitor at his house, I came to know a little about White Li. However, five years make a wide gulf between you when you are young. The brothers were as unlike as their nicknames—Black and White—for Black Li was the epitome of old China just as White Li was of the new. But the two did not quarrel on this account; they just saw things in a different light. Black Li was not really black. He was called Black Li only because he had a mole above his left eyebrow and the young brother was called White Li because he didn't have any mark. Nothing could be more logical to the middle school students who gave them the nicknames. Actually both of them had very light complexions and they looked much alike.

Both of them were pursuing the same girl—pardon me for not revealing her name. She wasn't sure which one she loved and would not say that she loved neither of them. We all expected trouble between the brothers on account of her, for though they were not inclined to quarrel ordinarily, love is a thing that does not recognize friendship or fraternity.

However, Black Li surprised everyone by withdrawing from the contest.

I remember it well. It was an evening in early summer with a light rain falling. I went to see him and found him alone in the room with four fine porcelain teacups decorated with red fish before him. As we never stood on ceremony with each other, I sat down with a cigarette while he went on studying the cups. He turned first this one and then that and went on doing that until he had all the fish exactly facing him. After he had arranged them to his satisfaction he leaned back and looked at them like a painter withdrawing from his canvas in order to get a better perspective of his work. Then he rearranged the cups so that the fish on the other side faced him and again leaned back to look at them. He turned and smiled at me with satisfaction.

He loved these hobbies of his. He was not expert in any of them but liked to play at them all. He never pretended to be a connoisseur; he took them up only as a form of relaxation. He was a very gentle soul and easily pleased. He could while away pleasantly an entire afternoon mending his books.

He turned to me and said with another smile: "I have given her up in favor of Four." White Li was Ssu-yeh, the fourth in his generation when you figure in all his first cousins. "I can't let a girl come between brothers."

"That's why you're not a man of this age," I said jokingly.

"It's not that, but you can't teach an old circus bear new tricks. I can't go in for these triangular affairs. I have told her; I said that I was not going to see her any more whomever she may love. I feel much better for having told her."

"I have never seen anyone in love behave like this."

"You may never have seen anything like it but it has troubled me enough as it is. She can do what she likes. The only thing I am interested in is that nothing should come between Four and myself. Should you and I find ourselves in a similar situation I hope either you would retreat or I withdraw."

"And then peace would reign?"

We both laughed.

Perhaps ten days later Black Li again came to see me. I had learned to read him. Whenever his brows were darkened, it meant that he had something on his mind, and whenever he had something on his mind we always drank a pot of Lotus White together. I got the wine ready, for his brows did not exactly radiate joy that day.

His hand trembled a little as we drank our second cup. He never could keep anything in his heart; he showed everything on his face in spite of his efforts to hide it. He was a most candid man.

"I have just come from her," he said with a wry smile.

I did not prompt him, for we were accustomed to each other's long silences and communicated more through them than the actual words themselves. That was one of the reasons why White Li called us hopeless when he saw us drinking together without saying anything.

"Four and I had quite a little row," he went on after a while, "because of her. It was my fault, because I know too little about a woman's psychology. Didn't I tell you that I had given her up in favor of Four? I did that in all sincerity and good faith, but she took it as a deliberate insult. You were right: I am not of this age. I thought that one can do what one thinks is right in this business of love between man and woman as in all other human relationships, but it appears that women like to be pursued by as many men as possible. So she felt insulted and decided to take revenge on me by refusing to see Four. Naturally Four blamed me for it. I had to go to her today and apologize. I had hoped that she would feel better after giving me a scolding and be friends with Four again, but she did not scold me. She only wanted both of us to continue to be her friends. I don't want to do such a thing, though I did not say that to her. That's why I have come to you. If I don't do what she wants, she will refuse to see Four and Four will blame me for it."

"And there is nothing you can do about it," I said it for him. After a while I said, "Should I see Four and explain the situation to him?"

"Yes, you might do that." He contemplated his wine cup for a moment. "It probably won't do any good. But I have made up my mind not to have anything more to do with her. I'll just say nothing when Four kicks up a row with me."

Our conversation drifted to other matters. He told me that he had taken up the study of religion. I knew, however, that it was just another hobby with him and it was not going to make any great difference in his life.

White Li came shortly after Black Li left. White Li had not yet graduated from college but you could easily see that he was a man of more experience and resolve than his elder brother. The minute you saw him, you knew that he was a born leader, a man who was always trying to bring you to his point of view and always ready to send you to the guillotine if need be. He was direct and forthright, quite unlike his brother.

On my part I always tried to avoid politeness and circumspection so as not to incur his contempt.

"I suppose Two has been here?" he asked. Black Li was Erh-yeh, the second of his generation. "And I suppose he must have told you all about it?" I waited for him to go on; the two "supposes" made any answer unnecessary. It was as I thought. He went on: "Did you know that with me it was only a pretext?"

That I did not know.

"Did you think that I really cared about that girl?" He laughed. The way he laughed was like his brother except that there was an undertone of contemptuousness which I never detected in Black Li. "I've been seeing her only to provoke Two; otherwise I would not have wasted my time. Since animal desire is at the bottom of relationship between men and women, why should I insist on her? Two, however, seems to think there is something sacred about it and insists on kowtowing before her. Now after he only got his nose smeared with dirt for all the kowtowing he did, he wants me to do the same thing. I am sorry, but I don't care for that sort of thing." He burst out into a loud guffaw.

I did not laugh and I did not break in, but only watched him and wondered how it was possible for two persons to be so much alike and yet so unlike.

"No, I don't kowtow, but I would kiss her whenever I had the opportunity. She likes it too, it is much more satisfying than being kowtowed at. However, this is not what I have come to see you about. What I want to know is this: do you think that I ought to live with Two always?"

I did not know what to say.

He laughed again, probably calling me a stupid fool in his mind. "I have my own future and my own plans and he has his. Don't you think that the best thing to do is for us to go our separate ways?"

"Yes, but what plans do you have?" I finally hit upon this after an awkward silence.

"I can't tell you that now. I want to divide up our inheritance first. You'll find out what my plans are in time."

"You have quarreled with Two only because you wanted to divide up the inheritance?"

He nodded and smiled but said nothing, as if he knew that I had another question. I did have another question: "Then why don't you speak to him openly instead of kicking up a row over nothing?"

"Because he would not understand. You two can talk with each other but I find it impossible to talk to him. The minute I mention dividing up he would probably weep and then give me the usual line about what mother said on her deathbed and how she wanted us to live together in harmony always. He is bound to give me that line, as if the dead were to rule the living. Another thing: when he hears that I want to divide up, he probably will offer everything to me. I don't want to take advantage of him. He is always so solicitous about me, his didi, always trying to work on my feelings, always pretending that he knows better about me than I do myself, but in reality he is way behind the times. I belong to this age, and can take care of myself. He doesn't have to worry about me." His face had suddenly become serious as he spoke.

As I watched the change that had come over his face I began to see White Li in a different light, I began to realize that this was not a case of the arrogance of youth but one of deep conviction born of a genuine desire to lead his own life. I began to see too why he had adopted his method of attack, for if he had tried to discuss the matter rationally with Black Li, there was, as he said, bound to be long and fruitless homilies on fraternal love. There was something to be said for making as clean a break as possible instead of dragging on in a relationship that only hindered his free development.

"Do you want me to talk to Two?"

"That's exactly it. I don't want any more rows." He laughed again. "I don't want to make it any more unbearable for Two than I have to. We are brothers, after all." The word "brothers" seemed distasteful to him.

I promised him that I would do what he wished.

"Try to make it as strong as you can. We can't be brothers for the next twenty years." He stopped and essayed a smile. "I have been thinking about Two. The best thing for him is to get married. It will make it easier for him to forget his didi after he gets a nice fat baby. After twenty years I shall be behind the times too and shall be ready, if I am still alive then, to come home and be an uncle. But tell him that to be successful in love he must kiss more and kotow less, he must chase after her instead of kneeling there and waiting."

So for a while I went to see Black Li every day. We drank Lotus White and talked but never got anywhere. This went on for at least half a month. He saw my point of view and was willing for Four to cultivate self-reliance and independence, but he invariably ended with the sentence: "I can't bear to give up Four."

"Plans? What kind of plans?" He paced back and forth and asked that again and again, his mole almost lost in the furrows of his brow. "What could they be? You ask him. I'll feel better if I know."

"He won't tell what they are," I said for the fiftieth time or more.

"If he won't tell, it can only mean that they are of a dangerous character! He is the only brother I have. Let him have his rows if he must. I don't mind. He didn't use to be like this. It is probably because of that girl after all! So he wants me to get married, eh? But how can I get married when we have rows like this even before I am married? I wonder what his plans are. As to dividing up, it is entirely unnecessary, for he can have whatever he wants."

Thus he rambled on, an hour at a time. He took up more and

more hobbies: he tried all kinds of fortune-telling games, but none of them helped him find out what Four's plans were; they only gave him more worries and fears. This didn't mean that he acted worried, for he was as unhurried and phlegmatic as he had always been. His outward behavior never quite caught up with his feelings; no matter how anxious he was inside, he was always outwardly calm and unconcerned as if life itself was to him nothing more than a hobby.

I suggested that by plans Four had in mind the future and not anything immediate and concrete, but he shook his head.

Things went on like this for about another month.

"Four can't have anything immediate in mind," I said in a sudden fit of inspiration. "He hasn't tried to hurry me at all during all this time."

Again he shook his head.

As time went on he took up more hobbies. One Sunday morning I caught him entering a church. Thinking that he might have gone in to see someone, I waited for him outside. He did not come out, however, and I gave up waiting for him. He had apparently decided to seek refuge in religion.

I found him home that afternoon. For more than a month now Four had been our sole topic of conversation, but on this occasion he deviated from that usual routine. His eyes gleamed and there was a serene smile on his face, as if he had just acquired a rare old edition of some book.

"I saw you," I spoke first.

He nodded and smiled, saying, "It is very interesting."

That was his invariable comment on every new hobby, on anything that people might tell him, including the most impossible ghost stories.

"The same philosophy is behind all religions and all systems of moral instruction," he said. "They all enjoin us to sacrifice ourselves for the sake of others."

"Haven't you sacrificed your own love?" I said, stating a matter of fact.

"That's hardly sacrifice in the real sense of the word. That was only a sort of passive relinquishment and involved no actual sacrifice of anything that was part of myself. I have been reading the Gospels during the past two weeks and I have decided that I ought to share some of Four's burdens instead of only trying to keep him for myself. Just think, if all he wanted was to divide up, why shouldn't he come to me and tell me about it openly?"

"He is afraid that you won't do it," I replied.

"No! that's not it. I have thought the matter over and I am sure that he has definite plans, plans that involve danger. That's why he wants to make a clean break: he is afraid to involve me. You thought it was the impetuosity of youth, didn't you? That's where you and I were wrong, and he has taken advantage of our mistake to fool us. What he has been trying to do is to safeguard me, to place me in a safe position so that he can do his work without worrying about me. It must be that! I cannot disregard him, I must make some sacrifice for him. Before mother died . . ." He did not go on as he knew that I was thoroughly familiar with that line.

I was not alarmed at the time, for I was inclined to think that he was merely indulging in noble generalities under the influence of his newly acquired religion. However, I decided to see White Li to make sure. I did not take Black Li seriously, yet I did not want to take any chances.

But White Li was nowhere to be found. I went to his school and made enquiries in the dormitories, in the library and on the tennis courts and I tried the restaurants around the school, but no one had seen him. That was typical of him. If Black Li had to go away for a few days, he would not only leave word at home but would even notify the more intimate of his friends. In my helplessness I decided to call on "her" and ask her about it.

She hadn't seen White Li either. She appeared to be still annoyed with the Li brothers, especially Black Li. However, when I asked her about White Li, she insisted on talking about Black Li. It dawned upon me that she at least preferred Black Li to White Li if she did not love him. She probably had placed a check mark against Black Li as a standard of comparison: she would scratch

him off the list if a better suitor came along but might marry him
eventually if she could find no better. It was only a fleeting thought,
but it made me feel disinclined to promote Black Li's suit. I was
too fond of him to think that any one short of an angel would be
worthy of him.

I found myself in a quandary after leaving her. I couldn't tell of
White Li's disappearance to Black Li. He was sure to place advertisements in the papers if he knew and to get up in the middle
of the night to consult the fortune-telling manuals. Yet I felt it
necessary to share the information with someone.

When I got near his window Black Li was intoning something to
himself, which he never did except when he was feeling pleased
and happy, but instead of such favorites of his as

> "In the maiden's chamber
> A piece of pure, flawless jade . . ."

I found that he was singing softly some Christian hymn. He had
no ear for music and intoned the hymns as he did everything else
in his customary singsong voice. But that was neither here nor
there; what interested me was that he was singing to himself and
that he was therefore pleased with something. What could it be?

He put the hymn book down when I entered the room.

"Good thing you came. I was just going to call on you. Four was
here. He asked me for a thousand dollars and said nothing about
separating, nothing at all about that!"

Obviously he did not ask his brother what he wanted the
thousand dollars for; otherwise he would not have been so happy.
All he wanted was that his brother should live with him, as if as
long as they lived in the same house nothing else mattered, no
danger could touch them.

"Prayer is a great thing," he said seriously. "I have been praying
every day and my prayers have been answered already. He said
nothing about separating at all. I don't care if he throws all the
money away as long as I have him."

I proposed that we drink a bottle of Lotus White on that, but he shook his head, saying, "You go ahead. I'll eat something with you, for I have sworn off alcohol."

I did not drink any either and I did not tell him that I had not been able to find Four. There was no use alarming him since Four had just been to see him. I mentioned my visit to "her," however, but he did not comment.

He told me some Bible stories. As I listened to him I could not help marveling at his attitude toward his brother and her and feeling that it was very odd to say the least. I could not put my finger on just what was wrong with it, but a sense that something was amiss troubled me even after I left him and went back to my own house.

One evening four or five days later, Wang Wu came to see me. He was the ricksha man of the Lis and had been with them more than four years. He was an honest and reliable man, about thirty years old, with a scar on his head from a nip by an ass when he was a child. He had no fault except occasional indulgence in liquor.

He had been drinking that evening, and the scar on his head was red.

"What has brought you, Wang Wu?" We were on friendly terms. He always tried to take me home when I stayed late at the Li house and of course I always tipped him.

"To see how you are," he said, sitting down.

I knew, however, that he had come to tell me something. "There is freshly made tea. Have a cup."

I gave him a cigarette. "What's on your mind?"

"*Heng,* something I shouldn't tell, but I have just drunk two pots of wine and it itches to come out." He took a strong puff at his cigarette.

"If it is something that concerns the Lis, you'll make no mistake in telling me about it."

"That's what I think too," he said but hesitated a while before he went on. "I have been with the Li family for four years and thirty-five days now. I find myself in a difficult position. Erh-yeh is very good to me and Ssu-yeh, why, he is just like a friend. That makes things difficult. Ssu-yeh forbids me to tell Erh-yeh about his

affairs and yet I do not feel right to keep things from him. If I
tell, I wouldn't be doing right by Ssu-yeh. That's what makes
things so difficult. By rights I should stand with Ssu-yeh. Erh-yeh
is a good man, true, but he is after all just my employer, and an
employer is an employer no matter how good he is to you. He
can never be like a friend or brother. Erh-yeh is really very good
to me. For example, when I go out with him on these hot days,
he is always stopping for little errands. It may be to buy a package
of matches or to look at bookstalls. Why? Because he wants to
give me a chance to rest and catch my breath. That's what makes
him a good master. And because he is good to me, I respect him
and am grateful to him. This is what people call to exchange good
with good. I understand such things; I have been around."

I offered him another cup of tea, to show him that I appreciated
his point of view. After he drank the tea, he pointed to his breast
with his cigarette and said:

"Here, but I love Ssu-yeh here. Why? because Ssu-yeh does not
look upon me as a ricksha man. Their attitudes—the way they
feel here—are different. As I have said, Erh-yeh tries to give me
a chance to rest on hot days. Now Ssu-yeh doesn't think about
such things. He makes me run for all I am worth no matter how
hot it is. But when we get to talking, he would say why should
one man pull a ricksha and another man sit in it? You see he
feels the injustice for us ricksha men, for all the ricksha men in
all the world. Ehr-yeh is good to me but never thinks of us ricksha
men as a whole. Erh-yeh only thinks of the little things but
Ssu-yeh thinks of the big things. Ssu-yeh doesn't care anything
about my legs, but he cares about my heart. Erh-yeh is considerate
and pities my legs, but he doesn't care anything about here." He
pointed to his heart again. I knew that he had more to tell and
being afraid that the tea might get the better of the stimulating
effects of the wine I urged him on: "Go on, Wang Wu! Tell me
everything. I can gossip just as well as any woman, don't you
worry!"

He reflected for a moment, stroking his scar, and then pulled
up his chair closer and said in a low voice: "You know, the streetcar

line will be finished soon. We ricksha men will be driven out of business the minute the cars start running. I am not worried about this myself; I am thinking about all us ricksha men." He looked at me, and I nodded.

"Ssu-yeh understands this, else why should we be friends? Wang Wu, we must think up something, Ssu-yeh says. Ssu-yeh, there is only one thing to do, says I, and that is to wreck the streetcars! That's right, Wang Wu, says Ssu-yeh, we must wreck them. And so a plan was adopted. However, I can't tell you about it. What I want to tell you is this," he spoke even lower, "Ssu-yeh is being followed by the detectives! It may not be because of the streetcar business but it is always bad business to be followed by detectives. This is what makes things so difficult for me: I wouldn't be doing right by Ssu-yeh if I should tell Erh-yeh, and if I don't tell I might get Erh-yeh in trouble too. I don't know what to do."

Black Li had guessed right, I thought to myself after Wang Wu had left. White Li did have immediate plans that involved danger, perhaps even more radical plans than wrecking the streetcars. That's why he wanted to live separately from his brother; he did not want to drag him in. White Li was not afraid to sacrifice himself and he would not hesitate to sacrifice others if necessary, but he did not want to sacrifice his brother when there was no occasion for it.

What was I to do? To warn Black Li would only cause him to worry more about his brother. It was not only useless to try to dissuade White Li from his dangerous undertaking, but it would get Wang Wu into trouble.

The crisis came when the streetcar company announced the date for the opening of operations. I had to forget my scruples and tell Black Li.

He was not home but he had not taken the ricksha.

"Where is Erh-yeh?" I asked Wang Wu.

"He's gone out."

"Why didn't he ride?"

"He has gone out without the ricksha for several days now."

"Wang Wu, have you told him?" I could tell from his manner that he must have.

"I drank a few cups too much and couldn't help it." Wang Wu's scar was purple.

"How did he take it?"

"He almost cried."

"What did he say?"

"He asked me only one question—'What are you going to do, Wang Wu?' I said, 'Wang Wu will follow Ssu-yeh.' 'That's all,' he said. After that he went out without the ricksha."

It was after dark and I had been waiting for fully three hours when he came in.

"How goes everything?" I asked, trying to lump together all the questions I had in mind in those three words.

"All right," he said, smiling.

I did not expect him to answer me like that, but I did not ask him any more questions since he did not want to confide in me. I should have liked some wine, except it was no fun to drink alone. As I got up to go, I said: "How about going away for a few days with me?"

"Let's talk about that after a few days," he said.

I have since realized that one is often coolest in one's outward manner when one is most agitated inside, but I did not expect him to behave that way to me.

The day before the streetcar line opened I went to see him again in the evening. He wasn't home. I waited until midnight, but there was still no sign of him. He was probably trying to evade me.

Wang Wu came back and smiled at me, saying, "Tomorrow!"

"Where is Erh-yeh?"

"I don't know. After you left the other day he burned his mole away with something or other and studied himself a long time in the mirror."

That meant the end of Black Li, for he was exactly like White Li without the mole. I decided to wait for him no longer.

On the threshold Wang Wu stopped me. "If anything happens

to me tomorrow," he said, stroking his scar, "I hope you'll take care of my old mother."

Around five o'clock the following day Wang Wu came running into my house, his clothes wet through with sweat. "We—we wrecked everything!" He stopped for want of breath. After recovering his breath, he seized the teapot and drank from the spout. "We wrecked everything in sight and did not disperse until the mounted troops bore down on us. I saw them grab Little Ma Liu. The trouble with us was that we had no arms; you can't do much with just bricks."

"How about Ssu-yeh?"

"I didn't see him," he reflected, biting his lips. *"Heng,* it was a serious business. Ssu-yeh is bound to be among them if further arrests are made. He is the leader, you see. But you can't tell, for Ssu-yeh is pretty smart though he is so young. Little Ma Liu is done for but maybe Ssu-yeh will get away."

"Did you see Erh-yeh?"

"He hasn't been home since he went out yesterday." He thought for a moment and said, "I have to hide here for a few days."

"That's all right."

The riot was reported in the papers the next morning. Li ——, ringleader of the rioters who wrecked the street cars, had been arrested on the spot together with a student and five ricksha men.

Wang Wu recognized only the character Li in the headlines, but it was enough to confirm his worst fears. "Ssu-yeh is done for, Ssu-yeh is done for!" Tears fell on the paper as he lowered his head over it, pretending to scratch his scar.

The news was soon all over the city that Li —— and Little Ma Liu would be paraded through the streets prior to being shot.

The burning sun beat down on the street and made the pebbles so hot that they scorched the feet, but that did not prevent a crowd. Two men sat in an open cart with their hands tied behind their backs. They were guarded by policemen in khaki and soldiers in gray, their bayonets glinting cool in the sun. Tied to the cart and dipping and swaying with its movement were two white cloth banners with the offense of the prisoners written on them.

The eyes of the man in front were closed, there were a few drops of sweat on his forehead, and his lips moved as if in prayer. As the cart rattled past close in front of me, I was overcome with grief. He did not once raise his head all the way to the execution ground.

When I went up to claim the body, his mouth was slightly open as if he had prayed to the last.

A few months later I met White Li in Shanghai. He would have passed me without recognition if I had not called to him.

"Lao Ssu!" I called.

"Oh!" he exclaimed, as if taken aback. "It's you! I thought Lao Erh had come back to life."

I suppose I might have sounded like Black Li. I didn't do it intentionally but perhaps Black Li, who still lived in my heart, spoke for me.

White Li looked older and more like his brother than ever. We didn't say much to each other, and he appeared to be disinclined to talk with me. I only remember his saying:

"Lao Erh has probably gone up to Heaven. That's the right place for him. I, however, have to go on trying to break down the gates of Hell."

The Glasses

By Lao She

Although Sung Hsiu-shen was a science student, he was not particularly scientific in his daily habits. He took no trouble, for instance, to keep away the flies from his food; he seemed to believe that they had been disinfected. He was near-sighted but never wore his glasses except when he did his studies, because he shared the traditional belief that the more you wear glasses the worse your eyes become. If he couldn't see what was going on around him, it was just too bad.

One morning he was walking close to the wall, as he always did to avoid bumping into people. He kept his glasses in their case, rolled up in a magazine that he was carrying. Evidently, he knew that they were not very safe, for he would stop once in a while to make sure that they were still there. It would be a great misfortune indeed if he lost them, for he was absolutely helpless without them and he was too poor to get a new pair. He had thought of putting them in one of his pockets, but his notebook, handkerchief, pencil, eraser, two small bottles, and a roll left over from his breakfast already filled them to capacity. So it happened that he carried his glasses rolled in the magazine. He would be careful, and he was sure to hear it if they dropped out.

As he turned the corner he ran into one of his schoolmates. The latter called to him and he had to stop and exchange greetings with him. Just then a motor car passed by. Instinctively he flattened himself against the wall. It wasn't really necessary, but since his eyes were bad he had to take extra precautions. He quickened his steps after both the car and his friend had gone so as not to be late to school. At the entrance of the school he stopped to make sure that his glasses were still there and to his horror found that they had gone! He turned back immediately to look for them, but of course he did not find them. None of the ricksha men at the corner admitted having seen them. He tried the stretch between the corner and school again, but all he succeeded in doing was to get his hands muddy. He was exasperated. He fished out his roll and threw it away angrily. If his pockets had not been cluttered up with these things, if he had not run into that wretched schoolmate, if he had not had to dodge that car! He was sure that one of the ricksha men had picked up his glasses but would not admit it. What a miserable world! It was not as if he were a stranger in those parts, he passed by every day. And of what earthly use could a pair of near-sighted glasses be to a ricksha man?

Wang Ssu, one of the ricksha men at the corner, did see Sung drop his glasses. His first impulse was to call the owner's attention to it, but when he saw who it was—for Sung had never used a ricksha—he suppressed the words that were on the tip of his tongue. He picked up the glasses and put them in his pocket without a word.

He could not examine his find carefully before the others, but he was pleased and wore a broad smile as he sat comfortably on the floor of his ricksha. He felt sorry for the poor student when the latter came back looking for his glasses, evidently very much distressed, and felt like giving them back to him, but it was embarrassing to spit out something once you had put it in your mouth. Moreover, he would probably get nothing for their return, while his fellow ricksha men were sure to chaff him for not having told them about his good luck. They were sure to say: "What's the idea of not saying a word? Afraid that we would snatch them from you? And how generous of you to give them back after having quietly picked them up!" It was better to keep still. It was just too bad for the student. He was better off than a ricksha man, however poor he might be.

After Sung Hsiu-shen had gone, Wang Ssu picked up his ricksha shafts and said ostentatiously, "I won't waste any more time here. I'll try my luck to the east." But to himself he said, "It won't matter if I don't get any fare today. I ought to get a dollar or so at least for the glasses." As soon as he got to a quiet spot, he put down his ricksha and examined his find.

The case was very old and worn, with the cloth covering almost entirely gone. He probably wouldn't get more than one box of matches for it from the match man. The frames seemed all right, of a dark color and very sturdy. Wang Ssu had a prejudice against light metal frames: he never even bothered to ask persons wearing such glasses whether they wanted a ricksha. He flicked his fingers against the bows and decided that they were not made of iron or of wood. Perhaps they were made of tortoise shell! His heart leaped.

There was a broken match in the case, which Wang Ssu struck off and threw away. The lenses were very dirty. He took a long time cleaning the lenses, breathing and spitting on them and wiping them again and 'again with his cloth duster. He tried the glasses on. He might have known that they wouldn't fit him, as the owner was a small man with a small face. Wang Ssu was somewhat disappointed; he had hoped that he might wear them for fun himself if he could not sell them. Then he comforted himself by saying that it would seem funny anyway for a ricksha man to be wearing glasses—and why shouldn't he be able to sell them?

He found a junkman with his wares spread out on the ground. "Hey! Sell this to you!"

"I don't want it," the man grunted without looking at the glasses, although he had quite a few pairs spread out, including some with old-fashioned embroidered cases.

Not in a mood for a quarrel, Wang Ssu did not even say "Mother's ——, how courteous you are!" loud enough for the junkman to have heard him.

He encountered another junkman carrying a basket at either end of a pole. "Hey, sell this to you! Frames made of tortoise shell."

"Never saw such tortoise shell in my life," said the man after a brief glance. "How much do you want for them?"

"How much would you give?" asked Wang Ssu.

"Twenty coppers."

"What?" exclaimed Wang Ssu, taking back the glasses.

"That's the best I can do. Plain and far-sighted lenses are easier to sell; these are near-sighted. The frames are made of chemical stuff and may break as I carry them about in my basket."

Wang Ssu's enthusiasm cooled off. Only twenty coppers! If he had known he would have given them back to the student. No, he wouldn't sell them; he'd give them back to their original owner the next day. He might yet get a dime or two as a reward.

The next morning Wang Ssu again parked his ricksha at the corner, but there was no sight of the student even after the bell rang. He waited until after ten; still no sight of the student. He got a fare and returned to the corner after twelve. The students all came out for lunch but the near-sighted student was not among them.

Sung Hsiu-shen did not go to school at all the next day.

He was lost without his glasses. He had not been able to see much of what was written on the blackboard, though he had sat in the front row and strained himself as hard as he could. By the time the first class was over, he had developed a splitting headache. He had no heart even for mathematics, his favorite subject. He wished he could go some place where no one could hear him and shout. He never had time to think about life and its implications; he was full of it now. He did not blame the ricksha men much, for to a poor man a stick of firewood was a godsend. He could not afford another pair. He had brought only seventy dollars with him at the beginning of the semester and did not know what to do about food for the next two months. The harvest had been good, but there was no market for grain. He thought of his father and his brother and how hard they had to work to reap the grain that they could not now sell. He had no time for these thoughts ordinarily; today the mathematical formulas that his head was usually full of seemed to have decided to make room for these thoughts. He wouldn't be able to do his assignments today and as long as he did not have his glasses, his head would ache and prevent him from his work. He did not want to withdraw from school, but he could not see how he was to go on.

The long hour finally came to an end. He decided that he could not bear another class. He did not ask for leave to be absent from the school the rest of the day; it did not even occur to him that it was necessary or that there were more classes to attend.

He did not stop to inquire among the ricksha men again, though the thought came to him when he passed by the corner.

He did not go to school the second day and so Wang Ssu waited in vain for him.

When it was about time for Wang Ssu to turn in his ricksha, little Chao, the son of the grocery man, appeared on the scene and soon they were all playing dice. Chao usually lost, but on this occasion luck was with him and he cleaned up all the ricksha men. When Chao refused to lend them any money to continue the game Wang Ssu suddenly thought of the eyeglasses, for he knew that Chao, though he put on no airs before them, had a secret hankering for a pair of spectacles to make himself look more important. His father had a pair, which he had bought second-hand for eighty cents and which he wore on state occasions.

"I'll give this to you, little Chao," Wang Ssu said, taking the glasses from the compartment under the seat and passing it to him. "Don't mind the box but look what's inside."

Chao took the glasses eagerly. They looked more stylish than his father's. He tried them on and found that they fitted him, that is, the size fitted.

"They are near-sighted," he said. "They make me dizzy."

"You'll soon get used to them," Wang Ssu said.

"Get used to them? I'll have to become near-sighted first." But he wanted a pair of glasses so much! He took a few steps and then took them off and looked at the men. They all agreed that the glasses added something to him, made him more dignified. Wang Ssu led in the general approval.

"They make you look like somebody all right."

"But they make me dizzy, too!" repeated Chao, though unwilling to relinquish the glasses.

"You'll get used to them soon," Wang Ssu again urged.

Chao put them on again and looked at the sky. "They won't do, they still make me dizzy."

"Keep them, keep them," Wang Ssu said generously. "I have no use for them. After a few years your eyes won't be so good and then they'll fit you."

"Give them to me?" little Chao said dubiously. "Really? But mother's ——, it'll cost me a few dimes to get a new case."

"Yes, I give them to you; I have no use for them. The most I can get is a dollar or so if I try to sell them." Wang Ssu was indeed generous with his friends.

"Let me count how much money I have," Chao said, taking out the dime notes. "Six dimes, that's all. Mother's ——, I won only two dimes."

"Don't forget the coppers!" someone reminded him.

"They'll at most make another dime," Chao said, though he did not take them out and count them. "Now, Wang Ssu, I don't want you to give the glasses to me for nothing. See now, here are six dimes. Now you take three and I keep three. That's fair enough, isn't it?"

That was more than Wang Ssu had hoped for, but since Chao was so generous, he might as well get all he could. "How about splitting the coppers too? You won them anyway."

"That's my lucky money. I want to keep them for tomorrow's game."

"All right," Wang Ssu said, pocketing the notes, "but you surely have a bargain!"

"Didn't you say that you wanted to give them to me for nothing?"

"All right, all right. What's money between friends."

Chao put the glasses in the case and went away, saying, "I'll play you again tomorrow." After a few steps, he stopped and opened the case, and put the glasses on when the ricksha men weren't looking at him. Everything blurred before him. He'd get used to them, he said to himself, agreeing with Wang Ssu. With a few more acquisitions such as a wrist watch and a gold front tooth he was sure that he would have no difficulty in impressing little Phoenix, the singer at Nankangtze.

Suddenly an automobile horn blared out as he turned the corner. Little Chao hurriedly took off his glasses so that he could see where he was going.

For some time now both little Chao and Wang Ssu, like the student who walked close to the walls, have disappeared from neighborhood of the school. "Wang Ssu is parking around Nankangtze nowadays," Li Liu explained.

Grandma Takes Charge

By Lao She

You couldn't blame old Mrs. Wang for wanting a grandson, for what was the use of getting a daughter-in-law if it was not to pave the way for a grandson? And you couldn't blame the daughter-in-law either. It is not that she hadn't tried, but what could you do if the baby didn't live after it was born, or was born without any life at all? Take the first birth, for instance. As soon as the mother became pregnant, old Mrs. Wang forbade her to do anything whatsoever, forbade her even to turn over in bed. You can't say that's not being careful. But after five months she had a miscarriage, probably because she blinked her eyes once or twice too often. And it was a boy, too! During her second pregnancy, she did not even dare to blink her eyes without due deliberation or indulge in a yawn without two maids on either side to make sure that nothing went wrong. Indeed, carefulness pays and the mother gave birth to a big, plump boy. But for some reason or other the child had lived barely five days when it took eternal leave of this world without so much as a cheep or without even a ghost knowing. That happened in the eleventh month. There were four open stoves in the nursery, without so much as a single pinhole in any of the windows. Not only was it impossible for any wind to get in, it would have been pretty difficult for the God of Wind himself to have found his way in. Moreover, the baby had piled on it four quilts and five woolen blankets. You can't say that he wasn't warmly covered, can you? But the baby died just the same. It was simply fate and no one could do anything about it.

Now young Mrs. Wang was again blessed. The size of her

belly was astonishing, like stone rollers that road gangs use. Was old Mrs. Wang tickled! It was as if her heart had grown two little hands that kept on tickling her and making her laugh. Judging by the mother's size it would be a wonder if it did not turn out to be twins! The Goddess of Children had answered her prayers and was going to reward her with a pair of them. She was ready to do more than offer prayers and burn incense; she could hardly have refused her daughter-in-law if she had wanted human brains for dinner. For midnight supper she gave her stewed fresh bacon, chicken noodles, and such rich delicacies. The daughter-in-law was very obliging on her part. The more she lay motionless the hungrier she became. She would eat a couple of pounds of moon cakes for a between-meals snack, so that oil fairly oozed out of her down the pillow, and you could have swept out mincemeat and crumbs from under her covers by the bowlful. How could a pregnant woman give birth to a plump baby if she did not eat as much as she could? Both mother-in-law and daughter-in-law were agreed on that. And of course maternal grandma was not to be outdone. She came every few days to "hasten the birth" and every time she came she brought at least eight trays of food. It has been discovered long since by philosophers that in-laws are implacable foes. And so the more things maternal grandma brought, the more convinced the other grandma became that the former was just trying to show off and shame her; and the more paternal grandma tried to press food upon her daughter-in-law the more convinced maternal grandma became that her daughter did not get enough to eat. The result of this wholesome competition was a boon to the young woman, who ate and ate until her mouth was worn thin.

The midwife had been on hand for seven days and seven nights, but to no purpose. They had tried all sorts of weird prescriptions and quantities of pills and powders and incense ash from the temple of the Goddess of Children, but nothing worked. On the eighth day, the young woman couldn't even be tempted with chicken broth. She just rolled and groaned with pain. Old Mrs. Wang burned incense to the Goddess of Children and maternal grandma summoned a nun to read the charm for hastening birth; still it was no use. Thus they struggled on toward midnight when the top of the reluctant child's head finally came into view. The midwife tried all her tricks but accomplished nothing more than to maul and bruise the young mother. The child just would not come out. The minutes, each as long as a year, dragged on until it was almost an hour, but still only the top of the child's head could be seen.

Some one suggested the hospital but old Mrs. Wang would not hear of such a thing, for that would mean that the mother would have to be disemboweled and the child "gouged" out by force. Foreign devils and foreign-devils-once-removed could do that if they wanted to, but not the Wangs. The Wangs wanted their grandchild to be born naturally, not "gouged" out by force. Maternal grandma didn't like the idea either. You couldn't exactly hasten the birth of a child. Even a hen has to take her time about laying an egg. Moreover, the nun hadn't yet finished incanting her charm and to slight the nun was to be disrespectful to the gods. What was the hurry?

Another hour went by. The child was as stubborn as ever. The mother's eyes became glassy. With tears in her eyes, old Mrs. Wang made up her mind to save the child and forget the mother. You could always get another daughter-in-law; the child was more important. It was time to be resolute and pull the child out by brute force if necessary. A wet nurse would do just as well in case the mother died. She told the midwife to pull hard. Maternal grandma, however, had a different reaction. To her a daughter was a daughter, much closer than a grandson. It was better to get her to the hospital, without waiting for the nun to finish. Who knows what she was mumbling anyway? What if it wasn't the birth-hastening charm after all? Wouldn't that be wasting valuable time? The nun was dismissed, but paternal grandma was obdurate against "gouging." There was little that maternal grandma could do. A married daughter is like water that has been thrown out of the pail. As long as her daughter lived she was a member of the Wang family and when she died she would still be a Wang ghost. The in-laws glared at each other, each ready to bite off a hunk of the other's flesh.

Another half hour went by, and the child was as unhurried and reluctant to come out as before. The midwife decided it was hopeless and sneaked off at the first opportunity. Her departure weakened old Mrs. Wang's position and gave more weight to maternal grandma's plea: "Even the midwife has sneaked off. What are we waiting for? Do you want the child to die in the womb?"

The juxtaposition of "death" and "child" made a deep impression on old Mrs. Wang, but still "gouging" would hardly do under any circumstances.

"Lots of people go to the hospital nowadays; they don't always resort to 'gouging,'" maternal grandma vehemently argued, though she was not so sure of it herself. As for old Mrs. Wang, she naturally did not believe it at all; to her going to the hospital meant only one thing and that was "gouging."

Fortunately, maternal grandpa arrived on the scene, immediately improving the position and morale of maternal grandma. He, too, was for going to the hospital. There was little else to do after that. After all he was a man and in a matter of life and death a man's word carries weight, though child bearing is strictly a woman's business.

And so the in-laws, the young mother and the grandson who had only his hair showing all went to the hospital in a motor car. The in-laws shed tears at the cruel fate of the grandson who had to be carted about in a motor car when he had just barely showed his hair.

Old Mrs. Wang exploded almost as soon as they got to the hospital. What, they had to register? What did they mean by registering? It was a case of childbirth, not as if they had come for their quota of rice at government price or to get a bowl of free gruel. Old Mrs. Wang was outraged and declared that she would sooner give up the idea of a grandson than to submit to such a humiliation. But when she found that if she refused to register they would refuse to let them in, she decided to swallow her pride, hard as it was for her to do, for the sake of her emerging grandson. If only her husband were living—it would have been a wonder indeed if he did not tear down the hospital then and there. A widow couldn't do that; she had to put up with things even though she had money. It was no time to ruminate over her grievances; the most pressing thing was to coax her grandson out. So she registered and was told that she had to pay fifty dollars in advance. That gave her her opportunity: "Fifty dollars? Even five hundred is nothing to me. Why didn't you come to the point? Why this nonsense about registration? Did you think my grandson was a letter?"

The physician came and again old Mrs. Wang exploded. It was a man, a man was to act as midwife. She wouldn't have a man attend to her daughter-in-law. Before she had a chance to recover from this shock, two more men came out and proceeded to lift up her daughter-in-law and put her on a stretcher. She was so outraged that even her ears quivered. Why, it was worse than revolution and rebellion! What did they meant by letting a crowd of men handle a young pregnant woman? "Put her down! Isn't there anyone here who knows what human decency means? If so, you'd better ask a few women to come out. Otherwise, we leave."

It happens that she had to deal with a very good-natured physician. "All right," he said, "put her down and let them go!"

Old Mrs. Wang swallowed hard and what she had to swallow burned her heart. If it were not for the sake of her grandson she would give him a few resounding slaps at least. But "an official in authority is not as important as a flunkey in charge," and what could she do since her grandson had decided to be difficult? All right, take her and waste no more words. As soon as the two men put the daughter-in-law on the stretcher, the physician began to press her abdomen with his hands. Old Mrs. Wang closed her eyes to the horror of it and cursed maternal grandma in her heart: "It's your daughter and you let a man press her belly without uttering a word of protest! Oh, the indecency of it!" She was about to say something aloud when her thought again turned to her grandson. For more than ten months he had never suffered any indignity or discomfort. Would he, with his tender skin and bone, be able to stand the physician's rough handling? She opened her eyes and was about to warn the physician when the latter anticipated her by asking: "What have you been feeding the mother? Look at her! I don't know what to do with people like you. You keep feeding the mother everything you can think of until the child is so large. You would not come for check-ups. Then you come to us when everything else fails." Then without waiting for old Mrs. Wang to say anything, he said to the two men, "Carry her in!"

Old Mrs. Wang had never suffered such a humiliation in all her life. It was as if the Goddess of Wisdom herself was being taught how to be wise! That was not the worst of it if there had been a grain of sense to what the man said. If a pregnant woman did not eat nourishing food how was she to bear a child, how was the child to grow? Did the physician thrive on northwest wind when he was in his mother's womb? But Western-style physicians are all foreign-devils-once-removed and you couldn't reason with them. She would take it out on maternal grandma, wherewith she glared at her. The latter was too busy thinking about her daughter to mind. She tried to follow the carriers. Old Mrs. Wang followed suit, but the physician turned around and said to them: "Wait here!"

Both women's eyes turned red with indignation. What, they would not let them in to watch? How were they to know where they were going to take her, and what they were going to do to her? After the physician left them, old Mrs. Wang unloosed the acrid smoke of her rage on maternal grandma: "You said they would not have to 'gouge' him out, but see now, they would not even let you go in and see what's going on! Why, they may even have her quartered twice over. It would serve you right to have your daughter cut up like that. But if anything should happen to my grandson, I shall not live, I'll match my life against yours!"

Maternal grandma was frightened. What if they really did cut up her daughter? It was not beyond these foreign-devils-once-removed. Didn't they exhibit a human leg and a torso in glass jars the last time the medical school was opened to the public? "Now you are blaming me! Who was it that kept on stuffing my daughter from morning till night? Didn't you hear what the doctor said? It was you who insisted on stuffing her. Now see what you have done. I have seen a lot of people in my time but I have never seen a mother-in-law like you!"

"Yes, I have fed her well, but that's because I wasn't sure that she ever got enough to eat before she was married into our house," sneered in-law Wang.

"And I suppose it's because we never gave her enough to eat in our own house that I had to bring eight food trays every time I visited my daughter at your house!"

"Now you have admitted it yourself. Yes, eight trays. Yes, I have stuffed her and you haven't!"

Thus the in-laws battled on, neither willing to weaken. Their jibes and retorts were highly original and effectively delivered.

The physician came back, and said, as paternal grandma had anticipated, that an operation was necessary. The term operation had an unfamiliar ring, but there was no question as to the implication: it meant that they were going to cut her up. If they operated, the physician said, they might save both mother and child; if not, both would probably die. The child was hours overdue and was definitely too big to come out without an operation. But a member of the family must sign before they could operate.

Old Mrs. Wang did not hear a word of what the physician had said. She was saying to herself that she would not stand "gouging."

"What are you going to do?" the physician said impatiently. "You must decide right away!"

" 'Gouging' won't do!"

"Are you going to sign? Hurry up and make up your mind!" the physician again urged.

"My grandson must be born the natural way!"

Maternal grandma became anxious: "Would it be all right if I signed?"

Old Mrs. Wang flared up at maternal grandma's presumptuousness: "She is my daughter-in-law! Who are you?"

The physician became more and more impatient. He shouted into old Mrs. Wang's ear: "This is a matter of two lives!"

" 'Gouging' won't do!"

"Then you don't care about a grandson?" the physician adopted a new line of attack.

For a while she was silent. Many ghosts presented themselves before her, and all of them seemed to say to her: "We want someone to keep on burning incense to us. We are willing to compromise on the issue of 'gouging.' "

She surrendered. Of course the ancestors must have an heir; let them resort to "gouging" if necessary. "But just one thing, it must be alive!" She had hearkened to the ancestors' wishes and given her permission to the physician to cut open her daughter-in-law and "gouge" the child out, but she must make it clear that she wanted a live baby. What good would a dead one be? As for the mother, it didn't matter so long as the grandson lived.

Maternal grandma, however, was not so indifferent to the patient's fate: "Are you sure that both mother and child will live?"

"Hush!" said paternal grandma.

"I believe that there will be no danger," the physician said, wiping his forehead. "But the birth has been very much delayed and we can guarantee nothing. Otherwise why should you be asked to sign?"

"You wouldn't guarantee anything? Then let us not go through all this for nothing!" Paternal grandma was very responsible in her attitude toward the ancestors; it wouldn't do anyone any good if only a dead child came out of all this horror.

"All right, then," said the physician, suffocating with exasperation, "take her back and do what you like. But remember, two lives!"

"What if it were three lives, since you would not guarantee anything?"

Old Mrs. Wang suddenly decided that perhaps she had better let them try. She would not have thought of this if the physician had not started to walk away. "Doctor, doctor, come back! Supposing you try what you can." The physician was so exasperated that he hardly knew whether to laugh or cry. He read the release to her and she signed it with a cross.

The grandmas waited and waited for they did not know how long. It was not until almost dawn that they succeeded in "gouging" the child out. What a big baby it was, fully thirteen pounds! Old Mrs. Wang was overwhelmed with happiness. She took maternal grandma's hands, laughing with tears streaming down her cheeks. The latter was no longer her enemy but her "dear elder sister." The physician was no longer a foreign-devil-once-removed, but a benefactor of the Wang family. She wished she could reward him with a hundred dollars at once. If he had not resorted to "gouging" her nice fat grandson might have suffocated. How would she then face her ancestors? She wished she could kneel down then and there and do some good old kowtowing but they did not have any shrine for the Goddess of Children in the hospital.

The baby was now washed and put in the nursery. The grandmas wanted to go in and take a look. Not only to take a look but to pat and fondle the child with their wrinkled hands that had not been washed all night. The nurse would not let them go in; they were only allowed to look through the glass partition. There was their own grandson inside, their very own grandson, and yet they were not even allowed to touch it! Paternal grandma took out a red envelope—which she had planned to give to the midwife—and handed it to the nurse. She would surely let them in after that! But nothing seemed to go right; the nurse actually refused to accept the gift! Old Mrs. Wang rubbed her eyes and contemplated the nurse for a long while. "She does not appear to be a foreign-devil girl," she said to herself, "then why is it that she would not accept a gift? Perhaps she is shy and feels embarrassed." She had it! She would strike up a conversation with her. Everything would be all right after she had broken down her shyness. She pointed to the row of baskets in the nursery and asked, "I suppose they were all 'gouged' out?"

"No, only yours. All the others were born naturally."

"Nonsense," old Mrs. Wang said to herself. "All those who come to hospitals must be 'gouging' cases."

"Only when you feed rich and fattening food to the mother is it necessary to operate," the nurse said.

"But would the child be so big if the mother didn't have enough to eat?" said maternal grandma, standing on a united front with old Mrs. Wang on the issue.

"A big, fat baby is better than a skinny monkey, though one may be 'gouged' out and the other born naturally," old Mrs. Wang said, beginning to feel that none but "gouging" cases had any business to come to the hospital. "And who ever heard of natural cases coming to the hospital? That would be as unnecessary as letting down the pants in order to break wind!"

But they remained on the outside of the nursery for all the talking they did.

Old Mrs. Wang had another idea. "Maid," she said to the nurse, addressing her as if she were a servant girl, "give the baby to us and let us take him home. We have a lot to do to get ready for the Third Day bathing ceremony."

"I am not a maid and I cannot give you the baby," said the nurse, none too politely.

"He is my grandson! You dare to refuse me? We can't invite guests to the hospital and do things properly."

"The mother can't nurse the child right away when we have to operate; we have to feed the child."

"And so can we! I am getting on toward sixty and I have borne sons and given birth to daughters. I should know more about such things than you do. Have you ever borne any children?" Old Mrs. Wang wasn't sure whether the nurse was married or not. Who could tell what these white helmeted women were anyway?

"We can't give you the child without the doctor's permission, no matter what you say."

"Then go and get the doctor and let me talk to him. I don't want to waste words with you!"

"The doctor has not yet finished; he has to sew up the incision."

This reminded maternal grandma of daughter, though old Mrs. Wang was still too full of her grandson to give any thought to her daughter-in-law. Before the birth of her grandson, her daughter-in-law always came to her mind when she thought of her grandson, but now that her grandson was born, it was no longer necessary to think of her daughter-in-law. Maternal grandma, however, wanted to see her daughter. Who knew what a big hole they made in her belly? They would not let anyone into the operating room and there was nothing for maternal grandma to do except to gaze at the child with old Mrs. Wang from the distance.

Finally the physician came out and old Mrs. Wang went up to parley with him.

"In operating cases it is best for mother and child to stay in the hospital for a month," the physician said.

"Then what are we going to do about the Third Day and the Full Month?" old Mrs. Wang asked.

"Which is more important, their lives or the feasts? How can the mother stand the strain of entertaining before her incision heals?" the physician asked.

Old Mrs. Wang undoubtedly believed that the Third Day celebration was more important than her daughter-in-law's life, but she could not very well say so with maternal grandma listening. As to how her daughter-in-law was to receive the guests, that was easily managed: she would let her receive them lying in bed.

The physician still refused. Old Mrs. Wang got another idea. "I suppose it is money that you are after? All right, then, we'll pay you, but let us take mother and child home."

"You go and take a look at her yourselves, and see if she is in a condition to be moved," the physician said.

Both grandmas hesitated. What if she still had a gaping hole in her, as big as a wash basin? Wouldn't that be horrible? Love of her daughter finally enabled maternal grandma to summon up enough courage to go in and there was nothing for paternal grandma to do but to follow.

In the sickroom daughter-in-law lay on the bed, propped up on a reclining rest, her face like a sheet of white paper. Her mother

cried out, not sure whether her daughter was dead or alive. Old
Mrs. Wang had more fortitude and shed only a tear or two, which
were immediately followed by an indignant protest: "Why won't
you let her lie down flat and proper? What kind of foreign torture
are you subjecting her to?"

"It would put a strain on the stitches to have her lie flat, understand?" the physician said.

"Can't you bind her up with plaster tape?" Old Mrs. Wang
could not get over her distrust of the physician's foreign ideas.

The physician would not even let maternal grandma talk to her
daughter, which made both grandmas suspect that the physician
must have done something or other to the patient that he was
anxious to hide. It was fairly evident that she could not be moved
out of the hospital for a while. In that case they could at least
take the grandson away so that they could plan on the Third Day
festivities.

Again the physician refused. Old Mrs. Wang became desperate:
"Do you observe the Third Day bathing ceremony in the hospital?
If you do, I shall invite all our friends and relatives here. If you
don't, then let me take him away. He is my first grandson. I
can't live and face people if I do not celebrate his Third Day
appropriately."

"Who is going to nurse the child?" the physician asked.

"We'll hire a wet nurse!" old Mrs. Wang said triumphantly.

The baby was brought out and surrendered to her. She began
to sneeze as soon as she got into the car and sneezed all the way
home, each sneeze being well aimed at her grandson's face. A man
was sent out immediately to find a wet nurse. Grandma kept the
baby so that she could sneeze into him. Yes, she knew that she
had caught a cold, but she would not relinquish her grandson. By
noon the infant had received at least two hundred sneezes and
was beginning to develop a temperature. That made old Mrs.
Wang even more reluctant to give it up. By three o'clock in the
afternoon, the child burned like fire. By night they had hired two
wet nurses, but the grandson died without having had one swallow
of milk.

Old Mrs. Wang cried a long while. As soon as she finished crying, her old eyes popped wide open with passion: "It is because they had to 'gouge' him out! Of course he couldn't live! I'll sue the hospital. Such a big, heavy child living only one day, who ever heard of such a thing! It's all the hospital's fault, the foreign-devils-once-removed!"

She got maternal grandma to go to the hospital with her and make life miserable for them down there. The latter wanted to get her daughter out of the hospital, too. You never could depend on hospitals!

The daughter-in-law was duly taken away from the hospital; you couldn't sue them before that was done. Her incision broke open not long afterwards. The "spring restoring plasters" for use after childbirth that they bound her up with did not do any good and she died without much ado.

Now old Mrs. Wang was able to sue the hospital on both counts. Life now held nothing for her except to avenge her grandson and her daughter-in-law.

The Philanthropist

By Lao She

She doesn't like to be referred to as "Mrs. Wang." She calls herself Miss Mu Feng-cheng and likes others to call her the same.
It gives her a sense of independence, though she has no compunction in spending her husband's money, of which he has a great
deal.

She is a very busy woman, so busy that she hardly has time to
catch her breath, especially since she has to carry the physical
weight of her prosperity with her. There is no meeting of any
consequence that does not require her presence, no welfare organization in which she does not have a hand. It would have worn
out an average woman just to get in and out of the motor car the
way Miss Mu—yes, Miss Mu, not Mrs. Wang—does, but she has
dedicated herself to society and she is not afraid to exert herself.
Even if her legs had been twice as large she would not have
shrunk from dragging them in and out of the car. It is not that
she cares nothing about herself, it is that she loves others more
and has given herself to their welfare.

She was still in bed when Freedom came in. Hadn't she told
the maids that they mustn't disturb her before she got up? That's
the way with bondmaids; it doesn't do any good to give them
such enlightened names as "Freedom." She wanted to throw the
lamp on the night table at Freedom but refrained since the lamp
was worth more money than the maid.

"How many times have I told you, Freedom." She looked at her
watch and found it was almost nine. That somewhat mollified
her, for she was pleased that she had slept so well, as only people

enjoying perfect health could. She had to look after herself for the sake of society; she needed her sleep.

"I have not forgotten, Madam—Miss!" Freedom tried to explain.

"What is it? Speak up!"

"Mr. Fang wants to see you."

"Which Mr. Fang? You should have enough sense to know that there are many Mr. Fangs."

"Mr. Fang the tutor."

"What about him?"

"He says that his wife has just died!" Freedom said sympathetically.

"I suppose that means that he wants more money!" She took a purse from under her pillow and took out twenty dollars. "Give this to him and tell him that I do not see any one before breakfast."

As Freedom was about to go, she stopped her and said, "Tell Humanity to run the bath and open the windows when you come back. I have to remind you people of everything! Where is the first young master?"

"He has gone to school, Miss."

"Without giving me a kiss!" Miss Mu said, nodding her head and causing her fat cheeks to quiver.

"The first young master said he would give you a kiss when he comes home for lunch." The maids all know a few words of English, such as "kiss," "pie," and "bath."

"Go about your business and don't stand there and wear me out with your chatter."

It suddenly occurred to Miss Mu that Mr. Fang's bereavement meant that he would not be able to give her second son his lessons. It annoyed her that Mr. Fang should be so inconsiderate as to lose his wife, for she was an enlightened woman and very much interested in her son's education.

Humanity knocked on the door and announced that her bath was ready. She went into the bath room and took evident satisfaction in its faultless appointments. The white porcelain tub was filled with clear water of just the right temperature and the air within the tiled walls had a pleasant mixture of steam and perfume. There was a large mirror, and several thick Turkish towels. The soap and bath salts containers all shone with cleanliness as did everything else. She stepped into the tub and was for a moment lost in thought. Her legs looked fatter than ever in the water and that made her feel a little sad. As she rubbed her neck she realized why—it was the memory of her youth. How slender she was twenty years ago and how pretty! She could hardly recognize herself now and her husband and her children had suddenly become strangers to her. To shake herself out of this dream of the past, she splashed herself with water and rubbed herself vigorously. It was more important for her to attend to the present. She was not only the wife of a rich man and the mother of two children, she was the mother of countless children and the leader of her sex. She had studied abroad and was familiar with world problems; it was her duty to serve mankind.

But it was not easy to serve mankind. She remembered how two years before she had started a campaign to promote bathing. "A home is not a home without a bathtub," had been her slogan. But what did she accomplish? Mankind is very stupid; you can't make them understand though you wear your tongue out. She mustn't care so much what became of the world, she said to herself as she rubbed her fat legs. Let it degenerate into a pigsty if it wants to, without bathtubs, without sanitation. But she must care, she must serve mankind to the end.

"Five minutes will be enough to air out the room," she shouted to Freedom.

"I have shut the windows already, Miss," Freedom answered.

Her bedroom had had indeed a complete change of air when she returned to it. She had made it a rule to take some breathing exercises in the morning. The air was too chilly in the courtyard, so she did it indoors after giving her room a thorough airing. She first bent down and touched the tips of her feet. It gave her satisfaction that she could still touch her feet, though she did not keep her legs very straight. She did this three times and then breathed deeply five or six times. She felt invigorated.

"Freedom, you may serve breakfast now."

Miss Mu was against overeating, so she had a simple breakfast consisting of a large plate of ham and eggs, two pieces of buttered toast, strawberry jam, and coffee with milk. She had once conducted a campaign for simple and wholesome meals such as they have in the West, with as much milk and butter as possible, instead of stuffing oneself with wowotou or black noodles. But like all good suggestions it was not followed. She had to be satisfied with carrying out her own advice, and so it happened that her kitchen was presided over by a cook trained in the Western style of cooking.

As she ate her ham and eggs, she thought of Mr. Fang. She paid him twenty dollars a month for tutoring her younger son. She did not believe in paying poor people too much money, for money is the seed of disaster in the hands of the poor, though it was safe enough in her own hands. It was not that she could not afford to pay Mr. Fang more but that she did not want to. In the first place she did not want to be looked upon as "easy" and then she did not want to plant disaster for Mr. Fang. He had lost his wife as it was. She felt sorry for Mr. Fang just the same and decided to do something for him.

"Freedom," she called. "Tell the cook to send ten of *my own* eggs to Mr. Fang. Tell Mr. Fang not to boil them too long but eat them soft boiled."

As Miss Mu sipped her coffee she told herself that the eggs ought to give Mr. Fang strength to bear the loss of his wife. Then it occurred to her that since Mr. Fang had now no one to cook for him it would be best for her to supply him his meals. She was always so thoughtful about other people. It was a habit that she could not do anything about. Of course she would pay him a few dollars less. But then Mr. Fang would get better and more wholesome food. He ought to understand that and be grateful for her thoughtfulness. She was always so solicitous about others and so understanding. But whoever thought of her, who understood her? The thought depressed her and made her realize the emptiness of life. She could not call back her youth, or make herself desired again. There was nothing left for her but to serve others. The pity of it was that the world was so ungrateful and unsympathetic.

She did not dare to dwell on these unpleasant thoughts; they would drive her mad. She must go to her study and set to work. Only work could make her life full, make her tired enough to sleep well, and make her happy and conscious of her own worth.

Miss Feng, her secretary, had been waiting in the study for more than an hour. She was just twenty-three and not bad looking. She got twelve dollars a month. Really she should be glad to work for nothing, for as Miss Mu's secretary she had many opportunities to meet the right people. If she should marry one of the rich people that she met, she would not have to worry about food and drink for the rest of her life. Isn't that better than to be earning fifty or even sixty dollars a month without such opportunities? Miss Mu is so far-sighted and thinks of everything.

"What's on today?" Miss Mu asked, sighing and depositing herself in a large comfortable chair.

"There is the exhibition at the school for the deaf and dumb, Miss Mu," said Miss Feng, looking at her notebook. "The opening ceremony begins at 10:20. At 11:10 the Women's Association, where you will preside; at 12, wedding at the Changs. In the afternoon—"

"Just a moment," Miss Mu said, with another sigh. "Have you had the present sent over for the wedding?"

"Yes, I have. A pair of flower baskets. Twenty-eight dollars. They look very smart."

"Is that not rather small?"

"At Mr. Wang's last birthday, the Changs sent only a silk scroll, not very—"

"It is different now. Mr. Chang has now a more important place in society. But we'll let that go for the present and wait for a future opportunity to make up. How about the afternoon appointments?"

"There are five meetings."

"H'm, don't tell me now. I can't remember them all. Wait until I return from the Changs." Miss Mu lit a cigarette. She was not satisfied with the wedding present for the Changs. "Miss Feng, make a note to ask the newlyweds for dinner next Friday or Saturday. Remind me of it Wednesday."

Miss Feng wrote it down rapidly.

"And don't forget to ask me what kind of banquet the Changs serve, don't forget."

"No, I won't forget, Miss Mu."

Miss Mu did not want to go to the exhibition but she was afraid that there might be pictures taken. It would not do not to show herself. She decided that she would be a bit late, timing herself to arrive just as the photograph was to be taken. She wanted to chat a while with Miss Feng, not so much because she cared anything about Miss Feng as because she felt bored and wanted to talk to someone. She suddenly thought of Mr. Fang.

"Feng, Mr. Fang's wife has just passed away. I sent over twenty dollars and ten eggs. The poor fellow." Miss Mu thought her eyes became a bit moist.

Miss Feng knew what had happened. However, she said what she was expected to say. "Yes, poor Mr. Fang! It is so kind of you to send him the money and so lucky for him."

A smile lighted Miss Mu's face. "I am always like that, but people are so unappreciative. What an ungrateful world."

"Who doesn't know of your generosity and your philanthropies?"

"Well, perhaps some do," Miss Mu smiled even more broadly.

"The second young master will have to neglect his school again for a few days," Miss Feng said, with some concern.

"That's true, unfortunately. It is always one thing or another."

"Perhaps I can tutor him for a few days, though I won't be much good."

"Why not? How stupid of me not to think of it. You can give him his lessons; you won't do it for nothing."

"Please don't give me anything for it. It will be only a matter of a few days."

Miss Mu thought for a while and then said, "Feng, how about working it out this way? Supposing you do both jobs and let me pay you twenty-five a month?"

"That would not be fair to Mr. Fang!"

"That's all right. He won't need so much since his wife is dead. I'll get him an eight- or ten-dollar job when I get a chance. So that's all right. I must be going now. Oh, how I wish I didn't have so much to attend to. Never a moment to myself!"

Liu's Court

By Lao She

In the Court where I live there was quite a commotion a few days ago because of a suicide.

But I must start from the beginning. Let me first introduce myself. I am a fortune teller. I used to sell peanuts, jujubes, and things, but that was a long time ago. I now have a stand and on good days I take in three or four dimes. My old woman died many years ago. My son is a ricksha puller, and the two of us live in a room on the northern side of Liu's Court.

There are over twenty rooms besides ours in the Court. How many families in all live there, I don't know. Most of them rent only one room and they move in one day and are gone the next. I can't keep track of them all. When you want to be friendly, you greet the neighbors with a "Have you had your dinner?" and no one takes offense if you don't want to say anything. Every one is busy from morning till night so that he may feed his mouth and has little time for idle gossip or passing the time of day. Of course there are those who like to talk, but a full stomach is necessary to put you in a conversational mood.

My son and I and the Wangs are reckoned old tenants; we have lived in the Court for over a year. We have thought of moving many times, but our room does not leak much when it rains and that's something, isn't it? Of course there are houses that do not leak, but they are not for poor people like us. Moreover, you have to pay three months' rent in advance every time you move. Better put up with it, I said to myself. The evening paper I take talks a lot about equality, but that's all nonsense so long as you don't have as many coppers in your pocket as the other fellow.

That's the truth. Take daughter-in-laws, for instance. They don't get beaten so often if their families do not take any bethrothal money. Isn't that so?

The Wangs occupy two rooms. Old Wang and I are considered the most what they call "civilized" [1] people in Liu's Court. But let me say right here that I don't put any stock in this trying-to-be-civilized business. In my opinion a man who tries to act civilized is three times a grandson. I am a fortune teller and I can read pretty well what is put in front of me. I spend two coppers a day on an evening tabloid. If that makes me civilized, then I am your grandson. Old Wang is a gardener in a foreigner's house and so may be said to be in the foreign business, but whether he knows any thing about gardening or not only he himself knows and he wouldn't tell if he didn't. Maybe you don't have to do more than cut grass in a foreigner's yard to be called a gardener. What I mean is that old Wang is the kind that likes to put on airs and act like so-called civilized folks. What's the good of that? There is nothing to be ashamed of in cutting grass, but old Wang doesn't see things that way. That's what makes the poor stay poor; they like to fool themselves by pretending they are somebody instead of trying to make something of themselves. There are lots of people like that in the Court. Any way old Wang does not make much, whether flower man or grass man.

Old Wang's son is a stone mason, with a head harder than a rock. I have never seen a man so glum and taciturn. But I must say, to be fair, that he is a good mason. It was his wife that committed suicide. She was ten years younger than her husband and looked like a stale, shriveled up wowotou, with a head of yellow hair, always sad and crying everytime she got a beating, which was often. Old Wang has also a daughter, around fourteen, as mean and wicked a girl as you can find. The four of them lived in the two rooms.

After us Chang Erh was the oldest tenant, having lived in the

---

[1] *Wen-ming,* the original expression, is a neologism introduced to translate "civilized" or "civilization" but was popularly used in the early years of the Republic in the sense of "new," "modern," "having 'class,'" etc.

Court over six months at the time he had to move. Though he owed two months' rent he managed to keep the landlord from evicting him until this thing happened. Chang's wife has a smooth tongue, which probably explains why they had not been evicted earlier. Of course she was only sweet·and smooth when the landlord came to collect rent. You should hear her swear the moment his back was turned! No one can help cursing the landlord, charging a dollar and half a month for a room no bigger than a doghouse! But no one curses as well to the point as she does. It makes you feel good to hear her curse, that is, if she happens to curse the right party. Even I can't help liking her—I mean because she can curse so well. But the rent remained the same in spite of all her cursing, which, when I think of it, makes me care less for her, for it shows that cursing doesn't get you anywhere after all.

Chang Erh is in the same line of business as my son, ricksha pulling. He doesn't have a very quiet mouth either; after a couple of coppers' worth of cat's-water he can talk until every one in the Court is dizzy. That's what I call a poor man's chew, something which I don't care anything about, though Chang is not a bad sort at heart. He has three sons; the first one is old enough to make himself useful by picking up coal that drops from passing carts, the second makes a nuisance of himself along the gutters, while the third is still in the crawling stage and has to limit his activities to the confines of the Court.

You can't begin to name all the children in the Court. There must be enough of them to make up a mixed regiment. It is easy enough to tell the boys from the girls, since all the children who can go naked do. You have to be careful walking through the yard if you do not want to step on someone, and there are bound to be words if you do. Everyone carries a bellyful of grudges with him and all welcome an opportunity for a quarrel. It is true that the poorer you are the more children you have. I am not saying that poor people shouldn't have any children, what I mean is that they should think of some way to take care of them. What are these naked brats going to do? I suppose they will all be like my son and pull rickshas. I am not saying that one should be ashamed of pulling a ricksha; what I mean is that it's not right to make a beast of burden of a human being. And lots of them do not live to be old enough to pull rickshas. A whole lot of them died of the measles epidemic this spring, and wailing was pretty general throughout the Court, including the most hardened child-beating fathers. But crying was about all they could do. Then they roll them up in matting and carry them out and that's that. What really matters is that there are that many fewer mouths to feed. "An empty pocket makes an iron heart," I have often said. That's no solution to the problems, of course; one should think of some way out.

There are many families besides us, but it is enough to mention only these three. As I have said, it was old Wang's daughter-in-law, the one that looked like a wowotou, who committed suicide. I am not trying to be funny when I say that she looked like a wowotou. It is not right to make fun of the dead. I feel very sorry for her and girls like her. I have often wondered by what right a girl is allowed to get like a wowotou. What can you expect of girls who never get enough to eat? Do you expect them to be plump and smooth? Of course you can't. But why should such things be?

It was like this, to make a long story short. Old Wang was most responsible for it; he was the worst of the lot. Didn't I say that he liked to put on airs? That's it. He was always trying to impress people with his importance and to act civilized. When he got a daughter-in-law he wanted to make the most of it and was always picking on her and finding fault with her. Because of three coppers' worth of oil or two coppers' worth of vinegar, he would make enough trouble to churn up the sea or turn back the rivers. I know, it's because we poor people have bad livers that we quarrel so much. But with old Wang it was not only that. With him it was a case of trying to show people that he was the father-in-law. Mother's ——, how many coppers is a father-in-law worth, let me ask you?

Another reason why old Wang was so mean to his daughter-in-law was that the girl's family took a hundred dollars for bethrothal money. He had to borrow the money and it will take him another two years before he can pay off the loan. It is quite a strain on him, of course, and so he tried to take it out on the girl. And since his old woman was no longer living, he had to work doubly hard to get all his money's worth.

When he went to work, he turned the job of torturing his daughter-in-law over to his daughter. That mean yatou! I don't have the least prejudice against poor girls. I don't care if they are bondmaids or concubines or even prostitutes. That happens frequently—though I am not saying that it is as it should be—and you can't blame the girls for it. But I detest that Erh-ni! She is just as detestable as her father. There was nothing that she would not do to "put small shoes" on her sister-in-law. She could tell the most outright lies in order to make her suffer. I know why she is so mean; it is because she attends a school at the expense of her father's foreign employer. That's what makes her look down upon her sister-in-law, though she wears the same kind of cloth shoes and a comb over her hair and does not look any prettier. If her sister-in-law was making a pair of new shoes, she would manage to step on them and soil them and then turn around and make her father scold the poor girl. I have no time to go into all her mean tricks. In a word, the poor daughter-in-law never had a day of peace and often did not get enough to eat.

The younger Wang works outside the city. He used to come home once in ten days or a half month, and every time he came home he never failed to give his wife a beating. Now it is quite the usual thing in the Court for a daughter-in-law to be beaten. Since they are dependent on the men and since their parents got money for them, you'd expect it. The younger Wang, however, did not really want to beat his wife. He did not want to look for trouble since he came home only once in a long while. But what could he do with his father and sister edging him on? Old Wang could only punish his daughter-in-law by making her go hungry or kneel in a corner, but he could not beat her himself. That would be "bad form" for a civilized person like himself. Therefore he made his son do it for him; he knew that one beating by his son was as good as five by some one else, he being a stone mason. After his son had done his chore, old Wang would be very nice to him. As for Erh-ni, she often pinched her sister-in-law's arms, but that was not enough for her. Nothing would please her more than to have her brother break her sister-in-law to pieces as he would a rock. Nothing can make a woman meaner to another than contempt, and how Erh-ni looked down on her sister-in-law! Wasn't she a student while her sister-in-law was only a poor wowotou bought for one hundred dollars?

There was nothing but misery in the poor girl's life and the more miserable she was the less cheerful she became. No one in the Court liked her. She even forgot how to speak. The only time she showed any signs of life was when she ran afoul of the evil spirits. This usually happened after her husband had given her the usual beating and gone away. She would cry and jabber away all by herself. That's when I came into the picture. Old Wang would asked me to slap her and drive away the evil spirits as he was afraid of ghosts himself. After I had gone to her in her room and quieted her down—I never did really slap her, for what she needed was sympathy and comforting words—old Wang would come in and dig his fingers in the middle of her upper lip and smoke her with paper tapers, though he knew perfectly well that she had come to. That's when old Wang and I always quarreled. Ordinarily I never interfered. What's the use? If I were to interfere, I would be sure to take the girl's part and that would only make old Wang torture her more. So I never interfered. But I couldn't avoid quarreling with old Wang when the girl ran afoul of the spirits, for I would be right there and I could not watch him torture her without saying a word. The strange thing was that everyone said that I was in the wrong on these occasions, including the women. It seems to be the general belief that a man should beat his wife, a father-in-law should discipline his daughter-in-law, and a daughter should make life miserable for her brother's wife. How does it happen that they believe such nonsense? Who taught them to believe in such things? It is all because of that turtle-egg and three-times-a-grandson business of trying to be "civilized" that makes them behave the way they do. Is there anything more absurd? With their bellies as flat as starved bedbugs they still talk about being civilized!

A few days ago the mason came home for a visit. For some reason or other old Wang was in a kindly mood and did not make his son beat the poor girl. The girl, on her part, was overwhelmed by the atmosphere of good will and you could almost see a smile on her face. But Erh-ni could not stand this. It was as if two suns had appeared in the sky. She was sure that there must be something behind her sister-in-law's happiness. Her brother might have brought his wife something. She went into the latter's room to search but could find nothing after a long time. By that I mean she searched pretty thoroughly, for there couldn't be much to look through in the poor girl's room. You can't find two tables in good condition among all the families in the Court. Except for this, you would be always hearing of thefts. If any one has bills, he puts them in his sock.

Erh-ni was furious. How dare her sister-in-law look happy? She must punish her whether she had done anything or not.

The daughter-in-law was cooking in the yard and was straining the excess water from the rice. Erh-ni gave her a vicious kick and caused her to drop the rice. Rice! It was only on such rare occasions as her husband's visit that they had rice. Her life seemed to have gone out of her with the rice. The water had not been strained off entirely and there the rice lay on the ground, a snow white mass of gruel. It was steaming hot, but the poor girl's first thought was to scoop it up, for even her life was not worth as much as that pot of rice, let alone her hands. But the rice was too hot for her. After two or three scoops the pain became unbearable. She dared not cry, she held her hands together, gritted her teeth and shook with pain.

"Pa! Look, she has spilled all the rice on the ground!" Erh-ni shouted.

Both father and son came out into the yard. Old Wang took one look at the steaming rice and became mad enough to kill. He gave his son only one look but it was enough. It said: "Do you want your wife or your father?"

The younger Wang's face became purple. He went to his wife and dragged her to the ground by her hair. The poor girl passed out without uttering a sound.

"Beat her! Beat her to death! Beat her!" old Wang shouted, stamping and kicking up dust.

To make sure that her sister-in-law was not pretending, Erh-ni pinched her on the thigh.

Everyone in the Court came out to see the fun. None of the men tried to put in a word for the poor girl, and naturally none of the women dared to utter a word. Men like to see other people's wives get a beating; it puts fear into their own wives.

Finally I interfered. Old Wang did not like it a bit and would have liked to give me a beating. But other men followed my example and we managed to drag the son away.

The next day both old Wang and his son went to work bright and early. Erh-ni did not go to school so that she could continue to torture her sister-in-law.

Chang Erh's wife happened to be in a sympathetic mood and went in to see the girl. Because she had a sharp tongue, she managed to offend Erh-ni in trying to comfort her sister-in-law. Words passed back and forth. Naturally Erh-ni was no match for Chang Erh's wife. "You'll end up in a brothel, yatou, as sure as my name is Chang," she said. "San Tu-tzu gave you two coppers and you let him kiss you. You thought no one saw you, but I did. Now is it not so? Is it not so?" She shouted her accusations in Erh-ni's ears, giving her no chance to reply.

Erh-ni fled from the Court and gave her sister-in-law no more trouble that day. Chang Erh's wife went in to take another look at the poor girl, and found her lying on the k'ang. She was wearing the red coat that she wore at her wedding. Chang Erh's wife said a few words to her but she turned away without replying. Just then Chang Erh's wife had to rush out to rescue her small boy, who had started a fight with another boy and had gone under.

Erh-ni did not come back until mealtime. She went directly to her sister-in-law's room to see if she had dinner ready. Erh-ni herself never cooked. She was a student, you know. No sooner did she open the door than she uttered a sharp cry, for she found her sister-in-law hanging from the door beam of the inner room. Her cry brought out the whole Court, but no one made a move to do anything about it. As the saying goes, "No one wants to spoil his good shoes by stepping on dog's manure." Who wants to get mixed up in a case involving life?

Erh-ni was scared to death. "Isn't it time that you went to fetch your pa?" some one suggested. Erh-ni turned on her heels and ran as if from a pursuing ghost.

Old Wang was helpless as the rest. It was too late to save his daughter-in-law. That did not matter anyway. What worried him was what his landlord might demand of him for defiling the rooms with violent death. You can always get another daughter-in-law if you have money. The thought of money reminded him that he had not yet paid off the loan and made him feel more cheated than sorry. He could have bitten the corpse.

The girl's family came but old Wang was not frightened by their shouts and threats. He had an answer ready: he had found from his daughter that it was Chang Erh's wife who had edged on his daughter-in-law to commit suicide. The Wangs had not done anything to her to drive her to commit suicide. Old Wang had copied civilized folks well; he could tell an outright lie without blinking an eye.

It is hard to shake off a thief's bite, particularly if no one minds your being bitten. That was the case with Chang Erh's wife. No matter how clever her tongue, she could not escape a beating when her husband came back. The case would not go to the courts, for poor people like us all shy away from the law. But what if the dead girl's family believed old Wang and his daughter and demanded satisfaction from her? It was all her own fault; it was that tongue of hers. She had made many enemies in the Court and now they all rejoiced in her predicament. They were pleased when Chang Erh gave his wife the beating.

The girl's family did not want to prosecute but they wanted

money. They did not want to threaten anything worse until they had failed to get satisfaction on that count. So old Wang had to promise to give what he could least spare. He could do no less, with a corpse right there in the room.

Then the husband came back. He was as glum as ever but I could see that he felt bad inside. He went into the room and sat by the corpse for a long time. If it had not been for his father, I am sure he would not have beaten her as often as he did. But since he did not want to be unfilial he had to beat her as his father wished. He forgot that his arms were accustomed to break rocks. He sat in the room for a long, long while and put a new pair of trousers—that is, without patches—on her. He paid no attention when his father spoke to him.

The girl's family wanted a hundred dollars, fifty for the funeral and fifty for themselves, and old Wang had to promise to pay. The latter went straight to Chang Erh and said to him: "It was your wife who brought this on me. There is only one thing to do: we must each pay fifty. Otherwise, I shall bring the corpse into your room." He spoke softly but he was firm.

Chang Erh's eyes were red as he had just drunk four coppers' worth of cat's-water and he had a ready answer. "You speak well, my Wang Ta-yeh. Did you say fifty? I'll give you everything I have. Look around the room now and take all you want. If you can't find anything of value, I'll sell my two older boys to you. Surely they ought to be worth fifty dollars. Mother of Hsiao-san!" he called, "take the two older ones over to Wang Ta-yeh's rooms. They are both old enough to run around and feed themselves. They'll be no trouble to you. You have no grandson. It's a perfect arrangement."

Old Wang looked around the room. Chang's furniture was not worth more than four coppers. He told Chang Erh to keep his children. But he could not let him off so easily. If he could not pay fifty, how about thirty?

"I cannot take advantage of you like that," said Chang Erh mockingly. "Let's stick to the original figure. Mark it down. You'll be paid when I get run over by the street car and the company pays my family."

Old Wang wanted to get his son to give Chang a beating, but Chang was a husky fellow and he was not sure that his son would be able to manage him. Chang's wife had kept still up to this point but she saw an opening and ventured to say something to redeem her lost prestige. "You whose name is Wang, just you wait! If I do not go to your room and hang myself I am no true woman. You just wait!"

Being a "civilized" man, old Wang could not bring himself to exchange words with a woman. Moreover, he knew that a woman like Chang's wife was quite capable of making good her threat. It was bad enough as it was with one suicide on his hands; he could not stand another. He decided to beat a retreat.

In reality old Wang had long ago made up his mind what to do. His call on Chang was only a feint. He went to the foreigner's house. His Excellency was not home but he knelt down before his ladyship and asked her for help. She gave him the hundred dollars, fifty was an outright gift, the other fifty to be deducted from his wages.

Old Wang went back to Liu's Court with his nose in the air. It cost him eight dollars for a charm from the exorcist. You can't tell what might happen without that. That was absolutely indispensable.

The girl did not die in vain. She got a brand new coat and a pair of trousers made of red imitation satin, new shoes and socks and a set of silver-plated hair ornaments. Her coffin cost twelve dollars. Five Buddhist monks were hired to chant prayers for her. Her family, however, got only a little over forty dollars, for try as they would they could not get old Wang to give them the entire fifty dollars.

So at last the affair was concluded. But Erh-ni got what was coming to her. She did not dare go into the room. No matter what she did, she could not dodge the sight of her sister-in-law hanging from the door beam, wearing her red coat and with a tongue sticking out at her. Old Wang had to move. But who would take

a defiled room? As long as he continued to live there, the landlord
was willing to say nothing. If he were to move, the landlord was
sure to demand damages. Yet what was he to do with Erh-ni, who
would not go into the room?

It was then that old Wang decided to get rid of his daughter.
He might get a couple of hundred dollars for her, enough to get his
son another wife and have something to put aside toward his own
coffin.

He came to me and broached the subject. At first I thought he
wanted to palm her off on me for a daughter-in-law, but I was
wrong. He only wanted me to keep my eyes open for some suitable
match. I did not say anything.

Just then a matchmaker proposed a girl for the younger Wang.
She was only eighteen, could wash and sew, and her family asked
only hundred and twenty for her. That made old Wang more
anxious than ever to get rid of Erh-ni.

Finally, the landlord came, having gotten wind of the suicide.
Old Wang had little difficulty with him. Wasn't he still living in
those rooms, he said. Moreover, it wasn't his fault. He was away
from home all day and could not have oppressed his daughter-in-
law. It was the fault of that wicked neighbor of theirs. If it had
not been for Chang Erh's wife, his daughter-in-law would never
have hung herself. And of what consequence was it any way?
Was he not negotiating for another match for his son? He was a
poor man but he worked for a foreigner, and the foreigner was
ready to come to his help. Did not his employer give him a hundred
dollars to settle the incident?

The landlord made enquiries of the other tenants and was assured by every one that old Wang did get his money from his
foreign employer. He found, too, that old Wang was respected by
his fellow tenants. The landlord decided to do nothing about old
Wang; he did not want to offend any one who worked for a
foreigner. However, he would tolerate Chang Erh no longer. He
was a bad character. He certainly had nerve to let his wife stir up
trouble when he owed two months' rent! For all his wife's clever

tongue, Chang had to pay up and get out. He was as drunk as a cat on the day he moved.

I am curious to see how much Erh-ni will fetch and what sort of wife the younger Wang will get. What is the world coming to! I am only sure of one thing: I am sure that a man who tries to act "civilized" is three times a grandson, as I have said before.

The Puppet Dead

By Pa Chin

As Jui-chueh's time approached, her condition caused Chen-yi-tai, the widowed concubine of the late head of the family, and some of the maid servants a great deal of concern. At first they only whispered among themselves but one day Chen-yi-tai brought the matter into the open. Her complaint was that should a birth take place in the same house in which the dead was still lying, the blood of birth would pollute the body of the dead and cause it to bleed. The only way to avoid this injury to the dead was to move the pregnant woman out of the house. It was not enough to move her out of the house; it was necessary to move her outside the city wall. It was not enough to move her outside the city wall, for the city gate would not shut out the blood emanations, it was necessary that a bridge should intervene. Even that was not absolutely safe; they must also seal up the coffin with bricks in a temporary tomb in order to safeguard for certain the dead from "the plague of blood,"

The first to approve of these safeguards was Shen-shih, Ko-ding's wife, and Wang-shih, Ko-an's wife, and later they were approved by Ko-ming, Ko-ding, and Ko-an, the bereaved sons. It was difficult to say whether they agreed to Chen-yi-tai's demands because they believed what she said, or because they did not want to incur the bad name of being unfilial, or perhaps even because they wanted to make things as difficult as they could for Chueh-hsin, the pregnant woman's husband and the chief mourner by virtue of being the first-born of his father, who was in turn the first-born of the dead. In any case they decided to follow Chen-yi-tai's suggestions. They insisted on Chueh-hsin's carrying out the require-

ments at once, since there was no question but that the welfare of
the grandfather, in life or in death, must be placed above everything else.

Chueh-hsin accepted these demands meekly, though they came
to him like a clap of thunder out of a clear sky. He did not say
one word in protest. He had, as a matter of fact, never uttered a
word of protest to any one in all his life, no matter how unjustly
he was used. Instead of manifesting any spirit of opposition he
would weep to himself and bury his indignation and his bitterness in his heart. He endured everything, not even stopping to
consider that in thus enduring things he might injure some one
else. That was the manner of man Chueh-hsin was; he was fated
to be always accepting unreasonable demands made on him as he
did in this instance.

When he returned to his own apartment and told Jui-chueh of
this development, she did not utter a word of complaint either.
She only cried, which was her way of showing that she did not
like the proposal. She was powerless to defend herself, and Chueh-
hsin was powerless to defend her. There was nothing for her to
do but allow herself to be twisted around as others wished.

"You know that I do not believe in these things, but what can
I do?" Chueh-hsin said, spreading out his upturned hands in
despair.

"I don't blame you; I only blame my own wretched fate,"
Jui-chueh said, sobbing. "Of course you cannot take upon yourself
the evil name of being unfilial. I could not let you do it even if
you wanted to for my sake."

"Forgive me, Chueh. I am weak and cowardly and cannot even
protect my own wife. We have shared our lives for several years
now . . . you ought to understand my difficulties."

"Don't say that," Jui-chueh continued, wiping her tears with
her handkerchief. "I understand your position. You have suffered
enough . . . You have been very good to me . . . I feel nothing
but gratitude."

"Gratitude? You must be joking! How much you've had to
put up with because of me! Now I have to let them send you out

to some lonely spot outside the city at a most difficult time, and you're not at all strong, and let you suffer the inconveniences of a strange place. It is unfair of me to shirk my responsibilities like this; it is I who have made you suffer. Tell me, can you think of any family that would treat a daughter-in-law like this? And yet you talk of gratitude!" He was overcome with sorrow and buried his face in his hands and began to cry.

Jui-chueh stopped weeping and stood up quietly and went out of the room without a word. A moment later she returned, leading Hai-chen, her son, by the hand and followed by Ho-sao, the maid servant.

Chueh-hsin was still weeping. Jui-chueh did not try to stop him herself, but pushed Hai-chen toward him and told the boy to speak to papa, to pull papa's hands away from his face, to ask him to stop crying and hold Hai-chen and play with him.

Chueh-hsin stopped crying. He took Hai-chen in his arms and looked at him with pity and affection. Then he kissed him and put him down before Jui-chueh, saying in a tone of bitterness: "There is no more hope for me, but take good care of Hai-erh and bring him up so that he won't be such a useless person like myself!" He started to go out, one hand still rubbing his eyes.

"Where are you going?" Jui-chueh asked with some anxiety.

"I have to go out to look for a house," he said with an effort, his eyes again filled with tears as he turned to look at her. Then he went out hurriedly, as though afraid that she might say something and cause him more grief.

Chueh-hsin returned very late. House hunting was not easy, but he managed to find a house with a little courtyard. It had a dirt floor and low papered windows and was dark and damp. The rent was cheap, but that was not the reason why Chueh-hsin had rented it; the reason was that he could not find anything better that would meet the two essential requirements: that it must be outside the city and that there must be an intervening bridge.

After the house had been inspected by Chen-yi-tai and then by Shen-shih and found satisfactory, Chueh-hsin began preparations to move his wife. Jui-chueh had planned to do her own packing, but he would not let her. He insisted on getting everything ready for her; he made her sit in a chair and watch him pack and would not let her touch anything. Not wishing to hurt his feelings, she acquiesced. He would pick out something that he thought she might need and bring it to her, asking, "How about taking this along?" She would nod her head with a smile and he would put it in the suitcase or net-covered basket. She almost invariably nodded assent or made encouraging remarks to his questions though they might be about things that she really had no need for, and he performed his task with enthusiasm. When he finished, he turned to her with a smile, saying: "See how well I have done! I know you well; I have come to understand you perfectly." She smiled back at him and said: "You have indeed; you have anticipated all my needs better than I know them myself. You are an excellent packer. Next time when I have to go on a long journey, I'll ask you to pack for me again." The last remark slipped from her before she realized its unhappy implications.

"Next time? Of course I'll go with you next time when you have to go away. I won't let you go by yourself. I won't let you leave me ever, wherever you may go," he reproved her good-naturedly.

They were both trying to fool each other, neither willing to reveal what was in their hearts. Both at heart wanted to cry but both assumed a smile, though their smiles did not conceal their sadness. He knew and she knew; he knew her heart and she knew his. But both deliberately hid what was in their hearts, both preferred to smile on their faces and cry in their hearts (though these deceptions only added to their sorrow) rather than to see the loved one shed tears.

When Shu-hua, Chueh-hsin's sister, came in with her cousin Shu-ying, they saw only what was on the surface; when Chueh-min and Chueh-hui, the two younger brothers, came in a while later, they too saw only what was on the surface,

However, the brothers could not maintain silence. Chueh-hui was the first to speak: "Da-ko are you really going to send saosao away?" He had heard about Chen-yi-tai's unreasonable demand but had not believed it. He had thought that it was only a sort of joke. But now when he saw the packing he realized that he had been mistaken.

Chueh-hsin nodded.

"Have you gone mad?" Chueh-hui asked in astonishment. "Could it be that you believe in those superstitions?"

"Do I believe in those superstitions?" Chueh-hsin repeated impatiently. "But what good does it do whether I believe in them or not? There are so many people in the family who do!"

"I think it's time that you resisted them," Chueh-hui said angrily, his eyes, which were not looking at Chueh-hsin but at the scene outside, full of hatred.

"Da-ko, San-di is right," Chueh-min said. "You should not give up without a struggle. Why don't you explain things to them first? They might realize· their folly. They are not devoid of intelligence."

"Intelligence?" Chueh-hsin said, still in a tone of impatience. "Since all the education they have had hasn't done them any good, what's the use of my explaining things to them? I have to do what they tell me because I cannot bear the evil name of being unfilial. But it is hard on your saosao."

"Why should it be hard for me? It will be quiet outside the city. Moreover, there will be the servants and you will all come to see me. I think I shall be very comfortable." Jui-chueh said this with a forced laugh which was almost indistinguishable from crying.

"You are again bowing to their unreasonable demands! I don't know why you are always bowing to them like this. You should remember the price that you have had to pay!" Cheuh-hui said passionately. "Take Erh-ko, for instance, he was almost sacrificed because of your submissiveness, he almost sacrificed his own happiness and that of some one else. It was only because he rose up in revolt himself that he won his final victory."

Chueh-min beamed with satisfaction when he heard Chueh-hui speak of him. He agreed with the latter that it was because he had the courage to run away that he won his happiness.

"Yes, you have won your battles," Chueh-hsin said with an air of self-deprecation. "You revolt against everything and sneer at everything and you have won your battles. But because you have succeeded in your revolts I have had to suffer all the more. They have always sought to take revenge on me for your opposition to them. They have heaped their hatred and scorn upon me and criticized me behind my back. . . . You can talk of revolt, you can renounce the family and run out . . . But what about me? Just think, what can I do? Can I run away as Erh-di did? Neither of you know what it has been like for me. There are so many things that you know nothing about. You have no idea how much I had to suffer because of Erh-di's refusal to marry the girl that Grandfather had picked out for him. You have no idea what I had to suffer because of San-di's friends and his magazine. I have kept all these things to myself. Only I myself know what I have had to go through. Neither of you will ever understand. You can indulge in such fine words as 'revolt' and 'struggle' but to whom can I use these fine words?" Here Chueh-hsin could no longer restrain his tears. He got up and went to his bed and slumped on it and covered up his face with his hands.

A wave of emotion engulfed every one in the room. First Jui-chueh broke down and began to weep. Shu-ying and Shu-hua tried to comfort her but their own voices were unsteady. Chueh-min's eyes too, were wet with tears. He began to regret that in his preoccupation with his own selfish interests he had overlooked his elder brother's suffering and to realize that he had been too inconsiderate of his feelings. He wondered what he could say to give him some degree of comfort.

Chueh-hui, however, did not shed a tear. He was, of course, affected by Chueh-hsin's tears and outburst, but he was over-powered by another passion which made it impossible for him to sympathize with his eldest brother: his heart was filled with hatred much more than with love. The placid lake in which Singing Phoenix[1] had drowned herself flashed before him and

[1] A slave girl whom the young man was fond of and who preferred death to becoming the concubine of a doddering old man, a friend of the late grandfather.

then the coffin in which she was laid. Then the present . . . and the future. These were things that he could not forget and they filled his heart to overflowing with hatred. He had, like his two brothers, inherited a capacity for love from his mother and he had, since his mother's death, tried to carry out her instructions, such as loving and helping others, reverence and obedience to his elders, and kindness to the servants. But how hateful his elders had turned out to be and how persistently the forces of darkness within his family had tried to destroy all feeling of love and affection! He had seen with his own eyes the unnecessary sacrifice of many young lives, and was even now being forced to watch helplessly the sacrifice of other young lives. He had, therefore, no sympathy to offer, and, though it was his own brother, he had nothing but contempt for his brother's non-resistance and hatred for the forces of oppression. "One woman has already died because of you," [2] he said coldly to Chueh-hsin, "I hope you won't be so spineless as to sacrifice another." He had a premonition of disaster as he uttered these words, but no one else in the room thought much about it. He stalked out of the room before any one had time to comment.

Back in his own room Chueh-hui was suddenly assailed by a feeling of loneliness which he had never experienced before. He saw life as a tragic stage, so full of tears and suffering. It appeared to him that there were entirely too many people for whom life was nothing but a process of weaving one's own destruction or the destruction of others. They could not avoid their own destruction in spite of all their struggle and suffering and often they dragged others down with them. His brother's fate lay clearly before him, but he was helpless to save him. Moreover, he knew that not only was his brother's fate like this, but that numerous others were headed along the same fatal road. "Why should there be so much bitterness in the world," he wailed to himself as instance after instance of such senseless suffering came to his mind.

[2] Referring to Chueh-hsin's sweetheart whom he gave up because of family opposition and who languished and died (so we are given to understand) after being unhappily married to a worthless young man.

"No matter what happens I shall not be like them. I must travel my own road, I must march ahead even though I have to walk on their corpses!" He finally thus encouraged himself. Wherewith he set forth for the Free Reading Room, there to meet his new-found friends in a common struggle.

At about the same time Chueh-hsin suppressed his sorrow and went to the new house with his wife. They were accompanied by Chou-shih, Chueh-hsin's stepmother, and Shu-ying and Shu-hua. Two servants were assigned to Jui-chueh, Chang-sao, a maid servant, and Yuan Cheng. Later Chueh-min and his cousin and fiancee Lute also went to see Jui-chueh settled in her new house.

The surroundings did offer many novelties, which, however, did not interest Jui-chueh. She had never lived in such a dismal house before and she had never been separated from Chueh-hsin since their marriage. Now on this occasion of their first separation it would last at least a month. She tried to comfort herself without any success. All she succeeded in doing was to affect an air of light-heartedness before the others, though she had to wipe off her tears when no one was watching.

It was soon time for the others to go back to the city.

"Why do you have to go all at once? Couldn't Sister Lute and Shu-ying stay a while longer?" Jui-chuch said.

"The city gates will be closed soon. We are quite a distance from the nearest gate. We'll come back to see you tomorrow," Lute replied.

"The city gate," Jui-chueh repeated, as if she did not know what that meant. But she knew all the time that she was not only separated from her husband by space but also by a gate that was closed from dusk to dawn, and that should anything happen to her during the night he would have no way of knowing and would not be able to come to her. She was like a criminal exiled to a strange land. "It is so quiet and lonely here," she said without thinking. "I am afraid."

"Don't worry, saosao, I'll move in tomorrow to keep you company," Shu-hua said.

"I'll speak to my mother and come to keep you company too," Shu-ying said.

"Chueh, be patient for a while. You'll get used to it after a few days. There are the two servants, both very reliable. The girls will move in tomorrow and I shall come to see you every day as long as I can. A month will soon pass." Chueh-hsin tried to comfort her with an affected optimism but at heart he only wished that he could hold her and cry.

Chou-shih also put in a few comforting words and then they all went. Jui-chueh accompanied them to the door and watched them get into their sedan chairs one by one.

Chueh-hsin had gotten into his chair, but he came out again and asked whether he could bring anything. Jui-chueh said that she had all she needed. "But bring Hai-chen tomorrow when you come," she said. "I miss him very much." She also said, "Take good care of Hai-chen." And again, "Do not write to my mother under any circumstances. She is sure to worry if she knew."

"I have written her already. I did not consult you because I knew you would not let me."

"Why did you have to write her? If she knew that I am now . . ." she did not finish because she did not want him to reproach himself.

"But we should let her know. If she should come to see you, you'd be better looked after."

They looked at each other in silence though they had so much to say to each other.

"I must go now," Chueh-hsin said after a few minutes.

"Come early tomorrow," Jui-chueh said, waving at him and watching him until the sedan chair turned the corner.

She thought of unpacking a few things, but she felt weak and faint and had to sit down. She felt the child stirring in her and seemed to hear its voice. In a fit of sorrow and irritation, she weakly patted her belly, saying, "You have brought all this on me!"

Chueh-hsin came early the next day and brought Hai-chen. Shu-hua moved in as she had promised. Shu-ying came but she could not stay because her father had not given her permission. Later on Lute also came. For a brief period the little courtyard was filled with gaiety and laughter.

But such moments of joy are all too brief; soon it was time to say goodbye again. Hai-chen did not want to leave his mother and they had to coax him to go away with Chueh-hsin.

"Come early again tomorrow," Jui-chueh said to Chueh-hsin as they parted at the gate, her eyes moist with tears.

"I am afraid that I won't be able to come tomorrow. The masons are going to come and I have to supervise them in the construction of the temporary tomb." He spoke sadly, but when he saw the tears in her eyes, he had not the heart to disappoint her. "I'll try to come tomorrow, I shall certainly come. Chueh, you mustn't cry. You must take good care of yourself. If anything should happen to you, I—" he did not go on for fear that he might burst out crying.

"I don't know myself why I am so easily grieved," she said, her eyes fixed on his face and stroking Hai-chen's cheeks with her hand. "I always feel as though we are not going to see each other again. I am afraid without myself knowing why."

"What is there to be afraid of? We are not so far away from each other and I can come to see you every day. Besides, you have now Shu-hua to keep you company."

"Is that the temple?" she suddenly asked, pointing to a rooftop not far to their right. I was told that Cousin Mei's coffin is stored there.[3] I should like to pay her a visit."

Chueh-hsin's countenance suddenly changed as he followed Jui-chueh's pointing finger. He quickly averted his eyes as a fearful thought occurred to him. He seized her hands and held them tightly as if afraid that someone might take her away from him. "Don't go, Chueh," he said. The tone of his voice was such that Jui-chueh could not forget it for a long time.

Without waiting for her to say anything he dropped her hands abruptly and said again, "I must be going now." Then bidding Hai-chen to say goodbye to his mother, he walked briskly to his

[3] Chueh-hsin's sweetheart.

sedan chair. The boy was still calling "Mama" when the bearers lifted the chair on their shoulders, but Chueh-hsin only forced back his tears in silence.

Back in their home Chueh-hsin met Chen-yi-tai coming out of the mourning hall.

"Da-shao-yeh, how is shao-nai-nai getting along?" she asked with a cunning smile.

"Not bad, thank you for asking," Chueh-hsin answered with a forced smile.

"Will it be soon?"

"I think it will be a few days yet."

"Remember, da-shao-yeh, you must not enter the birth-room!" Chen-yi-tai suddenly warned him solemnly. Then she left him with a kind of sneer.

This was not the first time that he had heard the warning; it had been given him three times already. But the state of mind he was in and the tone in which the warning was given all conspired to aggravate him and to rob him of the power of speech. He only stared after Chen-yi-tai, tears rolling down his cheeks, and was unheedful of Hai-chen, who was holding on to his hand and calling "Papa."

On the fourth day when Chueh-hsin went to see Jui-chueh, he was somewhat later than usual because of things that he had to attend to in the house. It was after three in the afternoon when he arrived.

He called to Jui-chueh as soon as he entered the gate, and hurried towards her room. But he had barely got one foot in the door when he was blocked by Chang-sao, the maid servant. "Da-shao-yeh, you cannot come in!" she said with an anxious expression on her face. He understood what it meant without another word from her.

Instinctively he withdrew his foot without the slightest protest and Chang-sao shut and bolted the door. After standing in the center room for a while, he went outside to Jui-chueh's window and stood there lost in thought. He experienced a variety of conflicting emotions, bitter and yet sweet, joy and sorrow, anger and satisfaction. A few years back he had had a similar experience but it was similar only in certain superficial details. She was now lying in bed as before, she was groaning with birth pains; as before there were light footsteps in the room and the sound of low voices. But now she was in a strange place away from home and was denied his presence. He was not allowed, as he had been before, to see her, to comfort and encourage her and thus to mitigate her pain. He was afraid and self-reproachful and kept repeating to himself: "I was the one who brought this upon her."

"Shao-nai-nai, how do you feel?" he heard Chang-sao's voice ask.

There was a silence.

Then suddenly the silence was broken by repeated groans and cries which made Chueh-hsin shudder and grit his teeth. He knew who it must be that the groans and cries came from, but it was so unlike Jui-chueh's usual voice that he found it difficult to reconcile himself to the obvious facts. He pressed his face against the window but could not see anything through it.

"Shao-nai-nai, try to bear it. It will be all right after a while," the unfamiliar voice of the midwife said.

There was another cry of pain, accompanied by the sound of some one violently rolling on the bed.

The door to her room suddenly opened and Chang-sao hurried out and went into another room. At first it did not occur to Chueh-hsin to rush in to his wife; he only stared at the open door and caught glimpses of people moving inside. When he did summon up enough courage to go in, it was already too late; Chang-sao had gone back and shut the door.

He pushed at the door a few times without receiving any attention from inside. He was about to withdraw to the courtyard when horrible cries again came from the room. He pushed hard at the door and pounded on it.

"Let me in!" he cried. There was fear, pain, and passion in his voice.

No one answered, no one opened the door. His wife continued to cry out in pain.

"Let me in! Let me in!" he shouted angrily, pounding the door with his fist.

"Da-shao-yeh, you cannot come in! I don't dare open the door to you. I have San-lao-yeh [4] and Chen-yi-tai's orders . . ." Chang-sao answered just inside the door.

"Where is da-shao-yeh? Where is he?" Jui-chueh wailed in a piteous voice. "Why doesn't he come to see me? Chang-sao, go and get da-shao-yeh to come!" She broke off into groans again.

"Chueh, I am here, I am here. I am coming to you. Open the door! Let me in quickly! She wants me! Let me in." He shouted at the top of his voice, forgetting entirely his usual reserve, and again pounded at the door with his fist.

"Hsin, where are you? Why can't I see you? . . . Oh . . . Where are you? Why don't you let him in? . . ."

"Chueh, I am here, I am coming in! I shall watch by your side and not leave you . . . Let me in. See how she suffers! Have you no pity for her?" He shouted hoarsely, pounding at the door with all his might.

Jui-chueh's voice now stopped and gave place to confused voices and footsteps; he knew that she must have fainted.

After an intolerable interval she began to call for him again, imploring him to come and rescue her from her pains, and he shouted back to her that he was right there and begged them to let him in. He called upon his sister to open the door for him, appealing to her intelligence, but no one opened the door for him.

Jui-chueh's voice again stopped and no one in the room spoke. Suddenly a baby's cries broke the silence.

"Thanks to Heaven and Earth," he said with relief. His fear and sorrow gave way to an indescribable happiness. "I shall love her and care for her more than ever from now on," he thought to himself, "and I shall love her second-born."

"Saosao!" A fearful voice suddenly came from the room and struck him like a rock. "Her hands have become cold!" It was his sister's unsteady voice.

"Shao-nai-nai!" Chang-sao, the maid servant, began to call also.

4 Chueh-hsin's oldest uncle, hence the head of the family.

Chueh-hsin knew that the worst was about to happen. He struck again at the door and shouted and implored them to let him in, but no one paid any attention to him. The door still blocked everything in the room from him, still unyielding, still denying him a chance to have a last meeting with his wife.

He kept on calling to his wife though the women inside had begun to wail. "Chueh, I am calling to you. Can you hear me? . . ." This was not only a cry of sorrow and grief; it was also the cry of life, a vain attempt to call back to this world one who was already well on the way to another. He was not only trying to stay some one else's life but also his own, for he knew what life would be like for him if she died.

But Death came.

Some one inside approached the door. He thought that they were going to open the door to him, but it was only the midwife with the newborn infant who spoke through the door: "Congratulations, da-shao-yeh. It is a young master." Then she walked away from the door murmuring to herself: "What a pity to be born without a mother to care for him!"

The last words lacerated his heart, robbed him of a father's joy at the birth of his son. The child was no longer his beloved son but his foe, a foe who had robbed him of his beloved wife.

He had resolved that he would disregard everything and go to his wife, confess to her his mistakes of the years past, and beg for her forgiveness. But it was now too late, too late because a flimsy door barred the way to love and stood between him and his beloved, refusing to let him have a last parting with her.

Then he realized that it was tradition and superstition, not the door, that kept him from his wife in her hour of trial and death, that it was these things that robbed him of his youth and happiness, robbed him of his future and of the two women that he had loved most. But at the very moment he told himself that the burden of tradition was too oppressive to bear and that it must be fought against, he also realized his own weakness and how hopeless it was for him to struggle against it. In his despair and helplessness he knelt before the door and abandoned himself to weeping, weeping not so much for her as for himself.

Two sedan chairs stopped outside the gate. Chou-shih, Chueh-hsin's stepmother, came in with Chueh-hsin's mother-in-law, followed by Yuan Cheng, the servant.

When Chou-shih heard the sound of weeping, her color changed. "Too late!" she said in a panic-stricken voice to her companion. They both hurriedly went into the center room.

"What are you doing?" Chou-shih cried in astonishment when she saw Chueh-hsin kneeling outside the door of the inner room.

Chueh-hsin glanced back and then stood up and said to Chou-shih: "It is too late." Then he saw his mother-in-law and greeted her in a voice that betrayed both shame and sorrow. He burst out crying anew. The bereaved mother said nothing but only wiped her eyes with her handkerchief.

The door was now opened to Yuan Cheng's knocking. Chou-shih said to the other woman: "Please enter, I cannot go in myself."

She went in and there immediately came from the room her loud wailing: "Chueh-erh, how could you have the heart to leave me like this? Why wouldn't you wait for a last meeting with your mother? I have come a long way to see you. Tell me everything. Come back and tell me everything, Chueh-erh. I am late, but why couldn't you have waited a little while longer. How grievously have you died, my bitter-fated child. See how lonely and abandoned you are here. You have been driven out of your house and abandoned. If I had come earlier, you would not have died. My bitter-fated child! It is my fault that you have died . . ."

Chou-shih and Chueh-hsin heard every word she said, and each word pierced their hearts like a needle.

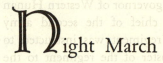

Night March

By Shen Ts'ung-wen

In the year 1919 I was living in a small town on the Hunan-
Kweichou border known as Yüshuwan. I have often described this
region and its life in my stories. Take, for instance, a piece I wrote
recently, entitled "My Education"; its setting was laid in Huaihua,
a town about forty li from Yüshuwan. I lived at both places for
some time and learned a good many things about life. The difference was that when I was at Huaihua, I was a private and my
life consisted largely of three things: cleaning my gun, watching
executions, and cooking and eating dog meat. But shortly before
I went to Yüshuwan, I was promoted from a private with six
dollars a month to a clerk in regimental headquarters by the military judge whose specialty was to extort confessions from prisoners.
My pay was increased to nine dollars and thirty cents a month.
I was put down as a first-class private in the official records, but
by courtesy I was referred to as a *shih-yeh,* a comprehensive honorific title given to non-combatant officers by the men. I got an
opportunity to write and draw and learned to sit at a desk for
indefinite periods without feeling tired. If I want to trace back
and find how I became what I am today, my life during this period
is worth careful consideration. As to that military judge, I shall
always remember his kindness to me though he was a rascal, a
ruthless extortionist of innocent but helpless prisoners, an accom-
plice of the executioner. The obvious reason why I was noticed
and promoted by him was my fondness for calligraphy, but there
was another reason, which makes me less grateful when I think
of it.

The reason was that in the midst of our carefree life of watching executions, eating dog meat and so on, an order suddenly came from a certain General Chang, the civil governor of Western Hunan and concurrently the commander in chief of the second army corps of the Ching Kuo Chün. Our regiment was instructed to send in within a specified time the roster of the regiment to the last man, together with a complete list of every piece of firearms. He needed this information for the military conference about to be convened at Chenchou. If the regiment did not comply with the instructions, it would jeopardize its present status and might face disbandment. With the order came a large batch of printed forms, which looked very complicated and confusing even to the most experienced secretaries and councilors at headquarters. They despaired in the face of these forms and blanks, not so much because they were incapable of making out the requirements (for even in such an irregular regiment like ours there was no lack of officers trained in advanced military schools) as because such work was distasteful to them. It seemed that the regiment had never had such a strict higher-up since it was organized during the expedition against Yuan Shih-k'ai in 1916. Though every month we had to send in a roster with a receipt properly filled out before the regiment's pay was issued, the figures had always been a matter of estimate and guesswork, always on the liberal side. But the printed forms made the customary laxity impossible. In the form to be filled in for rifles, it was necessary to give the make, serial number, and rounds of ammunition. The conference at Chenchou was only two months off, which meant that we must get the reports ready in about forty days in order that we, who had been occupied with the suppression of bandits, might not be looked upon as bandits ourselves. Since it was impossible to summon the various units to headquarters to conduct the investigation, agents had to be sent to the units instead. The outcome of this was a dearth of clerks, which in turn made the military judge think of me and thus brought about my promotion.

Three days after my promotion we were transferred to Yüshuwan, which was very much like Huaihua, the only difference being that it had a postal agency and a Christian church. As before we were stationed in a temple.

My new job was very agreeable. I copied what orders and other documents there were to be copied and used my spare time to practice calligraphy. Sometimes I would imitate the cursive writing of the commandant. Tiring of this occupation, I would watch my superiors play chess. I did not lack opportunities of speaking with my superiors, and they were not stingy in their commendation of my work.

Yüshuwan had also a fair, which came on days when the numerals four and nine occurred. Though I was now a *shih-yeh*, I still went to the fair on market days, being encouraged by the military judge to go and bring back dog meat. I would cook this myself for the greedy palates of my superiors. My old habits and interests had not changed. I liked to eat sometimes among the men, and I still liked to go out with some of my former comrades for a drink or to watch the women wash clothes along the river.

Unless I had something very pressing to do, I never missed an opportunity to see for myself how people actually cut out the hearts and livers of human beings. This performance I saw altogether eleven times. Once I saw a man inject fine powdered silver into a human gall bladder. I was told that thus impregnated that human organ became even more efficacious than bear's gall bladder in curing strange ailments such as only rich people can afford to have. But what I wanted to know most was how the heart looked in the frying pan. I had been told that it would quiver and jump about fearfully. I found that this was not true. Those stupid creatures! if their hearts had been living, pulsating things, they would not have allowed others to cut off their heads without a struggle. Since they died so meekly and never tried to cut off other people's heads, it was no wonder that their hearts did not jump in the frying pan.

One day the gatekeeper told me how he once ate a piece of a woman's tongue. He was serious and not just telling a tale. He said a friend of his had quarreled with his mistress, who later had relations with a tinsmith and plotted with the latter to murder his friend. When his friend found out about this (the tinsmith had betrayed her), he went to the woman's house, pulled out her tongue and cut it off. The gatekeeper happened to visit him at the time and was invited to partake of his solitary feast. It was not until later that he found out what he had eaten. He vomited for a whole month. Cannibalism is really not so extraordinary, though city people always connect it with savagery. That's because they are sentimental and ignorant of conditions in China. In reality cannibalism is very common; the difference lies only in the manner of eating. Even now I have frequent opportunities to see how certain classes of people are devoured by others. It is for this reason that I am able to talk, without undue show of emotion, about the strange and savage things that I have seen.

About twenty days after my promotion, it fell to my lot to go to the headquarters of one of the battalions and draw up a new report, as there were some mistakes in the one turned in. The battalion was quartered in a dismal village about twenty-five li away across the mountains. The clerk who went before did not want to make the wretched journey again. He knew that I was a relative of the major in command and that I would be glad to make the journey. He gave many very good reasons why I should go, among them the preposterous one that I alone was capable enough for the difficult task. There was some truth in what he said, for I did know something about guns as I had been promoted from the ranks. Another reason he gave for recommending me was that I was very young and needed the prestige that a mission such as this would give me. He fanned my vanity. Later he was responsible for goading me on to other foolish ventures which helped to make me what I am today.

My calligraphy was not very presentable at the time, certainly not as good as that of this experienced clerk. As far as filling out the forms was concerned, however, it was quite possible that I knew more than the bearded clerks, for I was young and curious and had pored over the forms with great interest.

I had to start immediately. I did not have to take many things with me, or perhaps I should say that I did not have many things to take with me. I tied a towel through my belt and took along my regulation tin cup. I had four companions, men who were returning to my destination with pay for the battalion. Among them was a corporal, a very estimable character. They were armed, and their company gave me courage. I was not worried about the leopard reported to be lurking in the mountains which we had to pass through.

We were having the heavy, gloomy weather characteristic of the south in February. Some people were already eating their suppers when we reached the outskirts of the town. We estimated that we would have made fifteen li before dark, but we were mistaken and total darkness came upon us when we had barely reached the bridge ten li from Yüshuwan. We warmed ourselves by the fire in the tea hut by the bridge, had some tea and food, lit our torches and lanterns, and continued our way.

We were soon in the mountains. Our torches crackled loudly in the stillness of the night, their flames glared and leaped. We brushed close against sheer rocks, passed over dangerous ledges, crossed chattering brooks. I did not feel lonely since I had my four companions. I put myself in the middle of the procession. I felt that there was a certain beauty to this night march, and this feeling made me forget the rigors of the journey. The path wound through ever-changing scenery. Sometimes it crawled up overhanging cliffs, sometimes wound its way into narrow canyons. Imposing stone walls rose on every hand, and everywhere dark, forbidding woods. Occasionally we passed by the ruins of ancient oil mills and long deserted houses, whose impressive walls recalled the glory of their erstwhile owners. We would lift high our torches for a better view of these ruins. Mystery lurked all around us, but marching between my four companions, who were all young and fearless and sang as they went, I had no occasion to be afraid; I was only intoxicated by the beauty of the night.

I don't know how they calculated distance in those mountainous parts, for it seemed a very long twenty-five li after we had marched for a good four or five hours. When I asked the corporal how far we were from our destination, he was not able to tell me but only told me the places that we must pass before we reached our goal. From what he told me I judged that though we had been marching half the night, we had not yet covered quite two thirds of the total distance. I began to feel tired.

We came to a stream. The water was swift and seemed deep, for no protruding rocks could be seen. If it had been day, we would have had no difficulty in contriving some way of crossing an even deeper and wider stream, for few of the soldiers in those regions did not know how to swim. But now it was different, for it was night and we had our guns and ammunition and the money we were carrying to think about. Besides, it was no weather in which to risk the cold of the water. Hence after a brief consultation we decided to follow the stream. The more experienced corporal favored our following the downward course on the chance that we might come upon a boat, but the other three men all favored an opposite direction, maintaining that there would probably be a bridge farther up at some narrow point, or, if luck was against us, we might walk across the lock of some water mill that we were sure to find. If the worst came to the worst, they further maintained, we could pass the night in the mill instead of exposing ourselves to the raw night wind. At the same time we heard a strange, persistent sound in the distance which suggested a mill. I threw my support to the majority. The corporal yielded with an air of a man who was convinced that he knew better.

None of us had any idea of what lay ahead of us; we were all strangers in that region. The corporal was the only one who had made the journey before—over ten times, as a matter of fact—but he had always followed the main road and was therefore as un-familiar with the course we had chosen as the rest of us. But we were all very young; we knew that it was unlikely we would be attacked by a large band of bandits and we were not afraid of wild beasts or ghosts. We had many opportunities to ford the stream, but passed these by as the sound that had attracted us came nearer and nearer. The corporal led the way, swinging and waving his torch. Suddenly one of my comrades discovered that our supply of torches would be exhausted in at most another three li. The lantern was totally inadequate on an inky night like this and on such an uneven road. We cursed and regretted our rashness.

We picked our way for another li, drawing nearer and nearer to the reassuring hum, which came full upon us as we rounded a corner. The absence of light disconcerted us. We pushed on for another half li before we came to what turned to be an unsheltered irrigation wheel. There was no mill, deserted or otherwise, and all our pleasant anticipations of a warm fire or even something more romantic (for one of the men had once had a piece of very good luck with a miller's daughter) came to nothing. We were too disheartened to go on. To turn back? No one had the courage to suggest such a thing. Besides, our torches would not last the return journey. It seemed that unless something unexpected happened we had to pass a night in the open. We could not find anything with which to make more torches. If the stream had been dry, we could have pulled off some pieces of bamboo from the huge wheel of the bucket pump, but it was now turning in the stream with mocking regularity, soaked through with water.

It was the corporal (who has long since rotted away. May he rest in peace, unperturbed by the recounting of this story!) who finally conceived the idea of climbing up the hill to see if we could spot any light. This suggestion gave us new hope and we eagerly made the ascent. We looked around carefully and soon spotted a light about a li away. After we had made sure that it was no will-o'-the-wisp we pushed on toward it through thickets and terraced fields filled with water. We reached the foot of the hill without any mishap. The corporal suddenly became cautious. He bade us remain about twenty meters behind, discard our torches, and turn down the wick of the lantern. He gave his gun to me and marched ahead of us. We could now make out the lonely house from which the light came. We fell upon our bellies and trained our guns upon the house while the corporal walked briskly towards it, waving his torch. We were tense, though we had no fear. If the corporal should suddenly throw away his torch or should cry out, I knew that I would be the first one to open fire, for I suddenly thought of the stories of bandits that I had heard and felt sure that this was a bandits' den. We had recently executed a notorious bandit chief and the revengeful inhabitants had cut him up and taken out his heart. The bandits might be holding a meeting to discuss measures of taking revenge, and our corporal might be caught and cut up and his heart made into a "broth for curing hangovers." I held the cold and damp rifle in position, my eyes fixed on the house. I could hear the breathing of my comrades, though they were spread out ten meters apart.

The corporal was now at the gate. He knocked. A dog barked. A man opened the gate and was talking with the corporal. We lowered our guns, somewhat disappointed now that there was nothing to fear and feeling a little foolish at our absurd precaution. The corporal called to us. We rushed over and found the corporal talking with a weary old man, who looked at us with sad eyes and ushered us in without further ado and led the way across the courtyard. The dog, which had bells around its neck, sniffed at us and having satisfied itself that we were respectable people, turned around and joined its master at the head of the procession. I was still a bit wary, for the man did not seem to be glad of our company, and I could not help thinking of stories of drugged wine and sausages made of human flesh. So I stayed behind in the procession, ready to spring back if those in front should fall into a camouflaged pit.

But when I entered the house, I felt ashamed of my suspicion. There were only three rooms. The door through which we entered opened into the center room. Scrolls of painting and calligraphy hung from the center wall. There was a lamp on the only table in the room and a large book and a teapot. To the left a door led into what seemed to be the bedroom. It was locked from the outside. To the right was the kitchen, with a large water jar near the door. The simplicity and the cleanliness of the old man's house turned my thoughts in another direction, causing me to play with the idea that this old man was perhaps a hermit sage, an immortal. The crackling of the torch we left outside attracted my attention; I left the room to stamp it out. One of the soldiers joined me and we looked through the window of the other room. There seemed to be a bed in it and some one seemed to be in the bed, but we did not have time to make sure as the corporal then called to us. We stamped out the fire and went back into the house. The old man took us into the kitchen and told us that we could suit ourselves if we wanted to build a fire and heat some water.

Upon enquiry we found that we were more than ten li out of our way. He invited us to stay for the night, saying that even with plenty of torches one often got lost in the mountains. He asked us where we had had our supper and when he found that we needed something to eat, he took us to a corner of the kitchen and showed us where the rice was. He gave us about a dozen eggs, and pointed out where the oil, salt, and things were. He even took down with a long-handled hook two dried fish that were hanging from the rafters. I held the lamp for him while he did this, so I had a chance to steal a glance at his book when I put the lamp back on the table. I did not know why I felt that there was something unusual about the old man, that an unearthly radiance seemed to emanate from his face. Though I found that the book was only a volume of the works of Chuangtze, I could not dismiss the notion that this old man was not of this mortal world. I said nothing to him of what I thought and I said nothing to my comrades. I only treated him with great reverence, expecting almost any time that he would say to me, as the Immortal Huang Shih-kung said to Chang Liang after the latter had retrieved his shoes for him for the third time, that I was a good boy, worthy to receive the book of heavenly secrets.

As we ate our late supper, the old man sat with bowed head as if deep in thought. To the questions of the corporal he gave what seemed to me enigmatical answers. Surely he was at least an estimable hermit if not an immortal, I said to myself. I became even more reverent towards him. I wished that the corporal would show more sense and ask questions that would throw some light upon this man of mystery, and I was irritated that he did not, he who had shown so much good sense and leadership while we were groping about out in the darkness. But why did I not ask the old man myself? Why did I not show off my learning before this mysterious hermit so that he might see that I was a boy worth salvaging? Many contradictory traits in my character showed themselves at that relished supper. Generally speaking, my nature is such that I feel very much like a man in love when I greatly admire some one; I feel inspired but at the same time awkward and tongue-tied. Because of this character trait I have suffered the ridicule of I do not know how many women and lost I do not know how many friends.

It was well past midnight when we finished our supper, but because we had no bedding with us and we knew that the new rice straw would make us itch, none of us thought of sleep. We could not all of us have gone to sleep anyway, as our military training forbade such a thing, in spite of the repeated assurance of our host that there could not possibly be any danger. We all agreed to the corporal's suggestion that we sit around the fire through the night. Our host went into the bedroom and brought out a bag of chestnuts and a basket of sweet potatoes for us to roast over the fire; he seemed to be planning to keep us company through the long winter night. Our corporal told him that he must not let us keep him from going to bed, but the old man only smiled sadly and shook his head, saying that he would not have gone to bed even if we had not been there, that he was glad of our company, that it was we who were keeping him company and not he us. No one understood then what he meant.

We chatted and ate chestnuts around the fire. After a while I suggested that we should pass the night telling one another true stories of our own experience, and that if every one was agreeable I would tell the story of my grandfather as an introduction. The soldiers were naturally enthusiastic; the old man also nodded indulgently. So I began.

My story was neither well delivered nor entirely authentic. I never did take the trouble to corroborate it. I only repeated what my father had told me about grandfather. My father said that grandfather was once fighting a tall and strong Taiping rebel. Grandfather was defeated and fled into a river, as he was a good

swimmer. The rebel, seeing that the water only reached grandfather's chest, followed, but went down immediately as he did not
know how to swim. Grandfather then turned around, caught the
rebel by the hair, and held him under water until he drowned.
Grandfather dragged him to the shore, cut off his head, and went
back to camp with it. For this he was made a general and later
became the garrison commander of Chaot'ung in Yunnan. I told
this story because I wanted to impress on the hermit that I was no
common soldier but was descended from a general. This childish
vanity has made me do many foolish things; even now I am not
entirely free from it.

This was only an introduction, and so I had no sooner finished
than it was again my turn. I told a ghost story wherein the ghost
turned out to be nothing more than a thief: I made the ghost a
very real one, a walking corpse, no less. I had my eyes on the old
man by the fire as I told the story. He smiled strangely, which
I interpreted as another evidence of the secret understanding between us. I pretended not to have noticed him and urged the
soldier sitting next to me to go on.

He was a dark, fat, and diminutive man in his early twenties,
very fond of talking about women. He told us that he had a mistress
once, a Miaotze woman whose husband was a medicine man. He
used to meet her night after night in the wood behind her house.
Needless to say, they met without the knowledge of the red-
turbaned husband, for the custom there was very much the same
as elsewhere: if the husband did not receive his wife's lover with
meat and wine, he received him with knife or spear. One night
the lover could not meet his mistress at the appointed time because
of important business that had suddenly turned up. He sent one of
his friends to tell the woman of the unavoidable delay. When he
had finished his business and hurried to the wood, he was incensed
to discover in the pale moonlight his mistress and his friend in close
embrace under a tree. He rushed up to them, but found, to his
horror, that they were pierced together by a long spear against the
tree!

The stories of the other two soldiers and the corporal were neither

exciting in themselves nor well told, so that our interest began to
lag until it came to our host's turn. We were all eagerness again,
especially myself, obsessed as I was with the idea that he was an
extraordinary man with a great secret to reveal. I wanted to hear
something from his own mouth, some sign, some hint that would
enable me to divine and reconstruct his secret.

The old man reflected a moment, but shook his head and said
that he did not have any story to tell, that it was getting toward
dawn, and that we ought to put on some water for our morning
wash. When I objected, he looked at me and said why didn't I
tell another? I can't help laughing when I recall my eagerness at
the time. I thought that surely this old man, this immortal in dis-
guise, was trying my worth. I told another story without any
hesitation. The old man seemed to enjoy it; he smiled and asked
for another, and like the fool I was, I again obliged, with growing
excitement as I felt more and more sure that the old man was no
common mortal.

It was getting light and cocks began to crow in the distance.
My comrades were dozing as I finished my story. I was wide awake,
however, and persistently begged the old man to tell me a story.
The latter looked at the fire and then at my dozing comrades.
"I want to go to my room and take a look," he said at last. "If you
insist on having my story, you can come with me." I followed him
with a palpitating heart. I had passed all the tests. At last he was
going to show me his treasures and reveal to me his secrets.

At first glance I could only see the usual jars and baskets with
provisions in them. When I turned my eyes to the bed that I had
seen dimly from the outside, however, I was shocked to find the
corpse of a woman in it, yellow like wax, dried and shriveled up
like a potato that has been exposed to the wind.

"What!" I exclaimed. "You have a dead person in the house?"

The old man did not lose his strange calm. He only looked at
me with sad eyes and sighed softly.

"This is my story," he said. "The dead one is my wife. I have
lived with her in this lonely spot for sixteen years. She died last
night at supper time. If you had not come, I would have had to

sit by her all by myself for the night. I am going to die myself very soon. I have no story to tell except this. It is getting to be broad daylight. Heat the water yourself. I do not want to prolong my existence any longer than is necessary, but I must go and dig a place for her . . . so that she can wait down there for me in peace."

I was too astonished to speak. I began to understand the look of sadness in the old man's face, why he had locked his bedroom door from the outside. The calm of the man chilled me now.

I got the hot water ready and woke up my dozing comrades. As we washed our faces, I heard, to the left of the house, the sound of digging as the spade fell slowly and weakly upon the damp earth.

It was then broad daylight.

Smile!

By Chang T'ien-yi

"Look, Chiang-san, what a pretty face Fa-hsin-sao has!"

Chiang-san laughed, sticking up one thumb: "Chiu-yeh has good eyes. You do have good eyes, I say."

"How strange that a country lout should have such a wife. It's like sticking a flower in a pile of dung for Fa-hsin to have such a nice morsel of white flesh in his mouth. Our Fa-hsin-sao is . . . What do you say, Fa-hsin-sao?"

As Chiu-yeh leaned toward Fa-hsin-sao the lamplight struck one side of his red face, showing up clear and distinct his large pores. He grinned and showed a row of irregular teeth, some yellow and some black. Two of them glittered in the light, the color of old brass. Li Tao-shih used to say that they were not real gold but only covered with yellow tin foil which foreigners use to wrap up their candy in.

That was what Li Tao-shih used to say. Now no one dared to say anything disparaging about Chiu-yeh. Even Li Tao-shih changed his tune: "That ring around Chiu-yeh's finger is made of solid gold."

Then he would sigh and comment upon the evil days that had befallen. "These are trying days, years of visitation. The bandits have not given us here any trouble only because of Chiu-yeh. If not for him . . ."

"Chiu-yeh has a few tricks. Formerly he . . ."

But formerly no one thought much of him. In the meantime he had somehow come up in the world: he had quite a few henchmen and had a monopoly of the drug traffic in the district.

And he commanded the local militia.

Chiu-yeh was a clever man. Otherwise why should His Honor Ming put so much trust in him? His Honor was the nominal head of the militia but actually Chiu-yeh had charge of everything.

"Leave everything to me," Chiu-yeh would say, thumping his chest. "Don't worry. I'll be responsible for anything that might happen in our district."

He wasn't boasting either. He had no difficulty in dealing with the people in the district, men or women. He had, for instance, dealt swiftly with that insolent egg Yang Fa-hsin, and he had no trouble with Fa-hsin's wife. All he had to do was to send Chiang-san to talk to her and there she was right in front of him.

He fixed his eyes on her and stuck his head closer and closer to her. His eyes were discolored with red threads, his left eye only about half the size of his right.

Fa-hsin-sao did not dare to look at his face; she only stared at the buttons on his coat.

But a hand seized her shoulder, a cold tongue cut at her chin like a chisel.

"Don't . . . don't . . ."

She twisted herself free and retreated to the door.

Chiang-san, who was in the act of conveying the wine cup to his lips, suddenly guffawed and almost dropped it.

Chiu-yeh frowned, his right eye growing larger still. In a shrill voice—

"Eh . . . !"

To tell the truth, he had not been thus rebuffed for a long time. The woman said in a trembling voice: "Chiu-yeh, Chiu-yeh, I beg you . . ."

"What, are you backing out?"

"Chiu-yeh, you are . . ."

Chiang-san decided that he had done enough laughing. He took a drink, wiped his thick lips with the back of his hand and stole a glance at Chiu-yeh's face. " 'Tisn't going right, 'tisn't going right," he thought to himself.

He knew Chiu-yeh: Chiu-yeh didn't like to be crossed in anything. If Fa-hsin-sao should refuse to do what was good for her, he, Chiang-san, would be held accountable.

"Hey! Fa-hsin-sao," Chiang-san stood up and approached her.

Her face was pale.

"Think it over, Fa-hsin-sao, think it over. I tell you, you had better be nice to Chiu-yeh, so that . . ."

He belched and stole another glance at Chiu-yeh.

"Hm, Hm, Hm."

The noise through Chiu-yeh's nose sounded partly as if he was trying to clear his throat and partly like a sneer.

"It was her own idea in the first place. Do I look as if I couldn't get all the women I want? What do I care whether she . . ."

It was true that Fa-hsin-sao meant little to Chiu-yeh. He had three concubines and several "regulars" in the city brothels, besides occasional purchases. He wanted her only because she was new and because . . ."

"And because I want to show Yang Fa-hsin what I, Chiu-yeh, can do to him. How dare he, a country lout, disturb the earth over my head? *Heng,* I'll show him. I'll make him suffer the consequences of the law and make a cuckold of him besides. I'll show him what it means to cross me!"

But just now Fa-hsin-sao had her sweaty hand on the door, ready to run away.

Chiu-yeh sat down, his right eye twitching. His huge shadow darkened the entire room.

The third person in the room first looked at Chiu-yeh and then at Fa-hsin-sao. He belched. Something came up, but he swallowed it down.

"Better think what you're doing, Fa-hsin-sao, think what you're doing. You mustn't . . ."

Suddenly the door opened and Fa-hsin-sao dashed out.

Chiang-san followed immediately and caught hold of her: "You can't run away, you can't run away!"

She struggled against him.

"Hey, hey, hey!" Chiang-san warned her in a low voice. "Do you want your Fa-hsin to live or don't you? Do you or don't you?"

Silence. Fa-hsin-sao stood still, panting.

"You know how Chiu-yeh is." Chiang-san spoke in her ear. He reeked of liquor and his voice made her ear ring though he tried to lower it. "Chiu-yeh has had your Fa-hsin arrested; he has his life in his hands. If you won't . . ."

"But I . . . but I . . ."

"*Hey,* listen to me, listen."

He looked around as if afraid of being overheard. He suddenly belched, frightening himself. He put his right hand to his mouth for a while.

"Chiu-yeh wants to have Fa-hsin punished as a bandit. Yes, as I have said, he can . . ."

Fa-hsin-sao wailed: "But how could he be a bandit!"

"*Hey,* don't shout."

After a brief silence, Chiang-san spoke slowly: "Listen to me. Chiu-yeh has often told His Honor Ming that the peasants are not very law-abiding nowadays and that Fa-hsin is their ring leader. Yes, Chiu-yeh said that to His Honor. Now let me see—yes, the other day Fa-hsin actually dared to talk back to Chiu-yeh, and cursed him and threatened him with physical violence. Of course Chiu-yeh had him arrested . . . Now Fa-hsin is suffering the consequences of the law, as you know. If you will be nice to Chiu-yeh, I assure you that Chiu-yeh will have him released, I assure you. If you . . ."

Chiang-san searched her face.

A ray of light shone through a crack in the door and played on Fa-hsin-sao.

"Think it over," Chiang-san said.

Fa-hsin-sao glanced at the door.

What was Chiu-yeh doing in the room? He might be drinking quietly inside, smiling with unconcern and twitching his right eye. But then it might be that he was being very angry, and thinking up ways of torturing Fa-hsin and then charge him with banditry and have his head cut off.

Then Fa-hsin's head would be hung up on a tree the next day

and His Honor Ming would give Chiu-yeh a banquet and slap
him on his shoulder—

"You have done it: You have rid the district of a great menace."
Fa-hsin and His Honor Ming have been enemies for a long time.

And then her entire family—her blind and deaf old mother-in-
law and her two children and herself—they would all . . .

Chiang-san knew that Fa-hsin-sao understood these things. He
belched and swallowed again and urged her repeatedly: "You think
it over, think it over. Let me tell you."

He waited for a sign of her yielding so that he could go to Chiu-
yeh and report the success of his mission.

But the other only bit her lips and said nothing.

Suddenly there was a crashing sound in the room, making both
of them jump.

Four eyes stared at the door, wondering whether there might be
a sequel.

Silence.

Chiang-san wiped his mouth with the back of his hand and began
to talk in a confidential tone to Fa-hsin-sao. After the warning
sound from the room he must finish his job as soon as possible.
He wanted her to know that Chiu-yeh could be a generous man if
she consented.

"Money means nothing to Chiu-yeh."

He asked her if it were not true that she needed money then
and again belched as if affirming his own question.

"You are short of money, aren't you? Isn't that right, eh?"

Of course he was right; he knew how it was with Fa-hsin-sao.
Her two children were waiting to be fed and were crying themselves hoarse for her; she could see her two-year-old daughter
crawling on the ground, sniveling and stuffing dirt into her mouth.
Then there was the old mother-in-law, mumbling no one knew
what to herself all day long. Her stomach, too, had to be filled. She
did not know yet that her son had been arrested and was suffering
the consequences of the law.

Fa-hsin-sao needed money, too, at the militia headquarters. A little money stuffed into the proper hands would make Fa-hsin suffer less.

Chiang-san sighed and urged Fa-hsin-sao solicitously to think it over.

"Think well, think well," he imitated the doleful manner in which His Honor Ming had urged the famine refugees to leave the district a few years back, as if he were about to cry any moment. "You are most pitiable. *Ai,* you are . . ." He shook his head, so sorrowful that he could hardly lift his face. "However, Chiu-yeh is willing to save Fa-hsin, yes, willing to save him, I tell you. If you would consent and be real nice to him, he will give you money and save your Fa-hsin. If you won't do what he wants, then . . ."

Then Chiu-yeh would be hard and everything would be finished.

Fa-hsin-sao shuddered. She glanced around with a scared look and went back into the room.

"Chiu-yeh, Chiu-yeh, Fa-hsin is only . . . please, honored one, let him off . . ."

Chiu-yeh said triumphantly: "Ha, ha. I knew you would come back. I knew. But why such a sad face? You must put on a more pleasant one."

He glanced in the direction of the door where Chiang-san stood. The latter knew that Chiu-yeh meant to commend him for the success of his mission but pretended indifference.

The woman's face was pale, her eyes filled with tears.

"Please raise high your honored hand and let him off. It is his bad temper that made him cross you. He is . . . A peasant is . . ."

"Come, give me a kiss!"

The huge shadow on the wall raised two steam shovels as Chiu-yeh clutched her face.

She did not struggle against him. Her tears streamed down her chin, glistening in the lamplight.

"Hey, hey, hey." Chiu-yeh warned, but not as harshly as he might. "As long as you've come here, you might as well put on a nice face. Did you think that I would spend good money for a sour face? What you want is money and what I want is pleasure. Come now, smile!"

The man at the door watched them, shifting his glance whenever one or the other of the two happened to look in his direction, and scraping his feet against the ground. He did not know whether to approach them or to go away. Finally he said with a sigh: "Ai, Fa-hsin-sao, think well, think over what I told you."

Fa-hsin-sao paid no attention to him but kept her eyes on Chiu-yeh's.

"Chiu-yeh, Chiu-yeh . . ."

"None of that, none of that. Come now, smile for me, smile!"

"Chiu-yeh, you must . . ."

"No, you must smile for me first."

Chiang-san had always had Chiu-yeh's complete confidence; he was a clever man and read Chiu-yeh's thought. Now he thrust out his chest, bracing himself for the important task before him: "Smile now, Fa-hsin-sao. It costs you nothing. Please smile once, please. Think well . . ."

He swallowed and wiped his mouth, and was about to continue when he was interrupted by Chiu-yeh—"Smile! It won't do otherwise!"

After an impasse of about a minute or so, Fa-hsin-sao gritted her teeth and forced a smile, while a large tear rolled down her face.

Chiu-yeh gave her wet face a pinch: "Ah, that's better!"

Chiang-san walked quietly out of the room, his face beaming because he had done a good job of persuasion. He peeped through the door for a while and then went back to his room.

"How much money would Chiu-yeh give her," he asked himself.

In any case country goods couldn't compare with city stuff; she shouldn't cost so much.

Money, however, did not really enter into the picture. What Chiu-yeh really wanted was to humiliate Yang Fa-hsin. The very next morning, he, Chiang-san, would go to Yang Fa-hsin and tell him all about it.

"All right, cross Chiu-yeh if you think you can get away with it . . . Now let me tell you, even your wife has given herself to Chiu-yeh . . . you bandit, you . . ."

He tried to think of something more adequate but could think of none. And a bandit deserved only one fate and that was to have his head cut off. Chiang-san knew all along that Chiu-yeh had no intention of letting Yang Fa-hsin off and that Fa-hsin-sao would not be able to save her husband after being nice to Chiu-yeh.

"You can't leave such a bandit around to terrorize the district, can you?"

Chiang-san crawled up on his bed and blew out the lamp. Suddenly he saw the shadowy figure of Yang Fa-hsin before him. He was covered with red and purple bruises and his legs tottered under him because they had been crushed in the press.

"Don't come to haunt me," Chiang-san said calmly.

The fellow's soul had wandered off his body because he was about to die. But could he blame anyone else?

"A good deed has its reward and an evil one has its proper punishment . . . This is fate, I tell you. Who told you to cross Chiu-yeh? Why must you run afoul of the law?"

Chiang-san recalled how Yang Fa-hsin had refused to pay his share of the assessment for the support of the militia, declaring that he had no money. He had argued with Chiang-san and even now the latter's ribs ached from the blow that he had received.

"Hm, you just wait."

Thus he pulled the covers over his head with a clear conscience.

Somewhere outside a woman was calling for the wandering soul of her child. Her voice was hardly human and made your hair stand on end.

A dog howled as if some disaster was imminent.

What strange days these were: the district was far from being peaceful in spite of the fact that such a clever man as Chiu-yeh was in control. His Honor Ming was always in terror of what might happen.

It was not even very peaceful in the house where he was sleeping. Twice during the night he was awakened by the shrieks and threats that came from Chiu-yeh's room . . .

When Chiang-san got up, Chiu-yeh was just ready to send Fa-hsin-sao away. Chiu-yeh picked out a silver dollar from his pouch and held it in his hand.

"Give me a smile, Fa-hsin-sao. You must give me a smile before I give you this. Ah, that's right!"

He threw the dollar on the table with a significant glance at Chang-san.

Fa-hsin-sao seized the dollar with a trembling hand.

"Now thank Chiu-yeh for the money," Chiang-san prompted.

But instead Fa-hsin-sao burst into crying, her whole body shook.

"Now, now," Chiu-yeh's lips were pressed together and his right eyelids twitched. "I don't like to see people cry. You mustn't cry here."

The woman turned and started to go, but Chiu-yeh caught her by the shoulder: "Come, let me . . ."

She ground her teeth and tried to struggle free.

Chiu-yeh jumped up. "That won't do! Remember I have spent a dollar on you! You must understand that you can't cross Chiu-yeh!"

He dragged her to him and pinched her on the thigh.

Fa-hsin-sao shuddered and shrieked. She did not scream a second time, but only shuddered when he pinched her again. Finally he gave her two pinches on her face, leaving two red marks.

"Go away." He gave her a push that sent her stumbling out of the room.

The two men in the room roared with laughter.

"So Chiu-yeh spent one milled-edge . . ."

"It was that dollar which Yu Pa had." Chiu-yeh could not help laughing again as he buttoned himself up, showing his discolored and irregular teeth and twitching violently his right eye. "She'll come back for another one."

Chiu-yeh was right. Fa-hsin-sao went to the tea house that afternoon to look for Chiu-yeh and asked him to give her another dollar.

"Please, honored one, give me another dollar for this one. This is . . ."

Her face was as pale as ash and swollen purple where she had been pinched.

Chiu-yeh first stared at her, then glanced at the faces in the tea house, and finally returned to the original object of his attention, and said in a loud voice: "Why?"

"This dollar is brass. I have shown it to . . ."

"How come that I'd give you a counterfeit dollar?"

Chiu-yeh again glanced all around him.

Fa-hsin-sao swayed. She gritted her teeth and put her hand on the table to steady herself.

"The dollar you gave me this morning . . ."

Chiu-yeh rolled his eyes and smiled.

"How does it happen that I, Chiu-yeh, should have given you a dollar? What kind of debt have I contracted? Tell me in front of every one here and I'll immediately give you another dollar in exchange."

Every one laughed.

"Now, tell us, why should Chiu-yeh give you a dollar all of a sudden?"

"A love debt, a love debt! Chiu-yeh must owe her . . ."

"Ah, there must be some reason for it. Ah, Chiu-yeh . . . ha, ha, ha!"

"So Chiu-yeh has a weakness for country stuff! oh . . ."

"Like husband, like wife," said an old man, looking at the gathering and repeating himself seven times to make sure that he was heard above the noise.

"Her man is that Yang something or other."

"Yang Fa-hsin."

"So? Nowadays even peasants are becoming difficult. He is . . ."

Chiu-yeh interrupted: "He took part in robbing the Wang family."

"What a team, what a team, with the man a bandit and the woman a prostitute."

The sound of voices and laughter became like one; the tea house was never so merry before.

"Tell me, Chiu-yeh: how much does she charge for a night?"

"Hey there! Are you trying to cut in on Chiu-yeh?"

Another thundering burst of laughter.

"I wonder if Yang Fa-hsin would try to cross Chiu-yeh now; even his woman has . . ."

Chiu-yeh took a sip of tea and then raised his hand to command attention: "What is this little widow to do after I am done with Yang Fa-hsin? Such a pretty face . . ."

"Let her come to Chiu-yeh, let her come to Chiu-yeh, that's what I say."

"If she wants to come to me . . ."

Suddenly a teapot flew through the air. Chiu-yeh dodged and the pot crashed to the ground.

All eyes were turned on Fa-hsin-sao. She picked up another pot, but her arm was seized by Chiang-san.

"*Hai*, what's the world coming to. Even women . . ."

Fa-hsin-sao's legs grew weak and she slumped to the ground. Her face was like quick lime and her mouth foamed like a crab's.

Reunion

By Chang T'ien-yi

It was an auspicious day according to the almanac, but the clouds and the darting dragon flies portended rain.

Da Gen's nose was definitely drippy. He was constantly sniveling and wiping his nose, cursing because it always seemed to need wiping.

"Your sister's brother, so much snivel!"

Erh Gen, his younger brother, glanced at him and said, "Koko has snivel but didi has none."

"You have to have snivel before you can be President."

Erh Gen gave Da Gen an incredulous look. Then he glanced around him and suddenly shouted, pointing to the bank of the river, "There's Doggie and Mangy Head!"

These two boys were throwing pebbles and making them skim over the surface of the water. They were Da Gen's schoolmates in the free night school and were two bad eggs. Mangy turned his mottled head on hearing the shout.

"Ah, there come the bastards. No wonder I can't make my pebbles skim; the bastards always bring me bad luck. Their mother is a dirty whore."

"What did you say?" Da Gen went up to him.

"I wasn't talking to you."

Doggie and Mangy walked away, with Da Gen and Erh Gen a few paces behind. Mangy began to tell a story to Doggie, loud enough for the other two boys to hear.

"Someone's mother is a dirty whore. The clerk at the bean-curd shop sleeps with her four or five times a month and gives her four dimes each time . . ."

"Hm." Doggie grunted through his nose, after a furtive glance behind him.

"Do you know who this fellow is?"

"No. And then?"

"And then, there are Ah Shui and Lao Niu and others, many, many others, for it is her business . . ."

Suddenly Da Gen rushed up to Mangy and caught him by the shoulder. When the latter turned his face, Da Gen smeared it with snivel that he had just wiped off his own nose.

"What is the idea?"

"This is the idea," said Da Gen striking Mangy in the face.

The two closed in on each other. Doggie tried to help his companion, but Da Gen's kicking feet kept him off. After he had disposed of Mangy, Da Gen went for Doggie but the latter ran without giving battle. Da Gen chased him for a distance and then stopped for Erh Gen to catch up with him.

Some girls were playing under a willow tree. Da Gen spat and put on the air of a grown-up.

"Go over there and see if Kuei Yuan is there. I have told her not to play with Ah Chiao."

Kuei Yuan was there, sure enough. She had been skipping rope with the other girls. She was holding San Gen in her arms, with Hsiao Yuan standing beside her. She was saying, "Ah Chiao, hold San Gen for a moment and let me jump."

"Kuei Yuan!" shouted Da Gen.

She came over to him and told him an important piece of news: "Papa has come back."

"What!" Da Gen was dumbfounded.

Erh Gen stared at Kuei Yuan. He had forgotten that he had a papa.

"Is papa like Grandpa Wu?" he asked, sticking his finger in his mouth.

"When did papa come back?" Da Gen asked, his face darkening.

"He came soon after you and Erh Gen left the house . . ."

That meant that his father had been home about three hours. Da Gen paid no more attention to his younger sister, who had gone back to "jump house" with Ah Chiao; he paid no attention to Mangy, who had gotten up and sidled off; he even forgot to wipe his nose. He was too busy wondering about papa.

Papa used to work in the Mukden Arsenal but had come to the South after the Japanese occupation of Manchuria. They managed to get along for a while, but later he lost his job and had to leave home to find work. He had been away over a year and had not sent a single word. But now he had suddenly come back.

Da Gen wondered about papa, he wondered whether he had grown older, whether he had come back with a fortune from the fabulously rich countries overseas.

"I'll go home and see," he said and started running.

"Papa has gone out," Kuei Yuan said.

Da Gen did not stop running until he reached home. Papa was not there. Mama was, and was wiping off tears. Granny Wu was with her and saying:

"Changshou is a sensible man. He ought to understand . . ."

"I can't face him. I shouldn't have . . ." Mama's face was a picture of misery. Da Gen went to the table and pulled out his Thousand-Character Lessons and pretended to study.

"It is best not to tell Changshou now. We shall all . . ." Granny gave mama a look which conveyed both pity and contempt and then they both stared at the mat on the bed.

"We can't keep it from him for long."

"Then let him find out. What of it?" There was a note of vehemence in Granny's voice. "Changshou is a sensible man. It has been more than a year since he went away. He did not send you a single copper all this time. What can he expect of you, with five little devils. You have been forced to . . . There is nothing for you to be ashamed of."

There were footsteps outside. Da Gen stood up, thinking that it might be his father. It was Lien Ssu-wu, the clerk in the bean-curd shop, and another man with him. Lien carried a bottle of wine.

"Please go away now, Lien Ssu-wu, please go." Mama was panicky.

"How's that?"

"Changshou has come back!"

"I am not afraid. You sell and I buy, and I have paid you already. I am not the only one who does business with you."

"Please be kind and do a good deed, Lien Ssu-wu. He does not . . ."

Granny Wu tried to intercede; her manner was both indignant and ingratiating. "You are a sensible man, Lien Ssu-wu. Changshou's wife has come to do this only because she couldn't help it. Her man has come back and you must try to understand."

"I understand all right, but I have spent good money. I have paid her in advance."

"Go away! Your sister's brother," Da Gen shouted.

"Little devil, you! But your daddy insists on staying. What can you do about it?"

"Didn't she say that she would pay you back?" Granny Wu's voice was shrill.

"All right, then let her pay me. She owes me one dollar and twenty cents."

"I'll pay you tomorrow. Please do a good deed and go away now."

But Lien Ssu-wu sat down on the bed: "No, that won't do . . . Lao Ying, let us have some fun tonight."

Da Gen picked up a stick of firewood.

Mama, however, went up to Lien Ssu-wu and knelt before him and implored him to leave.

"Smile for me, smile! I don't want to spend my good money for such a sour face."

Suddenly—whack! Lien Ssu-wu got a blow on the head. He pushed the woman away to take care of Da Gen.

Da Gen cursed and put his arms around Lien Ssu-wu's leg and sank his teeth into it. Somehow he was dragged away from Lien Ssu-wu. He gave the man a final blow with his fist and ran out, pulling a bench across the door to cover his retreat. Lien Ssu-wu stumbled over it and gave up the chase.

"Your sister's brother! I'll throw you in the dung pool and drown you," Da Gen cursed as he ran.

He had cursed Lien Ssu-wu and others like him before, but never to their faces. For the past year his mother had cried most of the time, and complained about papa's leaving her. But whenever Lien Ssu-wu or Ah Shui came to see her, she had to force herself to smile so as not to offend them. Da Gen hated to see her smile the way she did; he preferred to see her cry. Sometimes they held her in their arms and fondled her; sometimes she sent Da Gen and the other children out for two or three hours at a time; sometimes they would drag her away with them and keep her all night. Sometimes they dragged her up though she was sick in bed. After these things mama would have money to send Da Gen out to buy rice and pickled vegetables. When no one came to see her, she would cry and talk about papa and complain against her burden.

It had been like this for over a year.

Da Gen muttered another curse as he slowed his steps. The children had stopped playing under the willow tree and were chattering around a grown-up man. Who was he? He looked like papa, but seemed older. He was holding San Gen in his arms and talking baby talk to him, but San Gen did not want the stranger to hold him and was crying to get away.

Da Gen suddenly felt apprehensive.

"Come here, Kuei Yuan," he shouted to his sister. "Go quickly and tell mama that papa is here."

"Mama knows already."

"Don't you mind, go quickly."

Da Gen walked toward the direction of the willow trees. When the man saw him, he suddenly shouted:

"*Hey,* little devil! Where were you hiding when I came home? My, how you have grown! Do you remember me?"

"Papa!"

San Gen struggled to get away, reaching out for Ah Chiao. After the latter had taken him, he snuggled up against her and stole timid glances at papa.

Erh Gen grinned foolishly, his hand in his mouth.

Hsiao Yuan pulled at papa's leg, but laughed and ran away when papa looked down at her.

Papa squatted and put his hands on Da Gen's shoulders.

"I thought you were going to be a dwarf, but how you've grown, you little devil . . . How did you get your neck scratched, eh?"

Doggie and Mangy Head appeared a distance away. Da Gen followed them with his eyes, but papa did not notice them. He surveyed Da Gen from head to foot and asked him all sorts of questions. He asked him whether he missed papa, whether they had enough to eat, how come that his nose ran so much, how had mama's poor health stood up under the strain, when did they buy the two benches and how were the bedbugs, and whether mama had to beat him often. He asked Da Gen these and many other questions.

Now Doggie and Mangy began to shout loudly, one after the other.

"There is the turtle!"

"Changshou's wife, four dimes a night."

They retreated a few steps as papa turned to look at them.

"What did they say?" Papa's face darkened.

"Nothing decent ever came out of their stinking holes, their sister's brother!" Da Gen caught Doggie and threw him on the ground, spitting in his face and rubbing it in the dirt.

He turned to look at papa, but papa had gone! He let go of Doggie and ran in the direction of home, exchanging curses as he went. He picked up a rock; he was ready to fight papa is necessary.

Lien Ssu-wu had gone when Da Gen got home. Papa was holding mama's hands and pressing her with questions, with Granny Wu looking on embarrassedly and Kuei Yuan standing at the door and looking scared.

"I feel bad," Papa was saying. "Let me ask you, let me ask you. Tell me, have you deceived me?"

Mama was crying, and squirming because papa was squeezing her hand, hurting her. Granny Wu tried to drag him away.

"There, Changshou, don't be like that. You have just come back. This is your reunion. You mustn't . . ."

"I won't let you beat mama," Da Gen shouted.

The man paid no attention to him but said to Granny:

"You must know, Granny. She is your foster-daughter. She wasn't telling the truth. She was trying to fool me. How could she feed six mouths if she did nothing but sewing. Tell me . . ."

"Your brother's sister, papa!"

"Go away, little devil!"

"I won't let you beat mama."

Ah Chiao and the other children crowded outside the door. Kuei Yuan took San Gen from Ah Chiao, but the child stretched out its hands and cried for mama. Hsiao Yuan was sitting beside Granny, pressing her face against her thigh. Erh Gen cringed against the wall, wetting his pants without knowing.

"She must be deceiving me. How can she feed six mouths with what she gets from sewing. Besides, she is not strong . . ."

"Since you know I can't feed them, then why did you leave me with the five little devils? What can I . . ."

She suddenly cried out as papa struck her. Da Gen rushed up, but Granny had already dragged papa away from mama. Papa sat down on a bench and breathed hard and bit his lips until they became white. Granny Wu then told papa what it had been like for mama during the time papa had been away. She could not let the five little ones starve. She was not strong. What else could she do? And he had not sent her a single copper, not even a letter. Granny talked and talked until the wall turned gray and then black.

Papa had a great deal to tell, too. He had not been able to find steady work. Though he had not sent word, he was always thinking about mama and the children.

"I know she couldn't help it, it was all because . . . I understand. But think, Granny, my own wife! All the time I have been away I was thinking about her. How wretched I am, how can I . . ."

Then big papa broke down and cried like a child.

"I have nothing to say for myself, I . . ." Mama could not go on. Then she leaned upon her elbows and struggled up and got off the bed.

"It was my fault," she said after recovering her breath. "I was wrong to have done it. Changshou is right. But what could I do with the children starving?"

After a brief pause, she continued:

"Now you have come back, Changshou . . . I turn the five little devils over to you . . . I have done my part. From now on you take care of them. I'll not cause you more shame . . ."

Suddenly she dashed out of the room and ran away into the darkness.

"Mama . . ." Da Gen jumped up and ran after her.

"See what you have done, Changshou," Granny said.

"No, Granny, I cannot blame her. It was my fault. I cannot blame her." Papa spoke rapidly.

Granny got up and ran after Da Gen. Hsiao Yuan, who had been dozing off leaning against her, fell on the bed and began to cry, but no one paid any attention to her.

Papa ran out of the room, followed by Kuei Yuan, who had put San Gen down on the bed.

Papa ran faster than anyone else.

"Come back, come back! I don't blame you any more. I didn't really blame you . . . Granny, tell her that I don't blame her . . . I can't live after she is gone . . ."

He must overtake her and tell her that it was all his fault and ask her to forgive him.

He ran faster and faster, shouting, "Come back, Da Gen's ma! Come back, Da Gen's ma!"

Little Sister

By Feng Wen-ping

It was four years ago that my little sister died. Today memories of her have come back to me and I cannot put them out of my mind.

Sister was born June 30, the first year of the Republic [1912]. Her name was Lien. When my maternal grandmother, who was still living then, heard that it was a girl, she came over and told mother that she had found from old Mrs. Shih, the woman who sold eggs, that there was a carpenter living not far from our city who wanted to adopt an infant daughter-in-law. Though mother agreed with grandma that she should not take on the burden of raising another child, her voice did not carry much conviction. How could it be otherwise? As for myself, I was panic stricken and turned to grandma with a frightened look in my eyes. In an effort to placate me, she said, "I was told that the boy's grandfather was once a schoolmaster."

Of course the fact that my sister was to become the daughter-in-law of a carpenter was one of the reasons that I objected to the proposed match, but if she were not to eat and share everything with me I would feel that she was suffering greater hardships than I, even though she lived in the palace or the mansion of the prime minister, instead of going only into the family of a schoolmaster. At best he would be like my own poor teacher, and besides, this was the grandfather; the father was only a carpenter.

My grandmother seemed to take me for a grown-up whose objection had to be reckoned with. She remonstrated and argued with me earnestly and finally said impatiently, "Then you will

have to wash the baby clothes! Your mother must not be bothered."
I answered eagerly, "I'll wash them! I'll wash them!"

When I went to bed that night, I was unable to sleep for a long
while. It seemed as if I knew the carpenter well and had visited
the village where he lived. There seemed to be a tomb on the hillside nearby that had a monument decorated with dragons in front
of it. A herd of cattle was grazing and the cowherd was sister.
She was sitting under the monument with her back toward me,
digging at the earth and singing in a low voice. She turned when
she heard the rustling of my clothes and ran into my arms crying.
She told me that her coat was made over from something that our
elder sister no longer wanted and that her mother-in-law had
beaten her because she had made trumpets with the wood shavings
instead of taking them to the kitchen for fuel. "Don't cry," I said
to her. "I'll take you home." But I myself—

"Miao-erh, Miao-erh! Mama is here."

My pillow was wet with tears.

If I had thought about the matter, I should have known that
grandma's idea was unthinkable, for poor as we were, my father
was employed in the office of the commissioner of education. How
could we marry a daughter into the family of a carpenter? It was
probably because grandma did not have a good look at the baby in
mother's arms that she suggested such a thing, for when the baby
was shown at the Third Day ceremony she fell in love with it as
every one else did.

But because of this incident my sister and I were often teased
later on. If I were arguing with mother about something, she
would say when she got angry, "If you say another word, you can
wash the baby clothes!" Thereupon I would say no more. If sister
had done anything to displease her, she always intimidated her by
saying, "I should have taken grandma's advice and given you to
the carpenter!"

My grandfather did not like my mother and so did not show
as much affection for her children as he did for the children of my
aunts. (My father and his two brothers did not "separate house"
until sister was five years old.) He would buy fried dough strings

in the morning and stuffed rolls at noon for Eight and Nine, both
my third aunt's boys, one two years older and the other two years
younger than my sister. Though he bought only one apiece, yet
he never failed to do so a single day the year round. My sister?
It was as if she did not exist. Because she was only a girl? But
Ah Chu, my second aunt's daughter, was dearer to grandfather
than any of the other children. She was fifteen and got two rolls
at noon. Sometimes the peddler would remind grandfather of
sister's presence—for grandfather's eyesight was not good—if she
happened to be there when he passed the delicacies around, saying,
"Ah Lien is there, too." But being a sensible girl, sister would say
hastily, "I don't like to eat between meals," and retreat into the
house with bowed head.

Grandfather liked to go out with the children. After breakfast
sister, Eight, and Nine, the youngest children in the house, would
be playing at cooking in the yard, piling up earth and broken tiles
for stoves. After they got tired of doing that, grandfather would
take them out for a stroll. Needless to say, he carried Nine in his
arm and led Eight with his free hand. Sister would dust herself
off, saying in her birdlike voice, "Grandpa, are you taking them
outside the city? There are wildcats!" If grandfather should deign
to speak to her, sister would be so gratified and happy. She was
then only four years old.

How could a quiet and affectionate child like sister pick quarrels
with Eight or Nine? Yet if they should happen to have a quarrel,
grandfather would say, "Eight is a good child. It must be Ah Lien's
fault." If the quarrel was between sister and Nine, he would say,
"Nine is younger. Even if he did scratch or pinch her, Ah Lien
should overlook it." Sister would run to mother, holding back her
tears until she saw her, and then sob out her story. Mother would
say "It is a very small matter. It is not worth crying over."

I have never known any one who could cry so much as sister.
She knew herself that it was better not to cry, but her tears would
stream down her cheeks in spite of herself. Mother would knit
her brows, shake her head and point to the hall, where father used

to sit, as if to say that he would blame her for spoiling sister when he saw sister cry.

Sister had been afflicted with running ears ever since she was a year old. Many remedies prescribed by the village doctor were tried without any effect. My father used to have my younger brother do a sheet of calligraphy exercise every day. In the evening my sister would ask him for the sheet and give it to mother to clean the pus from her ears with. The boys would say, "Get away from us. You smell so." She was affectionate and liked to snuggle up to them, though a stranger could not induce her to come near him.

To my sister her ears were the cause of most of the trouble and sufferings that filled the seven years of her short life.

One evening while we were sitting in mother's room, I said to her, "Ah Lien, in the provincial capital there are foreigners that can cure all kinds of diseases. How would you like to have me take you there and have your ears looked into?"

It was, of course, beyond the question to take a little girl like sister on such a long journey, and sister, an intelligent girl, knew this. Mother, however, said with a serious air, "If they can really cure her, we'll let her go. Papa is willing to spend the money."

"How is she going to sleep?" my brother Three asked.

"With brother Miao," sister said without hesitation.

We all laughed and sister hid her face in embarrassment against mother's side and gnawed at the corner of her coat.

Sister, how your brother weeps when he recalls these things!

When I was six years old I almost died. As my father had to work all day in the district government office, my mother wore herself out running between my sick bed and the kitchen. I am sometimes troubled with a feeling that I was partly responsible for my sister's death. During the five years I was in middle school I was sick about three years and a half. I spent the last year entirely at home. Father seemed even more anxious about me than mother. His voice became tender and his austere face softened into a smile when he came in to see me. Sometimes mother would come in with sister and say, "They say that Ah Lien is getting thinner and weaker every day." But father never gave any thought about that; mother simply asserted a fact that was meaningless to him.

Sister's tears became even more copious as time went on. She cried on the least provocation. Afraid that father would get angry because she cried, she would say that she had a stomachache. My father never beat us; his displeasure was only shown on his face, which would darken like a beclouded sky. This was more terrible than beating, for if he had beaten us, we could have cried and forgotten our grievances afterwards. Fear and uncertainty were more unbearable. His anger had nothing to do with the merits or demerits of our behavior. If he happened to be in a bad humor, the least thing would cause him to explode like a cannon.

One day sister was crying again over something when mother called her to come in for the midday dinner. Mother, who was also in fear of father's moods, said, "Ah Lien is having the stomach-ache again." Father kept on eating without saying a word. I was nervous and said, "Don't cry any more, Ah Lien." She came in slowly, having dried her tears though her eyes were still red. I resumed eating without any further anxiety. After a few mouthfuls her tears began to flow again. I noticed it first and then father saw it, too. Sister took one glance at father and burst out crying even though she tried so hard not to. Father slapped his chopsticks on the table and dragged sister into the yard and left her standing there in the scorching sun. She writhed in agony like a skinned frog until my father's second sister came and took her away.[1]

It was evident that sister had lost her former liveliness. "Aren't you feeling well?" Mother would ask. Sister could not tell where her ailment lay. "Why don't you go and play with Eight and Nine?" mother would suggest, whereupon sister would say with irritation, "Must one be forced to play when one doesn't want to?"

One day I was lying on a wicker couch which my mother had placed in the hall where it was cool. Suddenly I wanted to have a pear and as there was no one whom mother could send at the moment, she looked appealingly at sister. She was not eager to go

---

[1] In a situation like this only a man's brother or sister can interfere, short of his parents.

but did not refuse. I did not protest either as I did not think that it would prove too much of a task. She was wearing only a vest and had a fan to shade herself from the sun. She left by the back gate, which was nearer to the main street, but came back through the front gate. I was facing the front gate and noticed that her footsteps were heavy and she seemed to have hardly enough strength to hold the fan over her head. After giving the pear to me, she sat panting on a bamboo stool and looked very miserable though she did not cry.

"Why did you have to take the longer way?" mother said to her. Sister burst into tears as she replied with some passion, "Because there is no shade outside the back gate!"

We did not know then that she was in the first stage of tuberculosis; she could not stand the heat.

She began to sleep a great deal. One day mother came to keep me company after dinner as she was wont to do. "Ah Lien has probably gone off to sleep again," she said, and sure enough she found her sleeping in bed. Mother scolded, "You have just eaten. You can blame no one if your stomach aches again." Sister did not answer. Mother tapped her gently with her hand and suddenly uttered a sharp cry. "How shiny are the child's feet! Are they swollen? Get up, precious." Sister was gratified because some one had at last noticed her troubles.

When the doctor called to see me, mother led sister in and said to father, "I'm afraid we shall have to ask the doctor take a look at Ah Lien."

"What a bother!" father said with a frown.

"But it is serious. Look at her feet!" mother said anxiously.

"It won't be very much trouble to take a look," the doctor mediated. Father gave in.

We looked upon the doctor as a deliverer at the time, but in reality sister's decline may easily have been due to his ill-prescribed remedies. He said that sister had malaria, and mother agreed with him because sister had complained of chills. And sister herself, gratified with the attention she was receiving, did what she was told. When the medicine was brought to her she would gulp it down without wincing, unlike myself who had to be watched carefully by mother until I had downed all the brew.

In the evening when my father returned with the two packages of medicine, he could not conceal his annoyance with sister. "She must have her share even in this," he said. Sister turned toward me and said, tears filling her eyes, "He wants to have only you treated!" When mother said that a clever girl like her ought to know that father was only joking, several tear drops had rolled down her cheeks.

Gradually my poor, sickly sister began to be bloated like a pig that had been plucked, but I did not think that she would die so soon. She gradually lost all appetite and it became more and more of an effort for her to lift her feet over the door sill when she came into the hall to keep cool.

A celebration in honor of the God of Thunder was being held in the temple near us, and the sound of drums and firecrackers proved irresistible to Eight and Nine. Sister never liked to follow noise and crowds; now she cared for them even less. But father insisted that mother should take her to the temple to see the festivities, probably thinking that the distraction would be good for her. I noticed that she walked with great difficulty but I did not expect the sharp cry she uttered when she tried to lift her foot over the doorsill at the gate. Mother said she would carry her over it, but she complained that she hurt all over. This was the last time that sister went near the gate.

In the last resort mother always turned to the gods for help. She said to sister, "My child, I shall go to pray to Tou Lao Niang Niang. You will be well soon." She went to the Tou Lao Temple outside the city while father went out to inquire about possible remedies. There was only my younger brother and myself home to watch over sister as my elder brother and his wife had gone to visit her people. Sister was lying in bed with her eyes closed and when she opened them on hearing footsteps they were only thin slits.

"Hasn't mama come home yet?"

"What do you want?" my younger brother asked, leaning over her bed. "I'll get it for you."

"I don't want anything," she said sweetly.

Finally mother returned, and the medicine prescribed by the fortune sticks was soon brewing over the stove. Sister, however, did not wait but went from us forever, three days before her birthday.

During the first few days father seemed more distressed than mother, but later on mother went almost insane with grief. When she saw Nine or his younger sister, she would take them aside and ask them, "Do you know where Ah Lien is?" In her superstition she was hoping that they might in their innocence reveal where sister's ghost might be. Nine was literal. "On the hill, aunt," he would say and offer to take her there. His sister did not even understand the question; she only shook her head and stared stupidly at mother. When the washwoman's little girl brought the wash, mother would take her in her arms and would not let her go. She gave her sister's clothes one by one, including a padded silk jacket that sister wore during the last New Year season.

On the Seven-times-Seventh Day after sister's death, father rose early, bought a string of spirit money, and went to the hill with my younger brother after breakfast. When they came home I asked my brother whether her tomb was on top of the hill or midway. He said that it was on top of the hill and that he could see the city wall and the roof of our ancestral temple from it. He said that he cried after he burned the spirit money but that father did not. "Father only said, 'Ah Lien, watch over your brother Miao and help him to get well soon.'"

I felt cold and a shiver ran through me when he told me what father said.

I have never visited my sister's tomb. I was told that mother asked Brother-in-Law Chuan to mark it with a large brick on which my younger brother had written an inscription.

The Helpmate

By Ling Shu-hua (Mrs. Ch'en T'ung-po)

Taitai had just awakened. She was lying in bed, recalling with chagrin how she might have mahjonged with the highest possible score of the evening if Chang taitai had not mahjonged on the same tile ahead of her, when her daughter came home for lunch and asked for money to pay her ricksha fare. Taitai cast an angry glance at her daughter and said, "You bring me bad luck by asking me for money the first thing in the morning. No wonder I always lose. Why did you have to ride today?"

"I cannot walk because my feet are frost-bitten," answered the girl, looking resentfully at her mother.

Tsai-ma, the maid servant, said, "It is now the eleventh month, time for padded shoes, which all the other young ladies at school have been wearing for some time. Taitai should have bought them for the young mistress before this. Leather shoes are not warm enough for such cold weather as we are having."

"You are always talking about buying and buying. Even if we were rich, we shouldn't spend money so freely. Didn't I tell you to buy a pair of soles? Wasn't that for making padded shoes?"

"But how can you make shoes without the uppers?" Tsai-ma said with a cold smile. "I have reminded Taitai to buy some material for the uppers but Taitai always forgets."

In a fit of irritation Taitai took her purse and threw it to her daughter, saying, "Count out some coppers to pay the ricksha man. He will be demanding more for being kept waiting."

The daughter was caught unawares and failed to reach out her hands to catch the purse, so that it struck her squarely on one of her frost-bitten feet. She uttered a sharp cry of pain and began to weep, nursing her foot. Not realizing what had happened and thinking that she wept because she resented the scolding, Taitai said as she got out of bed, "Tsai-ma, you go and pay the ricksha man . . . Such a big girl and yet she still knows nothing about trying to help mother to save money but cries upon the least scolding. You will be thirteen after the new year and in another year or two it will be time to think of your engagement, but you are still so spoiled."

Her daughter cried more inconsolably than ever, wiping her tears with her sleeve and wetting it through.

"Go on crying," Taitai said. "Cry all day if you want to. I am not like your aunt, who is accustomed to apologize to her daughter." Then she complained as she went into the living room, "Who is it that is always leaving the door open? Afraid to get his tail pinched?" She sat down in a chair. Her back ached and her eyes burned.

Tsai-ma came in with towel and soap and things, saying, "I left it open because my hands were not free."

"What did Lao-yeh have for breakfast?" Taitai asked as she washed her face.

"The tea-boiled eggs that we bought day before yesterday."

"Why did you give that to him again? Didn't he complain yesterday that those eggs were not fresh and that it gave him indigestion? He will blame me again when he comes home."

"What else was there for him to eat, since he would not eat sesame rolls or fried dough strings?"

"You better say that none of you want to bother. There must be something that you can cook. A bowl of broth with a poached egg in it would have done. Don't tell me that there are no eggs in the kitchen. You people think of nothing but money, money, day in and day out. When one buys anything, you must have your commission; when one plays mahjong, you have to have a percentage of the winnings; when one sends you out to deliver a present, you want a tip; but you never think of trying to save money for your employers."

"But reflect, Taitai, if it is not precisely because one is poor that

one leaves home to serve others," Tsai-ma said. She did not take
Taitai's complaints to heart because they were not specifically
addressed to her but to all servants.

Chang-sheng came in to dust off the tables. Tsai-ma said to him,
"Master Chang, who was it that telephoned twice for Taitai?"

"Huang taitai called to ask Taitai to go to her house as early as
possible. She said that they would be waiting for Taitai to begin
the game."

"Did she not say that Taitai should take some money with her
so as to recover her losses?" Tsai-ma said with a contemptuous
smile.

For a moment Taitai was silent. Then she said peevishly, "When
did I ever go to their games without taking money with me? As
for recovering my losses, she is positively insulting to mention it
since I lost only a trifling fifty dollars."

"It is really very unkind of Huang taitai to make such a point
of it to remind you of the money. And she is a relative of yours
too. I think Taitai ought to show her by paying everything you owe.
It makes us mad to have her talk the way she does."

As Taitai drank her strong tea, she did some figuring with
darkened brows. After a long while she said to Tsai-ma, "Find
Lao-yeh's fox fur robe and my gray squirrel fur robe and take
them to some pawn shop as far from here as possible and try to
get ninety dollars for them."

Presently Tsai-ma returned with the robes and asked, "Taitai,
how much are the robes worth altogether? I am afraid that they
won't fetch ninety dollars."

"The fox robe is worth seventy or eighty dollars at least, and the
squirrel robe ought to bring fifty or sixty dollars even though it is
second-hand."

"They will bring at most forty dollars," Tsai-ma said. "The
pawnshops give only about twenty dollars for things worth sixty
or seventy dollars. The marmot overcoat we pawned last time was
in better condition than these. Every one said that it was worth
at least a hundred dollars but as you remember it fetched only
thirty dollars."

Taitai thought for a moment and then said, "You can take Lao-yeh's red fox jacket also."

"That is worth only about twenty dollars. I think we'll have to take along a few more things."

Taitai went into the next room and after rummaging around for a while, she came back and said to Tsai-ma, "You can take this gold watch too. It cost over a hundred dollars. That ought to be enough, don't you think?"

"I shall try to get an even hundred for them," Tsai-ma said as she wrapped up the things.

When Taitai found that Tsai-ma seemed to be waiting for something, she said to her in a low voice, "Don't let people know about this. I see you need a heavier coat. I'll give you two dollars to get one."

"Thank you, Taitai. Chang-sheng is just outside. Don't you want to give him something so that he can get a pair of new shoes?" Then lowering her voice, she said, "He often talks to Lao-yeh about things when he waits upon Lao-yeh in his study."

Taitai did not like the implied threat and she did not want to seem afraid that Chang-sheng would tell her husband. "What if he does?" she said. "But if he needs a pair of new shoes, you can give him two dollars."

Half an hour after Tsai-ma went out, Lao-yeh returned. He was not feeling very well because of the stale tea-boiled eggs that he had eaten in the morning. Now when he found his daughter sulking in a corner with pursed lips and swollen eyes and his wife standing in the kitchen door berating the cook for grafting, he could not help feeling oppressed by the gloomy atmosphere as he sat in the dining room and waited for his dinner.

"Why did you stay so late at the office?" Taitai asked perfunctorily as she joined her husband in the dining room.

"We were discussing what to do about the birthday of the new commissioner's mother. This is her seventieth birthday."

"Have the presents been sent?"

"Yes. We were assessed fifteen dollars apiece. It is one of those things that you can't avoid. Will you have my fur robe and jacket laid out before dinner? I have to set out for the party immediately afterward."

The unexpected request embarrassed Taitai but she assumed a calm air and answered, "Didn't you lend them to your cousin?"

"When? Then send some one to get them immediately."

"He is probably not home now," Taitai temporized.

"I met him on the street just a while back," Lao-yeh said, looking steadily at Taitai. "He was not wearing my things. Please send some one to get them right away."

"Oh, I was mistaken. You did not lend them to your cousin. It was probably Mr. Chang who borrowed them when he was here the other day."

"Mr. Chang has gone to Tientsin. Besides, he is not my size. Now whom did you lend them to? Please think carefully. Ask the servants if they remember. I must leave the house at two o'clock; there isn't much time left. You know I can't go to the party in this robe. It will be impossible for me to borrow anything that will fit me. Besides, I don't know any one among my friends who has any decent clothes to spare."

Lao-yeh's sheepskin-lined coat was worn at the sleeves and there was a soiled patch on the front. Taitai did not know what to say. She wished she could cry.

"Couldn't you plead illness? I really can't remember whom I lent them to."

"Some one told me several days ago that the new commissioner is going to make some changes in the bureau and warned me not to give him any reason to find fault with me. I must go. I have no influential friends to back me. Now whom did you lend the clothes to?"

Taitai stared at the wall in silence, her eyes filled with tears. Lao-yeh kept looking at the clock and became more and more insistent as time went on.

"It is getting late. I shall certainly lose this job if I do not go to the party today."

Finally Taitai summoned Chang-sheng and said to him, "You go and try to overtake Tsai-ma and bring her back."

"What?" Lao-yeh exclaimed. "How does Tsai-ma happen to have them?"

"She has been gone for more than half an hour now," Chang-sheng said. "There is no telling where she is now."

"Look for her in the shops," Taitai said.

"But there is no telling which pawnshop she was going to; she only said that Taitai wanted her to go to some shop as far away from home as possible."

Lao-yeh suddenly realized the fate of his coats when he heard the words "pawnshop."

"Ah, so you have sent them out to be pawned! No wonder you would not say a word. What were you going to do with the money?" When she went on weeping without answering him, he put down his rice bowl and said, his eyes fixed on her, "Where have you sent Tsai-ma? We must find her and get the coats back."

Taitai suppressed her tears and said brokenly, "Chang-sheng, go and find Tsai-ma. Tell her to come back right away."

Somewhat relieved to know where his coats had gone, Lao-yeh picked up his chopsticks and resumed eating. But the food had grown cold. After a few mouthfuls he began to notice the pain in his stomach again and to recall the cold tea-boiled eggs that he had had to eat for breakfast.

"One should think," he complained to his wife, "that a woman of over thirty years of age like you would know enough to attend to her household duties instead of playing mahjong all day long."

The daughter had come into the dining room and was waiting for her mother to sit down so that she could sit down too.

"Sister had better come and eat," Lao-yeh said as his rising temper got the better of him. "Don't wait for your mother any more. *Heng,* what a mother!"

Taitai was on the point of drying her tears but at her husband's last remark, she jumped up and said angrily, "Do you mean to suggest that I am unworthy to be a mother? I don't care about the other things you have said, but I won't have you humiliate me before my own daughter!"

Lao-yeh shook with rage. He set down his tea cup with a bang, spilling some hot tea on Taitai's hand.

"*Ai yao!*" Taitai shouted, throwing herself at Lao-yeh. "He is trying to scald me to death!"

Lao-yeh fled out of the dining room, banging the door after him in revenge, put on his hat and went to a friend's house for refuge.

Taitai sat on the floor and abandoned herself to unrestrained weeping and wailing. Her daughter was too frightened to know what to do. She was hungry and the heat from the stove which she was standing by made her frost bites throb with pain. She, too, began to cry.

Hearing the sound of weeping, the old lady next door came over to comfort her. Taitai, as usual, complained of Lao-yeh's heartlessness, and the old lady tried to agree with her. By three o'clock peace had been restored and the neighbor gone home.

When Tsai-ma came back from her mission, Taitai was lying down in bed, after having washed her face and eaten some fried rice.

"Are you asleep, Taitai," Tsai-ma said. "Oh, what a time I had in trying to get the pawnshop to give a hundred dollars for the things I took there. At first they swore that eighty dollars was the most they could give for them." Then handing Taitai the pawn ticket and the money, she said, "Here is ninety-five dollars and twenty coppers. Taitai said that Chang-sheng and I could have two dollars each. I spent some money for ricksha fare and bought something to eat as I had to wait and became hungry."

"Why did you take such a long time?" Taitai said as she took the money. "I was worried to death because I did not know where to find you."

"The cook has told me about what has happened," Tsai-ma said. "But where could you find a family where husband and wife do not quarrel two or three times a month? You shouldn't take it so much to heart."

After a while the cook came to say that Huang taitai had just telephoned again and had said that they were waiting for her to begin the game.

Taitai rose from her bed, tidied up her hair, changed her clothes and set out for Huang taitai's house.

"If I don't go it would look as if I were trying to get out of paying them," she said at the gate. "But don't tell Lao-yeh where I have gone when he comes back."

"But Taitai," Tsai-ma said to her, "you had better leave some money for me to buy cloth for the young master's uniform so that he won't cry again when he comes home. He was crying this morning and refused to go to school because his teacher told him that if he did not get his uniform soon he would not only have to stand before the class for a punishment but that he would not be allowed to go to school any more. We had quite a time in coaxing him to go to school this morning. We promised him that he would have his uniform today. Then we must get some material for the young mistress's shoes."

"Oh, what bother," Taitai said, spitting in disgust. "You have to wait just as I am setting out for a game to ask me for money. Let us wait till tomorrow."

Thus speaking, Taitai got into her ricksha and went off.

Spring Silkworms

By Mao Dun

I

Tung Pao sat on a rock along the bank of the canal with his back to the sun, his long-stemmed pipe leaning against his side. The sun was already strong, though the period of Clear Bright had just set in, and felt as warm as a brazier of fire. It made him hotter than ever to see the Shaohing trackers pulling hard at their lines, large drops of sweat falling from their brows in spite of their open cotton shirts. Tung Pao was still wearing his winter coat; he had not foreseen the sudden warm spell and had not thought of redeeming his lighter garment from the pawnshop.

"Even the weather is not what it used to be!" muttered Tung Pao, spitting into the canal.

There were not many passing boats, and the occasional ripples and eddies that broke the mirrorlike surface of the greenish water and blurred the placid reflections of the mud banks and neat rows of mulberry trees never lasted long. Presently one could make out the trees again, swaying from side to side at first like drunken men and then becoming motionless and clear and distinct as before, their fistlike buds already giving forth tiny, tender leaves. The fields were still cracked and dry, but the mulberry trees had already come into their own. There seemed to be no end to the rows along the banks and there was another extensive grove back of Tung Pao. They seemed to thrive on the sunlit warmth, their tender leaves growing visibly each second.

Not far from where Tung Pao sat there was a gray white building, used by the cocoon buyers during the season but now quite deserted. There were rumors that the buyers would not come at all this year because the Shanghai factories had been made idle by the war, but Tung Pao would not believe this. He had lived sixty years and had yet to see the time when mulberry leaves would be allowed to wither on the trees or be used for fodder, unless of course if the eggs should not hatch, as has sometimes happened according to the unpredictable whims of Heaven.

"How warm it is for this time of the year!" Tung Pao thought again, hopefully, because it was just after a warm spring like this almost two score years ago that there occurred one of the best silk crops ever known. He remembered it well: it was also the year of his marriage. His family fortune was then on the upward swing. His father worked like a faithful old ox, knew and did everything; his grandfather, who had been a Taiping captive in his time, was still vigorous in spite of his great age. At that time, too, the house of Chen had not yet begun its decline, for though the old squire had already died, the young squire had not yet taken to opium smoking. Tung Pao had a vague feeling that the fortunes of the Chens and that of his own family were somehow intertwined, though one was about the richest family in town while his was only well-to-do as peasants went.

Both his grandfather and the old squire had been captives of the Taiping rebels and had both escaped before the rebellion was suppressed. Local legend had it that the old squire had made off with a considerable amount of Taiping gold and that it was this gold which enabled him to go into the silk business and amass a huge fortune. During that time Tung Pao's family flourished too. Year after year the silk crops had been good and in ten years his family had been able to acquire twenty mou of rice land and more than ten mou of mulberry trees. They were the most prosperous family in the village, just as the Chens were the richest in the town.

But gradually both families had declined. Tung Pao no longer had any rice land left and was more than three hundred dollars in debt besides. As for the Chen family, it was long ago "finished." It was said that the reason for their rapid decline was that the ghosts of the Taiping rebels had sued in the courts of the nether world and had been warranted by King Yenlo to collect. Tung Pao was inclined to think that there was something to this notion, otherwise why should the young squire suddenly acquire the opium habit? He could not, however, figure out why the fortunes of his own family should have declined at the same time. He was certain that his grandfather did not make away with any Taiping gold. It was true that his grandfather had to kill a Taiping sentinel in making his escape, but had not his family atoned for this by holding services for the dead rebel as long as he could remember? He did not know much about his grandfather, but he knew his father as an honest and hardworking man and could not think of anything he himself had done that should merit the misfortunes that had befallen him. His older son Ah Ssu and his wife were both industrious and thrifty, and his younger son Ah Dou was not a bad sort, though he was flighty at times as all young people were inclined to be.

Tung Pao sadly lifted his brown, wrinkled face and surveyed the scene before him. The canal, the boats, and the mulberry groves on both sides of the canal—everything was much the same as it was two score years ago. But the world had changed: often they lived on nothing but pumpkins, and he was more than three hundred dollars in debt.

Several blasts from a steam whistle suddenly came from around a bend in the canal. Soon a tug swept majestically into view with a string of three boats in tow. The smaller crafts on the canal scurried out of the way of the puffing monster, but soon they were engulfed in the wide wake of the tug and its train and seesawed up and down as the air became filled with the sound of the engine and the odor of oil. Tung Pao watched the tug with hatred in his eyes as it disappeared around the next bend. He had always entertained a deep enemity against such foreign deviltry as steam boats and the like. He had never seen a foreigner himself, but his father told him that the old squire had seen some, that they had red hair and green eyes and walked with straight knees. The old squire had no use for foreigners either and used to say that it was they that had made off with all the money and made everyone poor. Tung Pao had no doubt that the old squire was right. He knew from his own experience that since foreign yarn and cloth and kerosene appeared in town and the steamer in the river, he got less and less for the things that he produced with his own labor and had to pay more and more for the things that he had to buy. It was thus that he became poorer and poorer until now he had none of his rice land that his father had left him and was in debt besides. He did not hate the foreigners without reason! Even among the villagers he was remarkable for the vehemence of his anti-foreign sentiments.

Five years back some one told him that there had been another change in government and that it was the aim of the new government to rescue the people from foreign oppression. Tung Pao did not believe it, for he had noticed on his trips to town that the youngsters who shouted "Down with the foreigners" all wore foreign clothes. He had a suspicion that these youths were secretly in league with the foreigners and only pretended to be their enemies in order to fool honest people like himself. He was even more convinced that he was right when the slogan "Down with the foreigners" was dropped and things became dearer and dearer and the taxes heavier and heavier. Tung Pao was sure that the foreigners had a hand in these things.

The last straw for Tung Pao was that cocoons hatched from foreign eggs should actually sell for ten dollars more a picul. He had always been on friendly terms with his daughter-in-law, but they quarreled on this score. She had wanted to use foreign eggs the year before. His younger son Ah Dou sided with her, and her husband was of the same mind though he did not say much about it. Unable to withstand their pressure, Tung Pao had to compromise at last and allow them to use one sheet of foreign eggs out of three that they decided to hatch this year.

"The world is becoming worse and worse," he said to himself. "After a few years even the mulberry leaves will have to be foreign! I am sick of it all!"

2

The weather continued warm and the fingerlike tender leaves were now the size of small hands. The trees around the village itself seemed to be even better. As the trees grew so did the hope in the hearts of the peasants. The entire village was mobilized in preparation for the silkworms. The utensils used in the rearing were taken out from the fuel sheds to be washed and repaired, and the women and children engaged in these tasks lined the brook that passed through the village.

None of the women and children were very healthy looking. From the beginning of spring they had to cut down on their meager food, and their garments were all old and worn. They looked little better than beggars. They were not, however, dis-spirited; they were sustained by their great endurance and their great hope. In their simple minds they felt sure that so long as nothing happened to their silkworms everything would come out all right. When they thought how in a month's time the glossy green leaves would turn into snow white cocoons and how the cocoons would turn into jingling silver dollars, their hearts were filled with laughter though their stomachs gurgled with hunger.

Among the women was Tung Pao's daughter-in-law Ssu-da-niang with her twelve-year-old boy Hsiao Pao. They had finished washing the feeding trays and the hatching baskets and were wiping their brows with the flap of their coats.

"Ssu-sao, are you using foreign eggs this year?" one of the women asked Ssu-da-niang.

"Don't ask me!" Ssu-da-niang answered with passion, as if ready for a quarrel. "Pa is the one that decides. Hsiao Pao's pa did what he could to persuade the old man, but in the end we are hatching only one sheet of foreign eggs. The doddering old fool hates everything foreign as it were his sworn foe, yet he doesn't seem to mind at all when it comes to 'foreign money.'" [1]

The gibe provoked a gale of laughter.

---

[1] That is, the dollar coin. So called because the Chinese dollar is based on the Mexican peso, brought to China by European traders.

A man walked across the husking field on the other side of the brook. As he stepped on the log bridge, Ssu-da-niang called to him:

"Brother Dou, come and help me take these things home. These trays are as heavy as dead dogs when they are wet."

Ah Dou lifted the pile of trays and carried them on his head and walked off swinging his hands like oars. He was a good-natured young man and was always willing to lend a hand to the women when they had anything heavy to be moved or to be rescued from the brook. The trays looked like an oversize bamboo hat on him. There was another gale of laughter when he wriggled his waist in the manner of city women.

"Ah Dou! Come back here and carry something home for me too," said Lotus, wife of Li Keng-sheng, Tung Pao's immediate neighbor, laughing with the rest.

"Call me something nicer if you want me to carry your things for you," answered Ah Dou without stopping.

"Then let me call you godson!" Lotus said with a loud laugh. She was unlike the rest of the women because of her unusually white complexion, but her face was very flat and her eyes were mere slits. She had been a slave girl in some family in town and was already notorious for her habit of flirting with the men folk though she had been married to the taciturn Li Keng-sheng only half a year.

"The shameless thing!" some one muttered on the other side of the brook. Thereupon Lotus's pig-like eyes popped open as she shouted:

"Whom are you speaking of? Come out and say it in the open if you dare!"

"It is none of your business! She who is without shame knows best whom I'm speaking of, for 'Even the man who lies dead knows who's kicked his coffin with his toes.' Why should you care?"

They splashed water at each other. Some of the women joined the exchange of words, while the children laughed and hooted. Ssu-da-niang, not wishing to be involved, picked up the remaining baskets and went home with Hsiao Pao. Ah Dou had set down the trays on the porch and was watching the fun.

Tung Pao came out of the room with the tray stands that he had to repair. His face darkened when he caught Ah Dou standing there idle, watching the women. He never approved of Ah Dou's exchanging banter with the women of the village, particularly with Lotus, whom he regarded as an evil thing that brought bad luck to any one who had anything to do with her.

"Are you enjoying the scenery, Ah Dou?" he shouted at his son. "Ah Ssu is making cocoon trees in the back; go and help him!" He did not take his disapproving eyes off his son until the latter had gone. Then he set to work examining the worm holes on the stands and repaired them wherever necessary. He had done a great deal of carpentering in his time, but his fingers were now stiff with age. After a while he had to rest his aching fingers and as he did so he looked up at the three sheets of eggs hanging from a bamboo pole in the room.

Ssu-da-niang sat under the eaves pasting paper over the hatching baskets. To save a few coppers they had used old newspapers the year before. The silk worms had not been healthy, and Tung Pao had said that it was because it was sacrilegious to use paper with characters on it. In order to buy regular paper for the purpose this year they had all gone without a meal.

"Ssu-da-niang, the twenty-loads of leaves we bought has used up all the thirty dollars that we borrowed through your father. What are we going to do after our rice is gone? What we have will last only two more days." Tung Pao raised his head from his work, breathing hard as he spoke to his daughter-in-law. The money was borrowed at 2½ percent monthly interest. This was considered low, and it was only because Ssu-da-niang's father was an old tenant of the creditor that they had been able to get such a favorable rate.

"It was not such a good idea to put all the money in leaves," complained Ssu-da-niang, setting out the baskets to dry. "We may not be able to use all of them as was the case last year."

"What are you talking about! You would bring ill luck on us before we even got started. Do you expect it to be like last year always? We can only gather a little over ten loads from our own trees. How can that be enough for three sheets of eggs?"

"Yes, yes, you are always right. All I know is that you can cook rice only when there is some to cook and when there isn't you have to go hungry!"

Ssu-da-niang answered with some passion, for she had not yet forgiven her father-in-law for their arguments over the relative merit of foreign and domestic eggs. Tung Pao's face darkened and he said no more.

As the hatching days approached, the entire village of about thirty families became tense with hope and anxiety, forgetting it seemed, even their gnawing hunger. They borrowed and sought credit wherever they could and ate whatever they could get, often nothing but pumpkins and potatoes. None of them had more than a handful of rice stored away. The harvest had been good the year before but what with the landlord, creditors, regular taxes, and special assessments, they had long ago exhausted their store. Their only hope now lay in the silkworms; all their loans were secured by the promise that they would be paid after the "harvest."

As the period of Germinating Rains drew near, the "cloth" in every family began to take on a green hue. This became the only topic of conversation wherever women met.

"Lotus says they will be warming the cloth tomorrow. I don't see how it can be so soon."

"Huang Tao-shih went to the fortune teller. The character he drew indicated that leaves will reach four dollars per picul this year!"

Ssu-da-niang was worried because she could not detect any green on their own three sheets of eggs. Ah Ssu could not find any either when he took the sheets to the light and examined them carefully. Fortunately their anxiety did not last long, for spots of green began to show the following day. Ssu-da-niang immediately put the precious things against her breast to warm, sitting quietly as if feeding an infant. At night she slept with them, hardly daring to stir though the tiny eggs against her flesh made her itch. She was as happy, and as fearful, as before the birth of her first child!

The room for the silkworms had been made ready some days before. On the second day of "warming" Tung Pao smeared a head of garlic with mud and put it in a corner of the room. It was believed that the more leaves there were on the garlic on the day that silkworms were hatched, the better would be the harvest. The entire village was now engaged in this warming of the cloths. There were few signs of women along the brooks or on the husking grounds. An undeclared state of emergency seemed to exist: even the best of friends and the most intimate of neighbors refrained from visiting one another, for it was no joking matter to disturb the shy and sensitive goddess who protected the silkworms. They talked briefly in whispers when they met outside. It was a sacred season.

The atmosphere was even tenser when the "black ladies" began to emerge from the eggs. This generally happened perilously close to the day that ushered in the period of Germinating Rains and it was imperative to time the hatching so that it would not be necessary to gather them on that particular day. In Tung Pao's house, the first grubs appeared just before the tabooed day, but they were able to avoid disaster by transfering the cloths from the warm breast of Ssu-da-niang to the silkworms' room. Tung Pao stole a glance at the garlic and his heart almost stopped beating, for only one or two cloves had sprouted. He did not dare to take another look but only prayed for the best.

The day for harvesting the "black ladies" finally came. Ssu-da-niang was restless and excited, continually watching the rising steam from the pot, for the right moment to start operations was when the steam rose straight up in the air. Tung Pao lit the incense and candles and reverently set them before the kitchen god. Ah Ssu and Ah Dou went out to the fields to gather wild flowers, while Hsiao Pao cut up lampwick grass into fine shreds for the mixture used in gathering the newly hatched worms. Toward noon everything was ready for the big moment. When the pot began to boil vigorously and steam to rise straight up into the air, Ssu-da-niang jumped up, stuck in her hair a paper flower dedicated to the silkworms and a pair of goose feathers and went into the room, accompanied by Tung Pao with a steelyard beam and her husband with the prepared mixture of wild flowers and lampwick grass. Ssu-da-niang separated the two layers of cloth and sprinkled the mixture on them. Then taking the beam from Tung Pao she laid the cloths across it, took a goose feather and began to brush the "black ladies" off gently into the papered baskets. The same procedure was followed with the second sheet, but the last, which contained the foreign eggs was brushed off into separate baskets. When all was done, Ssu-da-niang took the paper flower and the feathers and stuck them on the edge of one of the baskets.

It was solemn ceremony, one that had been observed for hundreds and hundreds of years. It was as solemn an occasion as the sacrifice before a military campaign, for it was to inaugurate a month of relentless struggle against bad weather and ill luck during which there would be no rest day or night. The "black ladies" looked healthy as they crawled about in the small baskets; their color was as it should be. Tung Pao and Ssu-da-niang both breathed sighs of relief, though the former's face clouded whenever he stole a glance at the head of garlic, for the sprouts had not grown noticeably. Could it be that it was going to be like last year again?

3

Fortunately the prognostications of the garlic did not prove very accurate this time. Though it was rainy during the first and second molting and the weather colder than around Clear Bright, the "precious things" were all very healthy. It was the same with the "precious things" all over the village. An atmosphere of happiness prevailed, even the brook seemed to gurgle with laughter. The only exception was the household of Lotus, for their worms weighed only twenty pounds at the third "sleep," and just before the fourth Lotus's husband was seen in the act of emptying three baskets into the brooks. This circumstance made the villagers redouble their vigilance against the contamination of the unfortunate woman. They would not even pass by her house and went out of their way to avoid her and her taciturn husband. They did not want to catch a single glance of her or exchange a single word with her for fear that they might catch her family's misfortune. Tung Pao warned Ah Dou not to be seen with Lotus. "I'll lay a charge against you before the magistrate if I catch you talking to that woman," he shouted at his son loud enough for Lotus to hear. Ah Dou said nothing; he alone did not take much stock in these superstitions. Besides, he was too busy to talk to any one.

Tung Pao's silkworms weighed three hundred pounds after the "great sleep." For two days and two nights no one, not even Hsiao Pao, had a chance to close his eyes. The worms were in rare condition; in Tung Pao's memory only twice had he known anything equal to it—once when he was married and the other time when Ah Ssu was born. They consumed seven loads of leaves the first day, and it did not take much calculation to know how much more leaf would be needed before the worms were ready to climb up the "mountain."

"The squire has nothing to lend," Tung Pao said to Ah Ssu. "We'll have to ask your father-in-law to try his employers again."

"We still have about ten loads on our own trees, enough for another day," Ah Ssu said, hardly able to keep his eyes open.

"What nonsense," Tung Pao said impatiently. "They have started eating only two days ago. They'll be eating for another three days without counting tomorrow. We need another thirty loads, thirty loads."

The price of leaves had gone up to four dollars a load as predicted by the fortune teller, which meant that it would cost one hundred and twenty dollars to buy enough leaves to see them through. There was nothing to do but borrow the required amount on the only remaining mulberry land that they had. Tung Pao took some comfort in the thought that he would harvest at least five hundred pounds of cocoons and that at fifty dollars a hundred pounds he would get more than enough to pay his debts.

When the first consignment of leaves arrived, the "precious things" had already been without food for more than half an hour and it was heartbreaking to see them raise their heads and swing them hither and yon in search of leaves. A crunching sound filled the room as soon as the leaves were spread on the beds, so loud that those in the room had difficulty in hearing one another. Almost in no time the leaves had disappeared and the beds were again white with the voracious worms. It took the whole family to keep the beds covered with leaves. But this was the last five minutes of the battle; in two more days the "precious things" would be ready to "climb up the mountain" and perform their appointed task.

One night Ah Dou was alone on watch in the room, so that Tung Pao and Ah Ssu could have a little rest. It was a moonlit night and there was a small fire in the room for the silkworms. Around the second watch he spread a new layer of leaves on the beds and then squatted by the fire to wait for the next round. His eyes grew heavy and he gradually dozed off. He was awakened by what he thought was a noise at the door, but he was too sleepy to investigate and dozed off again, though subconsciously he detected an unusual rustling sound amidst the familiar crunching of leaves. Suddenly he awoke with a jerk of his drooping head just in time to catch the swishing of the reed screen against the door and a glimpse of some one gliding away. Ah Dou jumped up and ran out. Through the open gate he could see the intruder walking rapidly towards the brook. Ah Dou flew after him and in another moment he had flung him to the ground.

"Ah Dou, kill me if you want to but don't tell any one!"

It was Lotus's voice, and it made Ah Dou shudder. Her piggish eyes were fixed on his but he could not detect any trace of fear in them.

"What have you stolen?" Ah Dou asked.

"Your precious things!"

"Where have you put them?"

"I have thrown them into the brook!"

Ah Dou's face grew harsh as he realized her wicked intention. "How wicked you are! What have we done to you?"

"What have you done? Plenty! It was not my fault that our precious things did not live. Since I did you no harm and your precious things have flourished, why should you look upon me like the star of evil and avoid me like the plague? You have all treated me as if I were not a human being at all!"

Lotus had got up as she spoke, her face distorted with hatred. Ah Dou looked at her for a moment and then said:

"I am not going to hurt you; you can go now!"

Ah Dou went back to the room, no longer sleepy in the least. Nothing untoward happened during the rest of the night. The "precious things" were as healthy and strong as ever and kept on devouring leaves as if possessed. At dawn Tung Pao and Ssu-da-niang came to relieve Ah Dou. They picked up the silkworms that had gradually turned from white to pink and held them against the light to see if they had become translucent. Their hearts overflowed with happiness. When Ssu-da-niang went to the brook to draw water, however, Liu Pao, one of their neighbors, approached her and said to her in a low voice:

"Last night between the Second and Third Watch I saw that woman come out of your house, followed by Ah Dou. They stood close together and talked a long time. Ssu-da-niang, how can you let such things go on in your house?"

Ssu-da-niang rushed home and told her husband and then Tung Pao what had happened. Ah Dou, when, summoned, denied everything and said that Liu Pao must have been dreaming. Tung Pao took some consolation in the fact that so far there had been no sign of the curse on the silkworms themselves, but there was Liu Pao's unshakable evidence and she could not have made up the whole story. He only hoped that the unlucky woman did not actually step into the room but had only met Ah Dou outside.

Tung Pao became full of misgivings about the future. He knew well that it was possible for everything to go well all along the way only to have the worms die on the trees. But he did not dare to think of that possibility, for just to think of it was enough to bring ill luck.

4

The silkworms had at last mounted the trees but the anxieties of the growers were by no means over, for there was as yet no assurance that their labor and investment would be rewarded. They did not, however, let these doubts stop them from their work. Fires were placed under the "mountains" in order to force the silkworms climb up. The whole family squatted around the trees and listened to the rustling of the straws as the silkworms crawled among them, each trying to find a corner to spin its chamber of silk. They would smile broadly or their hearts would sink according to whether they could hear the reassuring sound or not. If they happen to look up and catch a drop of water from above, they did not mind at all, for that meant that there was at least one silkworm ready to get to work at that moment.

Three days later the fires were withdrawn. No longer able to endure the suspense, Ssŭ-da-niang drew aside one corner of the surrounding reed screens and took a peep. Her heart leaped with joy, for the entire "mountain" was covered with a snowy mass of cocoons! She had never seen a crop like this in all her life! Joy and laughter filled the household. Their anxieties were over at last. The "precious things" were fair and had not devoured leaves at four dollars a load without doing something to show for it, and they themselves had gone with practically no food or sleep for nothing; Heaven had rewarded them.

The same sound of joy and laughter rose everywhere in the village. The Goddess of Silkworms had been good to them. Everyone of the twenty or thirty families would gather at least a seventy or eighty percent capacity crop. As for Tung Pao's family they expected a hundred-and-twenty or even a hundred-and-thirty percent crop.

Women and children were again seen on the husking fields and along the brook. They were thinner than a month ago, their eyes more sunken and their voices more hoarse, but they were in high spirits. They talked about their struggles and dreamed of piles of bright silver dollars; some of them looked forward to redeeming their summer garments from the pawnshop, while others watered at the mouth in anticipation of the head of fish that they might treat themselves to at the Dragon Boat Festival.

The actual harvesting of the cocoons followed the next day,

attended by visits from friends and relatives bringing presents and their good wishes. Chang Tsai-fa, Ssu-da-niang's father, came to congratulate Tung Pao and brought with him cakes, fruits and salted fish. Hsiao Pao was as happy as a pup frolicking in the snow.

"Tung Pao, are you going to sell your cocoons or reel them yourself?" Chang asked, as the two sat under a willow tree along the brook.

"I'll sell them, of course."

"But the factories are not buying this year," Chang said, standing up and pointing in the direction of the buildings used by the buyers.

Tung Pao would not believe him but when he went to see for himself he found that the buyers' buildings were indeed still closed. For the moment Tung Pao was panic-stricken, but when he went home and saw the basket upon basket of fine, firm cocoons that he had harvested he forgot his worries. He could not believe it that such fine cocoons would find no market.

Gradually, however, the atmosphere of the village changed from one of joy and laughter to one of despair, as news began to arrive that none of the factories in the region were going to open for the season. Instead of the scouts for the cocoon buyers who in other years used to march up and down the village during this season, the village was now crowded with creditors and tax collectors. And none of them would accept cocoons in payment.

Curses and sighs of despair echoed through the entire village. It never occurred to the villagers even in their dreams that the extraordinarily fine crop of cocoons would increase their difficulties. But it did not help to complain and say that the world had changed. The cocoons would not keep and it was necessary to reel them at home if they could not sell them to the factories. Already some of the families had got out their long neglected spinning wheels.

"We'll reel the silk ourselves," Tung Pao said to his daughter-in-law. "We had always done that any way until the foreigners started this factory business."

"But we have over five hundred pounds of cocoons! How many spinning wheels do you plan to use?"

Ssu-da-niang was right. It was impossible for them to reel all the cocoons themselves and they could not afford to hire help. Ah Ssu agreed with his wife and bitterly reproached his father, saying:

"If you had only listened to us and hatched only one sheet of eggs, we would have had enough leaves from our own land."

Tung Pao had nothing to say to this.

Presently a ray of hope came to them. Huang Tao-shih, one of Tung Pao's cronies, learned from somewhere that the factories at Wusih were buying cocoons as usual. After a family conference it was decided that they would borrow a boat and undertake the journey of around three hundred li in order to dispose of their crop.

Five days later they returned with one basket of cocoons still unsold. The Wusih factory was unusually severe in their selection and paid only thirty dollars a hundred pounds of cocoons from foreign eggs and twelve dollars for the native variety. Though Tung Pao's cocoons were of the finest quality, they rejected almost a hundred pounds of the lot. Tung Pao got one hundred and eleven dollars in all and had only an even hundred left after expenses of the journey, not enough to pay off the debts they contracted in order to buy leaves. Tung Pao was so mortified that he fell sick on the way and had to be carried home.

Ssu-da-niang borrowed a spinning wheel from Liu Pao's house and set to work reeling the rejected cocoons. It took her six days to finish the work. As they were again without rice, she sent Ah Ssu to the town to sell the silk. There was no market for it at all and even the pawnshop would not loan anything against it. After a great deal of begging and wheedling, he was allowed to use it to redeem the picul of rice that they had pawned before Clear Bright.

And so it happened that every one in Tung Pao's village got deeper into debt because of their spring silkworm crop. Because Tung Pao had hatched three sheets of eggs and reaped an exceptional harvest, he lost as a consequence a piece of land that produced fifteen loads of mulberry leaves and thirty dollars besides, to say nothing of a whole month of short rations and loss of sleep!

"A True Chinese"

By Mao Dun

Lao-yeh always had his milk with two lumps of sugar in it promptly at seven while he was still in bed; it was brought him on a Fukien lacquer tray by Taitai herself, together with his morning paper.

Taitai always sat by him on the bed while he slowly drank his milk and rather hurriedly turned the pages of his paper. He always looked at the advertisements first, then the local news and then, finally, the national and foreign news. Having finished his paper and milk, he would turn to his wife and smile at her. That done, he would stretch himself with a yawn or rub his temples with his fingers and then fall back on his pillow and close his eyes so that he might review the business that he had to attend to in the course of the day. In the meantime Ah Wo, the maid, would have glided into the room like a shadow in answer to Taitai's ring and cleared the things away, and Taitai would follow her out, closing the door gently after her.

This had been the invariable routine in the household since Lao-yeh decided to adopt a more scientific mode of life two years ago. When Lao-yeh first began "to serve society" he did not insist on this ritual. He had milk in the morning as he did now, but he did not have to have it in bed nor did he have to have his wife bring it and put in the sugar herself and sit by him while he drank it. As a matter of fact, he used to get up first and open the windows and admit the servants while Taitai lay dozing in bed.

But since Lao-yeh's enterprises had prospered and he had graduated from "serving society" to "serving the Nation," he had come to feel that he should take better care of himself for the sake of the people and had decided that he would conserve his energies by taking things in a slower tempo and insure more wholesome food by sending his wife "back to the kitchen." Taitai, however, could only go back to the kitchen in a manner of speaking, for Lao-yeh had lunch home only two or three times a year and his supper about thirty or forty times and it was only in this morning ritual we have just described that Taitai was able to fulfill her duties as a wife.

One day Lao-yeh broke the rigid routine by opening up his paper at the section devoted to national news.

Taitai must have been preoccupied with her own thoughts, for she did not notice the change that had come over Lao-yeh's face until the rustle of the paper as he threw it aside recalled her to the present.

"Eh?" she turned to him enquiringly.

Lao-yeh only grunted but she knew from his tone and the frown on his face that there was something amiss. She felt his forehead with her hand and thought that it was slightly feverish. She was about to give utterance to her concern when Lao-yeh pushed her hand aside and reached for his milk.

"Oh, it's nothing," he said in a tone of irritation after sipping his milk. "Did you put more sugar in the milk than usual?"

"No, I put in the usual two lumps,". Taitai said, her eyes fixed on Lao-yeh's face. Then she laughed and said, "You must have something on your mind. The milk is all right but there is probably something wrong in the paper."

Lao-yeh was non-committal. He only smiled dryly and went back to his milk.

Taitai reached for the paper to see what had upset her lord, but Lao-yeh put one hand down on it while he gulped down the rest of his milk in one breath. Then he put down the cup and fell back on his pillow.

"Why distress yourself like this? After all it's the Government's—" But Taitai did not finish as she remembered just in time that her husband had now dedicated his services to the Nation.

"So the rumor I heard last night was true!" Lao-yeh murmured to himself. "All this nonsense about solution by peaceful means! Their mothers'——" He stopped short and glanced apologetically in the direction of his wife, for he had never indulged in this "national oath" before in the presence of such as his wife, though he resorted to it frequently in his office at the factory. Then addressing Taitai, he said: "You don't realize how important it is to maintain law and order. What is a few thousand lives if it is necessary to resort to military measures to put down these Communist bandits? But some of these people insist on peaceful compromise. Even Chien, the big banker, is for peace. It is most maddening."

"Now, now," Taitai said soothingly, for she did not want her husband to get upset so soon after breakfast. "You are right, of course, but what's the use of getting upset about it since they have decided on a peaceful solution? Moreover, our factory makes yarns. It is not as if you were a munitions dealer. Didn't you use to hope for peace during the One-Two-Eight War?" [1]

An impatient grunt from Lao-yeh made Taitai stop. Then diffidently she lifted her hand to feel Lao-yeh's brow, but the latter brushed her hand aside.

"I have no fever," he said. "But Taitai, how can you be so blind as not to see the difference? Let me explain by analogy: we should, of course, be as peaceable as possible with our neighbors, but what can we do except to take stern measures if cook and the servants should get impudent?"

Taitai smiled and nodded her head.

"Moreover," Lao-yeh continued, using Taitai as a foil, " 'One who does not attend the future is bound to have immediate trouble.' Haven't our neighbors [the Japanese] been talking about a united campaign against the Communist bandits? To forestall them we ought to suppress the bandits quickly and ruthlessly. How can we talk of peace at a time like this? What are we going to do if they should seize the excuse to land a few divisions and send over a few hundred airplanes? Can we offer any effective resistance? Do you think we can actually wage war against them? Remember, Taitai, that when that happens not only would our factory be

[1] The Sino-Japanese war of 1932 which broke out on January 28.

reduced to ashes, but we won't be able to chat in comfort and security as we are doing now!"

Taitai opened her eyes wide, completely acknowledging her mistake.

Lao-yeh did not take much comfort in Taitai's agreement with him, for she was after all only a foil to practice his devastating argument on. On the contrary, he was carried away by the force of his own arguments and became more worried and frightened than ever by the uncertain future. He buried his head deeper in the pillow and closed his eyes in weariness.

Suddenly hearing footsteps outside, Taitai tiptoed to the door and asked who it was.

"It is I," Ah Wo's voice answered. "I thought the bell might have got out of order as it did not ring."

The interruption recalled Taitai to the morning routine. "It is working all right," she said, subconsciously pressing on the button.

Taitai followed Ah Wo as the latter carried out the tray, and pulled the door shut gently behind her. She forgot the paper, however, and left it on Lao-yeh's bed.

At eight-thirty the children went to school in Lao-yeh's automobile; at nine the car returned and took Lao-yeh to his office, leaving Taitai to guard the house with her youngest daughter. At four in the afternoon Taitai telephoned Lao-yeh to ask whether to send their own car to get the children back from school or to send a servant for them in a taxi. This was Lao-yeh's rule, to guard against kidnapping.

Taitai was busiest around five, having to supervise the preparation of tea for the children, hear them tell of their activities at school (which she later relayed to Lao-yeh in the evening), and telephone around for Lao-yeh to find out whether he would be home for supper. Otherwise, however, Taitai had little to do the rest of the long day except to gossip with her friends over the telephone.

On this particular day Taitai had an early lunch, having decided to spend the afternoon with her youngest daughter in one of the department stores. Just as she was about ready to leave the house, Lao-yeh returned unexpectedly. He was sitting on the sofa in the living room with a cigar in his hand when Taitai went down. Remembering his bad humor that morning, she made a motion to feel his forehead.

But Lao-yeh intercepted her hand and thrust it aside none too gently, saying: "There is nothing the matter with me and I need none of your feminine doctoring. I was having lunch with some friends at Meijui's when I began to feel a little indisposed. But it's nothing. I'll be all right in a few minutes."

"Should I send for Dr. Huang?" Taitai said hesitatingly, sitting down on a low stool near the sofa.

"It isn't necessary," Lao-yeh said, shaking his head. He closed his eyes for a moment and then said with a grunt, "I can't understand it, Taitai. Even Mr. Lu is for peace. I was all alone at lunch, one mouth against four."

The beginnings of a frown appeared around Taitai's artifically elongated eyebrows, but she replaced it with a smile when Lao-yeh threatened to open his eyes.

"That's not all," Lao-yeh went on. "They told me that the *North China Daily News* had an editorial endorsing the Government's policy. Can you imagine a respectable British paper taking such a view of things?"

The youngest daughter now edged up to Taitai and looked at her, obviously asking her whether she was going to take her to the store. Taitai hesitated and then said to the maid: "Ah Wo, you take the young mistress to the store. Let her get a few playthings but don't let her buy anything to eat."

"Oh, were you thinking of going to the store?" Lao-yeh asked, noticing for the first time that they were dressed to go out. "Please go as you planned. I want to spend the afternoon in writing a letter to the *Daily News*."

"What do you want to write them for? You should not worry yourself since you are not feeling well!."

"I'll feel better after I get it off my chest," Lao-yeh said. "So please go as you planned."

Taitai stared at Lao-yeh in surprise, for he had always had a contempt for people who wrote letters to editors. Then it occurred to her that the editor might not publish the letter at all or might publish it with some ironical comment, neither of which was a pleasant thing to contemplate. One could never tell what one of these foreign papers might do. She decided that it was her duty to advise her husband against such a rash step.

"It is best not to bother," she said. "You are a man with a responsible position. It is not worth your while to get mixed up with these writing fellows."

"Never mind!" Lao-yeh said with some impatience. "You go on to the store." Then a little more gently, "Don't worry, Taitai; I am not going to sign my own name."

"What name are you going to use, then?"

"I am going to sign myself 'A True Chinese,'" Lao-yeh said, standing up. "But don't you worry. Go on to the store now and remember to bring me back two boxes of cigars."

Mrs. Li's Hair

By Yeh Shao-chün

Mrs. Li's hair had a history. Her husband had won her by writing pretty poems in praise of it, and her friends and relatives would always say, whenever they talked about her, that she had the hair of an authentic beauty. Her hair was indeed remarkable: it was long and soft, amenable to any kind of fashionable hairdress, and it was naturally more black and glossy, than pomades and oils could have made it. It was no wonder that every one identified her with beautiful hair, and beautiful hair with her. She herself paid a great deal of attention to her hair and would not suffer the least imperfection in connection with it. In other words, she was very careful in the matter of combing and brushing her hair and would do it over again without stint of time if a single strand was not quite in place or if the general effect could be improved in any way. This attention to her hair became almost a second nature with her so that even now she looked upon as her most pleasant task of the day combing and brushing it and achieving a satisfying arrangement, though she was now a middle-aged widow and the principal of the girls' middle school, and her hair had turned gray here and there.

One morning Mrs. Li was preoccupied in spite of the sunshine of the children's faces that streamed into her room and the singing of the birds sporting among the trees outside of her window. She had been preoccupied for several days and even nights. What worried her was simply this: was she to cut her hair as most of the girl students and many other women have done, now that the People's Revolutionary Army had taken over? The dilemma arose because she could not reconcile the pride that she took in her hair

and the sense of duty that she felt as the principal of the girls'
middle school.

Suddenly a new line of thought occurred to her and gave her
some comfort. It was this: since the 1911 Revolution had resulted
in men's cutting off their hair, it was but natural that the People's
Revolution should result in women's cutting off theirs. It was both
just and proper that they should do so unhesitatingly to show their
revolutionary spirit. Moreover, as the principal of a school, the
principal of the chief educational institution for women in the
region, it was her duty to set an example for the students and other
women. If she would not even give up a few strands of hair, it
was not at all impossible that people would say that she was opposed
to hair bobbing and therefore opposed to the Revolution. And it
would not be surprising in that case if her position would be . . .

Following this line of reasoning she should find it easy to make
up her mind. But unfortunately her position was complicated by
the fact that she had once posted a notice containing these uncom-
promising words: "It is both immodest and indecent for women to
cut their hair. No student in this school will be permitted to do so."
She even required the students in the primary grades to grow their
hair and do it up in queues or coiffures in the form of an "S" as
was then the fashion. That was, however, more than a year ago.

"Won't people laugh at me if I cut my hair now?" she asked
herself. "No, it doesn't matter. I would not allow them to cut their
hair last year because the time was not ripe for it; now that it is,
I must cut mine also. 'There is a time for everything.'" Thus she
pleaded for herself like a clever lawyer.

She picked up an oval-shaped hand mirror and studied herself.
How grey and thin her hair had become, showing patches of her
scalp as pale and white as the skin of a cat accustomed to doze in
the stove! How pitifully flat and loose the knot was behind her
head! How different it was from what she had always associated
with herself with joy and pride! As to the hateful thing she now
beheld in the mirror, there was nothing to do but to cut it off.

Another complication was where to have her hair cut. She could,
of course, go to a fashionable barbershop with a red-and-white-

striped pole painted on the window as so many women were doing, but the barbershops were crowded with customers within and curious spectators without, and if any one she knew should see her, he was bound to spread the news that Mrs. Li, the principal of the girls' school, had her hair cut today. If the informant was inclined to be clever, he might even use the word "tonsured" instead of "cut," thus comparing her to a nun. She did not mind that possible jibe so much as the telltale and specific "today," for that could only mean that she was a *new* recruit and new was a word complimentary in everything nowadays except when applied to a revolutionary.

She thought of asking one of her students to do it for her. They were all experts in the matter of hair and could do a different hairdress each day for ten days in succession without much trouble. But most of them were inclined to have clever tongues, clever to the point of cruelty. She knew them well, having lived among them so long. How humiliating it would be if her prospective candidate should say, with scissors poised over her, "You would not let us cut our hair last year and said that it was immodest and indecent. How is it that you have decided to join our ranks?" What should she do then? Should she put on a serious face and give the impudent thing a lecture or should she try to laugh it off?

She wished then that people had not noticed her hair so much and would not be conscious whether it was bobbed or not; she wished that she could dispose of her hair without incident and without arousing curiosity and that when people did notice they would think that she had perhaps cut it long ago but that they had not noticed before. That was, however, only an idle wish. The only thing that she could do was to dispose of her hair first and wait for developments. As to who was to cut it for her, she decided, after some hesitation, to send for her daughter, who taught a few classes in the same school.

She hesitated to take her own daughter into her confidence because she knew that the girl would not approve. This did not mean that her daughter was reactionary and valued her hair as much as her honor; she was, as a matter of fact, among the courageous

few who had cut their hair weeks before. (Mrs. Li had simply
ignored them, neither taking action against them nor expressing
approval.) But recalling recent remarks made by her daughter—
"It is so unbecoming of Mrs. Chang, a woman over thirty, to have
her hair cut," or "How ridiculous of Mrs. Wang to visit the barbershop with her daughter-in-law. It made me laugh so that my sides
ached when I saw her come out of the shop."—she could not help
hesitating. Her daughter's implication was clear: she regarded it
the exclusive privilege of young girls in their late teens and early
twenties to have their hair cut and thought it unbecoming for older
women to emulate them. It was obvious, too, that she held her own
mother in the same light, an old woman who should not try to
keep up with the times. Little did she realize that the tide of
progress would bring distress to her mother and place her in such
an awkward position.

"I am thinking of having my hair cut. What do you think of it?"
Mrs. Li tried to be nonchalant but the tone of her voice betrayed
her diffidence.

Her daughter laughed. Her bobbed hair shone in the morning
sunlight and formed a splendid setting for her sparkling eyes and
bright cheeks; she was as arrogant and self-assured as a flower
that had just blossomed out in the spring. She said, casting a contemptuous glance at her mother's head, "I am afraid that it won't
look very well for mama at her age to have her hair cut as the
young girls do." It was only a matter of rhetoric for her to have
said "I am afraid;" if she had been frank she would not have even
used the words "It won't look very well" but would have bluntly
said that it was *unbecoming* of her.

Mrs. Li did not weaken under the expected reaction of her
daughter. "Age has nothing to do with it," she said. "In these days
women should all have their hair cut. Haven't you done so yourself?
Moreover, my position . . ."

The reference to her position aroused an unpleasant reaction in
her daughter. These old dames! Always treated the students as if
they were their daughters or daughters-in-law! They would lecture
and coax by turns. How undignified of them to run a school on

those lines! Take her own mother, for instance. She apparently suffered not the least compunction after her ridiculously worded notice to the students the year before, but how humiliating it was for her daughter. If she would only relinquish her position, it would be easier for those related to her. With these thoughts in mind, the daughter said, assuming a childish innocence, "We children have often said among ourselves that the work at school is too strenuous for mama and that mama should take a rest. If they require principals to have their hair cut, it gives mama a good excuse to resign."

"What?" Mrs. Li was angry at the unexpected remark. "Why should I use this as an excuse to resign? Do you mean to say that my hair is so important that I should preserve it at the price of my position as the principal of a school? My ideas on the subject are just the opposite: I would much rather sacrifice my hair to maintain my position! And why do you suppose I want to make this sacrifice? I want you to understand, Miss, that it is all for the sake of you children!" There was a tremor in her voice as she said the last sentence. She felt hurt and sad because her children did not appreciate what she was trying to do for them but thought that she insisted on working because she was, like an old horse or ox, unhappy without occupation.

She understood only too well, thought the daughter to herself. Her mother's love amounted to only one thing: she insisted on keeping her daughter and son-in-law under her protecting wings and would not let them exercise their own. She insisted that they were unfit for the storms and dangers outside and that they must be sheltered in a safe harbor such as she herself provided, little dreaming that her daughter and son-in-law were like small but sturdy boats, eager to try the open and unknown seas, whatever the weather might be. Little did she realize that they hated most to lie idle in the harbor, which could only lead to rot and disintegration.

After a brief silence, the daughter said awkwardly: "Then mama might as well cut it off too." She always gave in to her mother when she assumed that it-is-all-for-you-children tone.

"You cut it for me," Mrs. Li said with the alacrity of one seizing upon an opportunity that comes only once in a lifetime.

"I'll cut it for mama." The daughter looked at her own hand as if unable to reconcile herself to the fact that it was about to take part in an awful crime. "But after it is cut off I hope you won't have to wear a wig one of these days, and make me do your hair for you."

"What nonsense," Mrs. Li replied with emphasis.

K-da! k-da! The scissors soon did their work. Mrs. Li's head felt extraordinarily light, as if a piece of her scalp had come off with the hair. Suddenly she realized how vain it was to imagine that people would not notice what she had done. She could see in her hand mirror how thin her hair was, how much more so it seemed than before she had it cut, how much more noticeable the strips of exposed scalp were and how impossible it was for even the near-sighted students to fail to notice it. She knew that she would be dubbed "new" and would be subjected to their laughter and ridicule.

To postpone the evil moment as long as she could, she decided that she would not go to the special training class in the principles of the Kuomintang which had been inaugurated only two days ago. She even closed her door for a while, thinking to safeguard the secret as long as possible, but she soon realized that it would only arouse their curiosity and bring more students to her room. She opened the door again and sat facing it, entrusting her secret only to the indifferent walls.

Many students passed by her door, some stopping to peep in. Some of the students in the primary grades were playing ball outside; several times the ball bounced into her room and when the students came in to get it she was sure that her secret had been discovered. She kept her eyes on a copy of the *Ladies' Journal* on her desk and her face reddened when she heard their titter. She became angry and wanted to get up and say to them what if she was "new," what if she had forbidden them to cut off their hair? She rehearsed her speech on the theme that there was a time for everything and that she was not ashamed to change her stand, but her courage failed her, and she only told them to leave her alone as she had a headache. To make her lie seem real, she awkwardly put her right hand on her temple.

"He, he, he!" They went off tittering.

She did not dare face them, for fear that the scorn in their eyes might be even more difficult to bear. Her eyes returned to the magazine. It was then that she made out the striking title of the article before her. It read: "I Am against Women Bobbing Their Hair!" The writer's name was not suffixed by the feminine title *nü-shih*. This meant that the article was probably written by a man, since very few women would forego the opportunity to publicize their sex when they got anything published. She read the article eagerly, for she who had just cut her hair was naturally eager to know why a man was against women's bobbing their hair.

The article was indeed written by a man, for the author said in the introduction that it was written from the point of view of a man and was based upon a man's conception of the special attributes of womanhood, that while he did not dare to insult women by regarding them like flowers in a vase or birds in cages, he believed it was permissible to express what a man admired in a woman, and that he, as a man, would certainly welcome any statement from the opposite sex as to what was expected of him, instead of regarding it as an insult or something equally unpleasant. Following this introduction he went on to describe how women's hair, in its unsheared state, appeals to all the senses of a man, the sense of sight as well as the sense of smell and the sense of touch, and how, especially when they share pillow and bed, it stimulates the most beautiful and tender feelings in a man and makes him think of strands of refined silk and puffs of clouds, and how it has a perfume of its own which is quite unlike any mortal extraction and which epitomizes womanhood itself. He gave many intimate details to illustrate what an important part hair in its unsheared state plays in the relationship of the two sexes and concluded by saying that for a woman to cut her hair short was to destroy all the things that distinguish her from and endear her to the other sex.

Mrs. Li pushed the magazine away, a little ashamed as if she had pried into something that she should not have. A thousand intimate details of her married life came back to her, details which had lain buried so long in her memory. She dwelt especially on the part that her hair had played in that long-lost past, and her reminiscences not only confirmed the views expressed in the article but underscored them and made the writer's exposition of the charms of long hair seem superficial and inadequate. Then she asked herself how her husband would have stood on the issue. There could be but one answer: he who had written so many pretty verses about her hair would certainly have begged her not to cut it off. Then there was her daughter. If the views expressed in the article represented the attitude of the majority of men, her son-in-law probably did not approve of his wife's bobbed hair and might cease to love her. She began to regret her rash act.

But these regretful thoughts were nothing compared to the feeling of panic occasioned some days afterwards by the report that the Revolutionary armies had suffered reverses and that Sun Ch'uan-fang, the Northern general, had recrossed the Yangtze with his horde. If Sun's forces should reoccupy the city, Mrs. Li would not only lose her position because of her bobbed hair but she might very well be shot as a revolutionary. She said to her daughter with some embarrassment: "I never thought that I would come to this, but under the circumstances it is best to be prepared. Take my hair to the shop and have it made into a wig right away."

"But you wouldn't listen to me," her daughter said triumphantly. "I am afraid that there isn't enough hair for a wig."

"What are we to do then?"

"Take some of mine."

"But, how stupid of us. You must have one made, too."

"I don't need one. I am not afraid and I can stay home when the worst comes."

"They may conduct a house to house search!" A nightmare of black chains and red blood rose before Mrs. Li.

"Then . . ."

"Then?"

The collapse of Sun's army ended Mrs. Li's fears for her life, but at the same time she received her dismissal notice from the Bureau of Education. No reason was given for her dismissal; she was simply instructed to get things in good order and await the arrival of her successor.

Neighbors

By Yeh Shao-chün

One day toward evening my younger brother and I were playing outside our gate. He walked in front of me with his hands stretched out behind him holding mine and pretended that he was pulling a ricksha. I followed him, swaying a bit from side to side, while he shouted: "Here comes a ricksha, here comes a ricksha!"

Suddenly a bicycle rider turned into the alley, and though I was not noticing him especially, I knew for certain that it was the Japanese boy who lived to the west of us. In a flash he was alongside of us. He tried to dodge, but in his excitement he turned into us instead and knocked down our little ricksha man.

"*Wah.....*" didi burst out crying. He lay flat on his chest and hands and kicked his feet up and down.

I was a bit angry as I helped didi up and I was frightened to see blood streaming down his lips.

"I am very sorry, very sorry," the Japanese boy said in Chinese, jumping off his bicycle and leaning it against the wall. When he saw the blood, he was frightened too and his face became flushed down to his neck. Then he said, "I'll go and get some cold boiled water," and ran into his house.

A moment later he came back with the water and some sterilized cotton. He squatted down, dipped the cotton in the water, and began to wipe the blood gently off didi's lips, while I acted the part of a physician's assistant by supporting didi's head from the back so that he could lift up his face. Didi was still crying, shedding drops of tears as big as beans. I tried to quiet him, saying, "Don't cry any more. What's a little bit of pain."

"It's not bad, it's not bad," the Japanese boy said with relief after he had cleaned off the blood. As a matter of fact, it wasn't bad at all. There was a slight cut on the inside of both lips with the blood still oozing out.

Mama had heard the cry and came out. When she found what had happened and was satisfied that didi was otherwise unhurt, she patted didi and said to him: "Don't cry any more. The blood will not stop flowing if you keep your mouth open. Let's go in and look at picture books. There are camels with large humps and deers with long necks in them."

Didi gradually stopped crying and went in with Mama, holding onto her with one hand and wiping off his tears with the other.

The Japanese boy stood up and again apologized with evident sincerity: "I am very sorry, very sorry."

By that time I was no longer angry and I replied: "Don't let it worry you. You did not do it intentionally."

"Of course it was not intentional but just the same I was responsible for what had happened." He spoke in stilted Chinese and looked like a repentant student before his teacher.

Toward evening on the second day he came to our house to see didi, bringing with him a present of four cakes of a light green color. Didi's cuts had already healed, leaving only two discolored spots. He was delighted with the cakes and took one of them.

Our visitor said: "These are Japanese cakes, made entirely of soya beans, including the stuffing. Try them."

I asked him to have one too. They were indeed very good. Compared to our moon cakes they were not quite so sweet or so heavy.

From then on I often chatted with him when we met. I found that he was born in Shanghai and was an apprentice in a Japanese book store. His father was a clerk in some Japanese shop and had lived in Shanghai close to twenty years. He told me about Japanese customs, the meaning, for instance, of the split bamboo poles at their gate and of the fish-shaped bags that they hang on their roofs. He told me too about how hard life was for their friends and relatives in Japan: how clerks could not find work and how peasants did not have a chance to eat the things that they grew in the fields.

I also told him about our own family, how we lost practically everything in the One-Two-Eight War,[1] how we have had to furnish our new home stick by stick like a bird building a nest, and how even now we were still far from having everything we needed.

"It is the same with us," he said with some passion. "We were living in one of the side streets off Paoshan Road then and the bombardment destroyed everything in our house. It is even worse for us to undergo the calamity, for you may be said to have sacrificed for your country but as for us what did we make the sacrifice for?"

"For your country, too, of course," I said off-hand.

"You are being sarcastic now. Why should we sacrifice for them, those robbers and bandits?" His voice trembled, his eyes filled with anger.

I said apologetically: "Please forgive me, I shouldn't have said that. We can all mark our sacrifices off against those robbers and bandits."

"That's the way to put it," he said, nodding his head, and then continued with passion: "It is a shame for us Japanese to have that kind of people among us. As I am a Japanese, I feel very apologetic for the acts of these people."

We shook hands warmly and assured each other that we must all nourish our strength so that we could stand up against those people.

Our neighbors to the east moved away and three days later new tenants came to occupy the house. Among the furniture there were low tables and thick floor mats, which told us at a glance that the new tenants were Japanese. Soon we found that our new neighbors consisted of husband and wife without any children. The man had thick eyebrows, high cheekbones, and a short moustache. The woman was a sickly and pathetic looking creature, her face heavily powdered.

We rarely saw the man, but the woman was often seen going out to shop or washing the pavement outside their gate with a pail

[1] See footnote on p. 161.

of water. The Japanese boy who lived to our west told me that the man was a high-salaried employee of some large Japanese concern.

One night I was suddenly awakened out of a sound sleep by a violent banging that sounded like a carpenter tearing down a wooden wall with a hammer. Mama was up already when I opened my eyes, holding didi in her arms. I heard Papa's voice in the room overlooking the back door saying:

"What do you want? what do you want?"

The answer was more banging and an indistinct mutter which sounded like profanity.

I dressed hurriedly and ran toward the back in spite of mama's protest. I looked out of the window and found that it was our new neighbor and that he was banging away at our door like a barber pounding away at a customer's back. He was not very steady on his feet and had to lean against the wall with his hands when he was not banging at the door.

"What do you want, knocking at peoples' doors in the middle of the night?" Papa shouted in a loud voice, unlike his usual self.

More banging and then kicking, probably because his hands were beginning to hurt. The door shook in its frames and the walls rocked as if they were about to collapse. A stream of words rushed out of his mouth but we could not make out anything as he spoke in Japanese.

By this time a crowd of about twenty persons, both men and women, had gathered in the alley. Among them were some Japanese, including the father of the Japanese boy who was our neighbor to the west. He went up to the man who was making the noise and talked to him. The latter answered him, gesticulating and pointing to us and shaking his fist.

After finding out what the trouble was, the father of the boy I knew told us about it in Chinese. The man wanted satisfaction because a boy in our house had called him a Japanese turtle.

The accusation made me very indignant, for there were only two boys in our family and since didi was too young to go out by himself, the offending boy could only have been I. But why should I have cursed him? I was not the kind of boy that indulged in that kind of pastime. I told papa that I wouldn't lie about it and that I had not called the man any names.

Papa then asked our neighbor to the west to tell the man that on his honor as a Chinese he could assure him that no one in our family had cursed him. The man did not appear to believe it and resumed his banging. The Japanese spectators talked among themselves and then went up to the man and half urged and half dragged him away and escorted him to his own back door.

The crowd dispersed, followed by the sound of doors shutting. We could hear the man mounting his stairs with a heavy tread and cursing incessantly in Japanese.

We couldn't fall asleep for a while, for the incident had upset all of us. Suddenly we heard two sharp slaps and then a woman weeping. Two more slaps even heavier than the first followed and the woman's weeping became shrill and loud and tremulous, suggesting that she was probably rolling on the floor.

As I set out for school the next morning I encountered the Japanese boy just starting out on his bicycle. When he saw me, he got off his bicycle and walked alongside me and told me that his father had told him about last night. He said the man was drunk and that most of the Japanese in the alley thought that he was in the wrong to bang at people's gate in the middle of the night when he had no proof for his accusation.

I was inclined to forget the episode when I heard that the man was drunk and was not responsible for his actions. I did not, therefore, immediately grasp the significance of the presence of a police sergeant and three policemen in our parlour when I returned home in the afternoon. The sergeant tilted his head at me and asked, "Are you the one who called people names?"

"Call whom names?" I said, still uncomprehending.

"The Japanese next door," the sergeant said, twisting his mouth in the direction of our east wall.

Mama answered for me: "None of us called him names, as I have told you already."

"But it is not enough just to deny it. He went to the Consulate and said that some one in your house had called him names and the Consulate complained to us."

I lost my inclination to forgive the man. I said indignantly: "He was drunk and came to bang at our door in the middle of the night without any justification. He should be punished for disturbing the peace."

"He should be punished? But he demands that you people be punished. Let me tell you, little didi, you should understand that we are living in a difficult time and that we must try to be as courteous to the Japanese as possible. It's the Government's orders that we should live in peace with them. You must watch out what you say and where you throw a tiny piece of pebble or bamboo, for we must avoid any incident whatever. It's orders, my little friend."

The sergeant was not very severe in his manner; he was more like a teacher trying to admonish a student. But it was a kind of admonition that I could not accept with grace. I looked away from his pockmarked face and began to unpack my school case.

Papa came back at this juncture and the sergeant repeated what he had just said. He said further that he had come only to warn us for the present.

Papa's face was far from genial when he replied: "We have never called him names and shall not call him names in the future. You can be sure of that."

The four of them left but after supper another two policemen came and said that they had instructions to guard us, one at the front and one at the back door. They were apologetic as well as sympathetic but they had their orders and they paced the street at either end of our house throughout that night. In the morning they were relieved and returned again that night.

The next day Papa decided to move in order to avoid possible trouble in the future and Mama seconded his proposal. Papa found a flat the same day and we started moving right away. After the last cartful of things had been sent off and as we were about ready to leave the house ourselves, the policeman at the front gate said to Papa with some embarrassment: "I am glad that you have decided to move. You school people are different, you understand things.

What's the use of bucking against them? Well, it's easier for us, too, I guess we won't have to come back to morrow."

Papa said nothing.

I stopped for a moment in front of the door of our neighbor to the west. It was closed. The boy had not yet returned from work and so I did not have an opportunity to say goodbye to him.

What's the Difference?

By Lusin

Fang Hsuan-cho has recently got into the habit of saying "What's the difference?" The expression is not only constantly on the tip of his tongue but has become an integral part of his psychological make-up. He used to say "It's all the same," but he decided that was too positive and hence potentially dangerous and modified it to "What's the difference?" which has served him to this day.

The rediscovery of this banal expression gave him a new point of view and a new source of comfort. For instance, he used to get very indignant when he saw youth oppressed by age, but now he comforts himself by saying that when youth grows to old age and has children and grandchildren of its own it will in all probability behave exactly the same way. Again, he used to become very indignant when he saw a soldier beating up a ricksha man, but now he reasons that if the soldier and the ricksha man changed places one would be beating the other just the same. Sometimes he has an uncomfortable feeling that he is not being honest with himself, that he has adopted this process of reasoning because he does not have courage enough to fight the evils of society, that it is nothing but an excuse and an escape, that it comes very close to being without a sense of right and wrong, and that he should, therefore, change this cowardly attitude. However, he has not changed it, but, on the contrary, has allowed it to take a firmer hold of himself than ever.

It was in the classroom of the school where he was teaching that he first propounded his thesis that "nothing makes much difference." He had been discussing certain events in Chinese history and was prompted to remark that "the ancients and moderns are not

far apart" and that "people are very much the same by nature."
That naturally led to the subject of students and government
officials, on which he held forth thus:

"It is the fashion nowadays to abuse public officials, and of those
who criticize them there are none so vociferous as students. But
we must remember that officials are not a race by themselves but
have come from the people. There are many officials today who
were once students; so what is the difference between them? 'It is
their positions that make them appear different.' Otherwise there
is no difference between them whether in thought, speech, action,
or manners . . . Is it not generally admitted that even the various
enterprises sponsored by the student organizations have not been
free from corruption and malpractices and that many of these enterprises have collapsed as a result? There isn't much difference. But
in this fact lies the cause for the dark future of China . . ."

Of the twenty-odd listeners in the room, some were reflective
and seemed to agree with the speaker; others were indignant because he had blasphemed sacred youth; still others only smiled
mockingly, probably because they regarded his speech as a self-
defense—for Fang Hsuan-cho was an official as well as a teacher.

In reality all these suppositions were wrong, for with Fang
Hsuan-cho it was only a matter of adopting a new pose, of championing a new cause that involved no danger. He knew himself
that he was no agitator but a very law-abiding citizen at heart,
though he was not sure whether this was due to laziness or futility.
His minister had maligned him by saying that he was a psychological case, but he would never make any protest as long as his
position was secure; it was now more than six months since the
teachers got their last pay, but as long as he drew his other salary
he would never complain. Not only did he not complain, but when
the teachers held a mass meeting to demand payment of their
salaries he even privately expressed the opinion that the step was
too blatant and ill-advised. When his fellow officials became too
critical of the teachers, however, he felt drawn towards the latter's
cause. Then he told himself that he felt this way probably because
he happened to be short of money and that his fellow officials did

not feel the way he did because they were not at the same time teachers as he was.

Although he was in need of money, he did not join the teachers' organization. When a strike was called, however, he did not go to his classes. The government's stand that there would be no pay unless the teachers went back to their classes first made him a little angry, for that was, he said, like teasing a monkey with fruits. He was even more angry when a prominent educator expressed the opinion that it was undignified for the teachers to hold a briefcase in one hand and hold out the other for money.

"*Wey,* how does it happen that there are only two dishes?" he complained to his wife that evening, looking at the food on the table.

They had not received the newer brand of education, and his wife did not have any school or pet name which he addressed her by. He might have called her "taitai" according to the old custom but he did not want to be old-fashioned. He adopted, therefore, the exclamatory *wey.* Taitai did not even use that; he was able to infer that she was talking to him by the fact that she was, at the moment, facing him.

"We have spent all the 15 percent payment that we received last month . . . I had considerable difficulty in getting credit for rice yesterday."

"And yet they say that it is undignified for the teachers to demand their pay. These people don't seem to understand even the elementary fact that a man must eat, that he must have the rice grain in order to cook rice [1] and that he must have money before he can buy the grain."

"That's right. How can one buy rice grain without money and how can one cook rice without . . ."

His wife's remarks served only to irritate him further and he puffed out his cheeks as if annoyed at her because her ready agreement with him showed a deplorable lack of independent spirit, between which and obsequiousness "there isn't much difference."

---

[1] There is a saying that even the cleverest housewife cannot cook rice (*fan*) without the grain (*mi*).

He turned his face away from her, which was his way of announcing that he did not want to pursue the discussion further.

The teachers did get some of their back pay after staging a demonstration in front of the presidential palace on a certain dismal and rainy day, during which some of them were roughly handled by the soldiery and sustained injuries. Fang Hsuan-cho, however, got his share of the money without having taken any trouble about it at all. But after paying some of his more urgent debts he was again without funds; for now his salary as an official had also become irregular. When this happened, the high-minded officials began to feel that salaries should be paid. How much stranger must have been Fang Hsuan-cho's feelings since he was at the same time a teacher. Therefore he adhered faithfully to the decision of his colleagues to continue the strike although he still absented himself from their deliberations.

Again the government paid and the schools opened. A few days earlier the Students' Federation had submitted a petition to the government asking it to withhold the teachers' pay until they went back to their classes. The petition did not have any effect, fortunately, on the teachers' position, but it did remind Fang Hsuan-cho of the government's previous declaration that there would be no pay until the teachers went back to their classes, and it convinced him again that "there isn't much difference" between students and government officials and caused him to give public utterance to this theory of his.

Soon something else happened to confirm Fang Hsuan-cho in his thesis that "there isn't much difference," for the government now ignored the lesser officials as it once ignored the obstreperous teachers. It allowed their salaries to fall further and further in arrears until some of the high-minded officials who had criticized the teachers now became some of the most outspoken exponents of the movement to demand back pay. These officials were in turn criticized and satirized by the newspapers. This did not surprise Fang Hsuan-cho in the least, for according to his thesis the newspapers adopted their sarcastic tone because they were still receiving their subsidies. He was sure that should their subsidies stop, the journalists would also be holding mass meetings.

It was natural that Fang Hsuan-cho should approve the action of his fellow officials, since he had already expressed his sympathy for the teachers in their demand for back pay. Yet as before he sat in his office and did not take part in the meetings and demonstrations. This was not because he was trying to be different, as some people thought, but because, as he explained, he had been only dunned by others for debts but had never in his life dunned others for debts owed to him, the latter being one of the things "he was not good at."

Thus by staging frequent demonstrations the teachers and government officials managed to pull through festival after festival, though Fang Hsuan-cho found it much more difficult to make ends meet than formerly. He found that even his wife grew rebellious, to say nothing of the servant that they kept and the shopkeepers that they had dealings with. He noticed that his wife no longer agreed with everything he said as she used to but would often venture opinions of her own and act without asking his leave. For instance, when he returned home at noon on the day before the Dragon Boat Festival, she pushed a pile of bills unceremoniously right under his nose, and said without so much as looking at him, "It will take at least 180 dollars to pay these . . . Has it been issued yet?"

"*Heng,* I don't want to be an official any more. The check has been received, but the committee has decided to hold it, first saying that those who did not join the demonstration would not get anything and then that they must go before the committee in person to receive their salary. So as soon as they hold the funds in their hands they assume the face of the King of Hell. I don't like to see such faces . . . I don't want their money. I'll give up my post. Such humiliating tactics . . ."

Mrs. Fang was taken aback for a while at this outburst, but she recovered her self-possession almost immediately.

"I think it would be best that you go in person as they want you to. What does that amount to?" she said looking at him.

"I sha'n't go! It is my salary, not a tip, and it should be sent to me by the treasurer's office as it has always been."

"But what are we going to do, since they are not going to send it to you?—By the way, I forgot to tell you yesterday that the children said their school had repeatedly asked them to bring their tuition. They said that unless it is paid soon . . ."

"Nonsense! How could they have the brazenness to demand tuition from the students when they do not pay their fathers for their services?"

Realizing that there was no use to argue with a man who was getting unreasonable and who was not above venting upon her the displeasure that he felt against the principal of the school, she said no more.

After lunch, during which neither one said anything, he thought for a while and then went out, still in an irritable mood.

It was his usual custom in recent years to come back home around midnight on the eve of a festival and to say in a loud voice as he entered the room, *"Wey,* I've got my salary!" and hand over to her a bunch of Bank of China and Bank of Communications notes, not without an air of complacence. But on this the fourth day of the Fifth month he came home at the unprecedented hour of seven in the afternoon. Mrs. Fang was surprised and thought he might have really given up his job, but searching his face carefully she could not detect there anything so disastrous.

"What is it? . . . Why so early?" she asked with her eyes fixed on him.

"They can't issue the salaries today. The banks have already closed and we must wait until the eighth."

"How about the question of appearing in person before the committee?" she ventured timidly.

"That? Well, they have decided to spare us that humiliation. I was told that we'll be paid through the treasurer's office as usual. But the banks will be closed for three days over the Festival and we'll have to wait until the morning of the eighth." He sat down with his gaze fixed on the ground and then said slowly after taking a few gulps of tea, "Fortunately there is absolutely no more question of our being paid. We'll get our money on the eighth for certain . . . It is no easy matter trying to borrow from so-called friends and relatives. This afternoon I went to see Chin Yung-sheng, after a hard struggle with myself. We chatted for a while and he praised me for my not joining the demonstrations and for refusing to appear in person before the committee. He said that I took the right line of conduct for a dignified and self-respecting individual. But when he learned that I wanted to borrow fifty dollars from him, he acted as if I had stuffed a handful of salt into his mouth and his face wrinkled up in a manner which no one would have thought possible. He told me how he had not been able to collect his rents, how he had been losing money in his business, and that it was no great humiliation to appear before the committee in person. He got rid of me quickly enough."

"Who would want to lend money out at a time when people are expected to pay their debts?" Mrs. Fang said indifferently as if suggesting that it was unreasonable to expect people to behave otherwise.

Fang Hsuan-cho bowed his head in silence. He realized that his wife was right. Moreover, he was not a very close friend of Chin Yung-sheng. He recalled a similar incident which had happened at the previous New Year festival. A fellow provincial of his had come to borrow ten dollars from him, and he had sent him away empty handed by saying that he "was willing but unable to help" since he had not received his salary either from the school or the bureau, though as a matter of fact he had already received his certification from the latter. He remembered that he had assumed an air of embarrassment at the time. He could not recall now just what sort of face he made, but the recollection of the incident made him feel uncomfortable, and he compressed his lips and shook his head.

But after a short time he suddenly came back to life as if he had just had an inspiration: he commanded his servant to go out immediately and get a bottle of Lotus White on credit. He reasoned that the shop would probably not dare to refuse for fear that they might not get their portion of the Fang family's salary check. If they did refuse him credit, he said to himself, he would not pay them a single copper when he got his money, and that would just serve them right.

The servant did come back with the Lotus White and after two cups his pale face became flushed with red. After dinner he was again in good spirits. He lit a "magnum"-size Hatamen cigarette, took a copy of Hu shih's *Experiments* from his desk, reclined on his bed, and began to read.

"But what are we going to do about the shopkeepers tomorrow?" Mrs. Fang followed him relentlessly and asked, standing before the bed and looking at him.

"The shopkeepers? Tell them to come on the afternoon of the eighth."

"I cannot say that to them. They won't take that for an answer."

"They will have to. They can go and inquire. No one in the ministry has got his salary. All have to wait until the eighth." His hand described an arc as he opened *Experiments*. Mrs. Fang's eyes followed the movement and decided to say nothing as she perceived that he was in an unreasonable mood.

"I am afraid," she said after a while, "that we can't go on like this. We must find some other way out . . ."

"What do you suggest? What else can I do?"

"Didn't you use to write things for the Shanghai publishers?"

"The Shanghai publishers? Why, they figure your manuscript by the word and would not count the punctuations and blank spaces. But see how much blank space there is in the free verse that I have written. I am afraid it would only fetch three hundred coppers. Moreover, you're lucky if you received anything in six months on the royalty basis. 'Distant water will not safe a near-by fire.' I haven't that much patience."

"Then how about the newspapers here . . . ?"

"Their rates are even worse. One of my students is the editor of one of the biggest papers in town but he can't do anything. I couldn't support the family even if I should write night and day. Besides, I haven't got so much in me to write about."

"Then what are we going to do after the festival?"

"After the festival?—I'll keep my job at the ministry . . . When the shopkeepers come tomorrow, just tell them that they'll have to wait until the afternoon of the eighth."

He was about to turn to *Experiments* again, but Mrs. Fang did not want to miss the opportunity and so she said hastily and with diffidence:

"I think that after the festival, when the eighth comes around, we—it might not be a bad idea if we got a lottery ticket . . ."

"Nonsense! how can you say such an . . . ?

But as he chided his wife, he recalled that after his unsuccessful interview with Chin Yung-sheng that afternoon he had passed by the Rice Fragrance Village and that his attention had been arrested by the huge posters saying so many ten-thousand dollars first prize. He recalled that he had had a sudden impulse, that he might have even slackened his pace, but that he had passed on resolutely after he decided that he could not afford to gamble with the last six dimes he had. However, Mrs. Fang knew nothing of this and she concluded from her husband's sharp tone that he must be thinking what an ignorant and uneducated woman she was. She retreated hastily, while Fang Hsuan-cho settled himself down in a more comfortable position and began to read *Experiments* aloud.

Peking Street Scene

By Lusin

Everything was still on a street in the western part of Peking, the nation's capital, for though the sun was not yet directly overhead, the sand-and-gravel roadway was already afire with its rays, and the heat-laden atmosphere was everywhere proclaiming the power and tyranny of summer. The dogs lolled with their tongues hanging out, and even the crows in the trees panted for breath with parted beaks. The stillness was not, of course, absolute. There was, for instance, the distant sound of two brass cups being struck together, reminding one of iced plum water and suggesting cool delight. The monotony of this metallic sound, however, only emphasized the stillness.

There was also the sound of the soft footsteps of ricksha men, grim and silent, as though intent on running away from the scorching sun overhead.

Then there was the sleepy and hoarse voice of a fat boy shouting before a shop, his eyes half closed and his mouth cocked to one side:

"Hot *bautze-a-a!* Just out of the steamer . . ."

On an old and rickety table at his side there was a pile of twenty or thirty cold stuffed rolls with not the least suggestion of being hot.

Then like a rubber ball that had been thrown against the wall and had bounced back, the fat boy flew across to the other side of the street where two men had just stopped by a telegraph pole, One of them was a lean, sallow policeman in a faded khaki uniform, with a sword hanging at his side. He held in his hand one end of a rope, while the other end was tied to the arm of a man in a long blue cotton gown with a white vest over it. The man's eyes were covered by the turned down rim of his new straw hat. When the boy peered up at him, however, their eyes met and the boy was disconcerted to find the man's eyes apparently fixed on his head. He quickly lowered his gaze to the white vest and discovered written on it line after line of characters.

In another instant a semicircle of spectators had formed in front of the policeman and his prisoner. By the time a bald old man had joined the semicircle there was very little space left; almost immediately even that space was filled by a big fat man with a red nose, naked to the waist. The fat man was so broad he took the space of two, so that the spectators who continued to arrive had to stand on the second row and stick their heads out between the necks of those in front.

The bald man was standing almost directly in front of the man with the white vest. He leaned forward and began to study the characters written on the vest and ended up by reading them aloud.

The fat boy noticed that the man in the white vest was, on his part, studying the shiny bald head, so he looked too, but could discover nothing of interest on the shiny scalp except a few patches of gray hair. In the meantime a nursemaid with a baby in her arms was trying to squeeze in, as the posture assumed by the old man offered her an opportunity. The man was, however, loath to lose his place and forestalled her by standing up straight. He had not yet finished reading, but that could not be helped. He turned his attention to the face of the man in the white vest and saw beneath the rim of his straw hat half of a nose, a mouth, and a pointed chin.

Again like a rubber ball that had been thrown against a wall and had bounced back, a schoolboy dashed up and set about burrowing his way into the semicircle, holding his hand over the white cotton hat that he was wearing. But when he reached the third—or it might have been the fourth—row, he struck something gigantic and immovable. Looking up, he discovered, above the waist of a pair of blue pants, a very broad naked back with quantities of sweat trickling down along it. He realized the futility of trying to break through such a wall and turned to the right alongside the waist of the blue pants until he discovered, at the end, a strip of empty space through which light was coming. But just as he lowered his head and was about to bore his way through, he heard a "What do you want?" and observed a yawing movement of a pair of buttocks below the waist of the blue trousers. The empty space was immediately sealed up and with it the gap of light disappeared.

But after a while the schoolboy managed to emerge beside the policeman's sword. He looked around wonderingly: beyond him a crowd of people, above him a man with a white vest, opposite him a fat boy naked to the waist and behind the fat boy a big fat man with a red nose, also naked to the waist. It then dawned upon him that this was the man whose back had presented such an insurmountable obstruction to him on the other side, and he could not help fixing his eyes on the man's red nose in wonder and admiration. The fat boy had been watching the schoolboy and he now followed the latter's line of vision and turned his head around. He could not see, however, beyond the fat man's breast where the chief attraction was a pair of nipples with a few long hairs around them.

"What's the man, er, guilty of?"

The voice that broke the silence and startled everyone came from a man who appeared to be a laborer. He had humbly directed his question to the bald old man.

The bald man did not answer but simply stared at him steadily until he lowered his eyes. When he looked up again after a while, the bald man was still staring at him. Moreover, he felt that everyone else was staring at him, too. This made him feel as uncomfortable as if he had committed a crime himself and in the end forced him to back out and slink away, whereupon, a long fellow with an umbrella stepped up and filled the place he had vacated, while the bald man again turned his attention to the white vest.

For a while the long fellow bent over to get a better view of White Vest's face under the rim of his straw hat, but when he sraightened up his back it again became necessary for those standing behind him to stretch out their necks. A thin man had to stretch out his neck so much that his mouth dropped open like that of a dead fish.

Now the policeman suddenly lifted a foot without warning. At this the crowd stirred and focused their eyes on the policeman's feet. But as the feet remained inactive, the interest shifted back to White Vest. The long fellow now bent his waist once more to investigate under the straw hat but once more he straightened up, only this time he lifted one hand and scratched his head violently.

Bald Head now appeared annoyed, for he had just become conscious of a disturbance of the peace behind his back, followed by the sound of munching and smacking. He looked back with a frown and caught sight of a black hand in the act of stuffing a large hunk of roll into a mouth set in a catlike face. Bald Head decided to say nothing and turned his gaze on White Vest's new straw hat.

Suddenly the fat man staggered forward as a hand just about as big and fat as his own reached over his shoulder and struck a blow on the fat boy's cheek that resounded like a clap of thunder.

"Having a good time, eh? Your mother's——" a man with a round Laughing Buddha face said back of the fat man.

The fat boy staggered forward four or five steps but did not fall. With one hand on his cheek he turned about and tried to escape through the space alongside the fat man's leg, when the latter steadied himself and filled up the space with a yawing movement of his buttocks, saying angrily, "What do you want?"

The fat boy darted hither and yon in confusion like a trapped mouse, but suddenly he made a straight dash in the direction of the schoolboy, pushed him aside and broke through. The schoolboy turned and followed.

"Hey, the idea of the boy . . ." said five or six men with one voice.

When, after quiet had been restored, the fat man again looked at White Vest's face, he found White Vest looking at his own chest. Hastily he looked down to see what was wrong but found only a patch of sweat between the protrusions. He brushed the sweat off with his hand.

The crowd began to get restless. The nursemaid with the baby in her arms happened to turn her head to look around during the general excitement incidental to the fat boy's exit and unintentionally brushed the tip of her elaborate hairdress, shaped like a magpie's tail, against the nose of a ricksha man. The latter gave it a push and brushed his hand against the child in the process. Thereupon the child squirmed and clamored to go home. The push had also caused the nursemaid to stagger a little, but she steadied herself and then tried to interest the child in White Vest by pointing to him, saying, "Look! Goody, goody!"

A young man wearing a stiff straw hat and looking like a student stuck in his head through an empty space, but withdrew after putting a melon seed in his mouth and cracking it between his teeth. His place was taken by a man with an oval face covered with dirt and grease.

Now the long fellow with the umbrella appeared annoyed at something. As he was looking over his shoulder and staring at the man with the mouth open like a dead fish, it was likely that the hot breath which came from the open mouth was not an easy ordeal to bear, least of all during the height of summer. The bald man was now studying with great interest a placard nailed on the telephone pole, while the fat man and the policeman were studying the sicklelike feet of the nursemaid out of the corners of their eyes.

Suddenly there was a shout somewhere. As this held out promise of new excitement for all those present, everyone turned around, including even the policeman and his prisoner.

There was nothing new in the immediate neighborhood. As before, the fat boy was crying sleepily with his mouth cocked on one side, and the ricksha men were running grimly as if trying to escape the hot sun overhead. The crowd was about to give up hope entirely, when perseverance was finally rewarded with the discovery, ten or fifteen houses away, of a standing ricksha and a ricksha man just getting up from the ground.

The semicircle immediately broke up and straggled off in that direction. The fat man stopped to rest under a locust tree before he had gone halfway, while the long fellow, who walked faster than either Bald Head or Oval Face, was the first to reach the scene. The passenger was still sitting in the ricksha. The ricksha man was now on his feet and rubbing his kneecaps. Around them there were five or six men laughing and grinning at them.

"Can you go on?" the passenger asked, as the ricksha man started to pick up the shafts. The latter nodded, pulled up the ricksha, and went off, the crowd following him with their eyes. For a while they were able to tell which was the ricksha that had had an accident, but soon it got lost among the other rickshas.

The street became quiet again. The fat man, who was still resting under the locust tree, was now watching the bellies of the dogs that rose and fell rapidly as they panted with their tongues out.

The nursemaid hobbled off under the shade of the eaves with the child in her arms. And the fat boy, with his head cocked to one side and his eyes half closed, went on crying in a sleepy and hoarse voice, "Hot *bautze*-a-a! Ho-a-a! *Mantou bautze* just . . ."

Yuchun

By Yang Chen-sheng

I

It was a moonlight night early in autumn, and the sky outside was as clear and limpid as water. Sitting alone in my room with no one near except my own shadow on the bookcase, I could not help thinking about the time before I went away to school, when both my parents were living and my elder sister not yet married, when friends and relatives were always coming and going and filling the house with bustle and activity. Now I lived alone in the house except for a few old servants. As I was thus thinking of the past I was suddenly awakened by the sound of the knocker against the gate.

Chang Lao-tou, our old servant, went to open the gate and announced when he came back: "Mr. Tu is here to see you."

Tu Ping-fu burst into the room before I could go out to meet him. Throwing his hat on the table and flinging himself into a chair heavily like a rock, he put his head between his hands and tapped his feet on the floor without saying a word.

He did not answer my questions. I sat down in a rocker and watched him as I rocked.

Suddenly he jumped up, walked around the room a couple of times, took a cigarette, lit it, and threw the match savagely on the rug. Then he sat down again, puffing violently and staring at the smoke that he blew out. I went over to stamp out the match and then returned to my rocker and watched him as before.

After smoking his cigarette half way down in silence, he threw it on the floor and stamped it out with his feet. Then throwing himself back in the chair, he laughed scornfully and again lapsed into silence. I continued to rock and watch him as before.

He closed his eyes as if reliving some experience. Suddenly he opened them wide and said, "Ha, ha, Beard, Beard! You would not let your daughter marry the son of an enemy but it happens that he would marry no one else. Yes, he would marry no one else." He stamped his feet for emphasis.

He stopped for a moment, then leaned forward and asked me in a low, weak voice, his head resting between his hands and his eyes fixed on the ground, "Do you remember Chou Yuchun?"

"Chou Yuchun?" I exclaimed, my heart beating violently.

"Yes, the daughter of Chou the Beard who lives on Flower Market Street," he answered slowly.

"What about her?" I asked as the vision of a bright-eyed girl that I used to know more than ten years ago rose before my eyes.

"I met her when I was a student at the Peita and she a student at the Women's Normal College." He got up as he spoke and pounded on the table with his fist. "Today I went to her family to propose marriage but the Beard had nothing but unkind words for me."

I looked down and said nothing for a while. Then I said, "I should think your families are well matched. Why should the Beard object?"

"That's what I thought, too," he said, beating the table; "but who'd think that he would bring up an old score? He said that years back my late father had impeached him for something or other and that he could not give his daughter in marriage to the son of his old enemy. Unfortunately, Yuchun's mother is dead and there is no one to speak up for her, her stepmother being totally indifferent. Moreover, the Beard got on the subject of freedom of marriage and compared it to 'flood and wild beasts' and that sort of thing. He even summoned Yuchun and berated her and forbade her to go back to school.

"I saw Yuchun tonight," he said after a pause. "Look, this handkerchief is wet with her tears!" His eyes became red. He went back to the chair and sat down in silence. There was no sound in the room except for the purring of the cat curled up in the corner of a chair, sound asleep and oblivious of everything.

After a long, long while he got up and said: "I have to set out for Shanghai tomorrow to catch a boat for France. I want you to take care of Yuchun after I am gone. I have told her about you. She is going to see me off at the boat tomorrow. You must come." With this he took his hat and departed.

Sitting alone by the lamp my thoughts went back to the time when I was about sixteen years of age. My grandmother was still living then and she used to be fond of entertaining the daughters of friends and relatives at our house and used to listen to the ballad singers with them. Among these girls, Yuchun, the daughter of Chou the Beard, who was a friend of my father's, was the best liked. She was only eleven or twelve years old, with bright eyes and sparkling teeth, her hair as black as a raven's and her complexion as white as snow. She was always smiling, showing two rows of fine teeth and a dimple on each cheek, and used to come with bunches of flowers to visit my elder sister.

Once, while she was watering flowers with my sister in the inner court, she stumbled over the root of a tree and fell, spilling the water kettle she was carrying and soiling her new dress. I went to her and pulled her up, but she only held up her muddy hands and cried, and kept on crying even after my sister had cleaned her hands and dried her clothes for her. I went and got an axe and began to bring it down on the offending root with all my might. Then she turned from crying to laughter, with gratitude in her tear-stained eyes.

I used to dream all kinds of vain dreams about her as only a boy could. Though she was only a little girl of eleven or twelve, she was the axle around which all my thoughts revolved. As I studied my lessons I saw myself pass the examinations and come back in triumph to impress her, and I was always filled with indignation and schemes for revenge when she was reprimanded by her tutor. I dreamed of rescuing her from bandits at the cost of my life and of luxuriating in her tears and gratitude and her visits to my tomb, year after year even after she was married.

Traces of these silly dreams had not been effaced after more than ten years, though deaths and marriage had gradually cut off intercourse between our families. Not only had I not seen her at all during the ten years or so that I was away at school, but I had not even heard anything about her until now when she was being courted by Tu Ping-fu, one of my closest friends!

The meowing of the cat suddenly broke the thread of my thoughts and caused me to look in its direction. Its front paws stretched toward me, its nose lifted, and its teeth bared, it made a deep yawn and then purred loudly as if to remind me that it was getting late and time to go to bed.

2

As I went out of the city gate at six o'clock the next morning, the sun had just risen above the trees and the mist was hovering over the grass still wet with dew. In the distance smoke from chimneys rose straight into the cloudless sky. I headed for the beach, skirting a stretch of vegetable gardens. I thought over what Tu Ping-fu had told me the evening before, and my heart leaped as I thought of meeting Yuchun after so many years. I was glad for her because Ping-fu was a fine man, but when I recalled Ping-fu's request, I wondered what I could do to help her in a country where a Milky Way is drawn between men and women.

Cutting across a field, I came upon a couple strolling along the beach. They gradually slowed down and then the woman stopped and looked down at the ground with her face turned away. The man stood before her with outstretched arms as if in supplication, but the woman refused and the man dropped his arms.

Not wishing to disturb them, I went toward a little girl picking up pebbles at a distance from them. Just then Ping-fu's voice said behind me: "I-tsun, Yuchun and I have been waiting here for you a long time."

They were walking toward me when I turned to look. Yuchun was tall and slender, and even more lovely than I remembered her. I wanted to go up to meet her, but my feet refused to move.

"Mr. Lin, do you remember Yuchun after all these years?" she walked up slowly and said to me, smiling and blushing a little.

"I remember well your smile and the way you used to cry," said I.

"You talk as if I cried a great deal," she said.

"You did not cry very often, but when you did cry it was quite difficult to pacify you. Do you remember about the tree that I had almost to cut down in order to make you stop crying?"

She laughed, the fur collar of her cape quivering against her cheeks.

"When my brother was still living, we used to get news of you, but nothing about you has reached us since his death," she said, her head bowed a little. "You had gone abroad when I went to Peking to study. I was told that you wrote to no one!"

"One writes only when one has something to rejoice over with friends or when one has some sorrow and needs consoling," I said. "I have not written because I've had nothing to rejoice over with my friends and because I do not want them to grieve on my account."

She turned her head and looked at the sea.

Pointing to the little girl, I asked, "Who is she?"

"That's my sister Lingchun," she replied, beckoning to the girl. "Meimei, come over and meet Mr. Lin."

Lingchun came running over and transferred all her pebbles to her left hand and held them against her breast so that she could shake hands with me, tiny, plump hands with a dimple at the base of each finger. I spoke to her but she only held onto her sister's short skirt and stared at me with her big, round eyes.

Yuchun said to her, stroking her head, "What's the matter with you, chatterbox? Why have you become like the golden image with sealed lips all of a sudden?"

Suddenly we were startled by a steam whistle. When we turned to look, we saw a boat flying into the harbor from the west. Ping-fu cast a savage glance at the boat and drew closer to Yuchun, his face suddenly grown older by ten years.

"Yuchun!" he said, his eyes afire and his throat choked with emotion so that he could not go on.

Yuchun took one of Ping-fu's hands, her eyes filled with tears of hope and regret. After looking at him for a while with slightly parted lips, she said in an unsteady voice:

"You'll be back after three years?"

"I don't want to go!" Ping-fu said, stamping his feet and dropping his eyes as if to avoid hers.

"Nonsense," Yuchun said, with a forced smile. "Of course you must go."

"I want to wait . . ." Ping-fu began but broke off.

Yuchun searched his face for a long while and then dropped his hand and was silent. Suddenly she blushed and said with some embarrassment:

"Go now, you can depend on me to wait for you."

I hastily turned away and went to get a porter. Ping-fu and Yuchun did not move even after the luggage had been put aboard. It was not until the whistle blew that they awakened from their trance. Reluctantly Ping-fu went aboard, whereupon the boat gave out a loud shriek and puffed off toward the east.

Yuchun stood motionless even after the boat had become a mere speck on the horizon. The wind from the sea scattered her silky hair and chilled her snowy cheeks. She was like a goddess carved out of jade.

I wandered back and forth to one side with my eyes on the ground, not knowing whether to go up and speak to her or leave her alone. After a while I called Lingchun to me and told her to take her sister home. Lingchun looked up at me as if she wanted to say something to me. I stooped down and she whispered in my ears:

"Why did chieh-chieh let Mr. Tu go and then be sad after he's gone?"

"Don't you know?" I said, smiling. She shook her head.

"I don't know either. Let's ask the seagulls," said I.

She stared at me incredulously and then ran back to her sister and said, taking the latter's hand: "Chieh-chieh, let's go home."

Slowly Yuchun walked away with her sister with bowed head and I myself also turned toward home in a depressed mood.

3

As Chin-erh, Chang Lao-tou's only daughter, was putting the books back on the shelves after they had been put out to dry in the sun she kept up a stream of chatter and gossip about this and that neighbor. I only half listened to her until suddenly she said something about a Miss Chou's frequent visits to the beach.

"Is it the Miss Chou who lives on Flower Market Street that you are speaking of?" I asked anxiously. She only nodded without looking at me and went on arranging the books. "What about Miss Chou?" I asked again.

She turned her head and glanced at me but returned to the books, pretending not to hear me.

"What a wicked girl you are getting to be, Chin-erh," I said. "You keep on chattering away without the slightest encouragement, but become dumb when I ask you a question."

"Don't get angry, shao-yeh," Chin-erh said without haste. "I'll tell you. Hsiao-jun from across the street and I went to the beach this morning after breakfast and saw Miss Chou standing there gazing at the sea. She did not move for the longest time. Hsiao-jun told me that Miss Chou goes to the beach very often. She used to go with her little sister but now she goes there herself. People say that she will jump into the sea one of these days."

"Nonsense!" I said, standing up unconsciously as I fancied I saw Yuchun being dragged down into the sea by silvery claws that rose out of the waves. Chin-erh stared at me and wondered at my abstractedness. Embarrassed by her gaze, I was about to step out when I suddenly heard Chang-ma's voice outside the window:

"Chao Ta-niang, so it's you! What wind has blown you here?"

"Is your shao-yeh home?" Chao Ta-niang's voice said.

"What do you want to see him for?"

The two women whispered among themselves and laughed.

Chang-ma came in and said to me, "Chao Ta-niang wants to see you about some important business." She gave Chin-erh a wink as she went out.

Presently Chang-ma ushered Chao Ta-niang in. The latter was

a woman about fifty years old with a thin face and thin lips; she
was neatly dressed. I bade her sit down but otherwise paid no
attention to her. Standing before the bookcase, I pretended to read.

After looking me up and down, Chao Ta-niang said, "You have
grown up quite a tall man, shao-yeh."

Still I paid no attention to her.

After a while she went on, "I used to come over quite often
when your grandmother was still living. *Hai,* was I not matchmaker for your aunt? See what a fine family she has now, the
envy of every one. When I first went to the Ho family to propose
the match . . ."

"Chao Ta-niang, are you still a matchmaker?" I interrupted her.
"According to the new laws you ought to have your tongue cut
out and thrown into the sea."

"Don't be afraid, I have not come here for matchmaking."

"That's better! Have some tea."

Chin-erh served her tea. She followed me with her eyes as she
drank the tea and then said laughing:

"If not for us matchmakers, you'd never get your wives."

"Thank heaven for that. Only fools want to get married."

"What? You don't want a wife?" She put down her tea cup and
said reproachfully to Chang-ma: "Your late master and mistress
were very good to you and your husband. How could you let your
young master get such strange ideas without doing something
about it?"

"We have talked ourselves hoarse, but Heavens, what's the
use!" Chang-ma answered. "A few days ago his aunt was here and
talked to him about it but he paid no more attention to her than
to the breeze that blows by his ears. When she became insistent, he
even argued with her and made her cry. *Hai,* you have no idea
what strange notions this shao-yeh of ours has!"

After a while Chao Ta-niang said, assuming a serious expression:
"All jokes aside, this young lady I have in mind is really out of
the ordinary. She is not only pretty but more beautiful than anything you can find in pictures. She can write and figure and is
kind and considerate. Every one in the family from the servants

up has nothing but praise for her. Moreover, she has been to school, exactly suited to your . . ."

"Since she has been to school, she ought to be able to take care of her own marriage without your meddling," I said, interrupting her.

"*Aiya,* what sort of family do you take hers to be to let her find her own husband!" she said with impatience. "Only half a month ago they had quite a row over freedom of marriage."

"Whom are you talking about?" I asked hastily.

"If you are not interested at all I am not going to mention their name," she tantalized.

"How can I say whether I am interested without knowing who it is?"

"You know the family," she said with an important air. "I am talking about the daughter of the Chou family on Flower Market Street."

Suddenly my head grew large and everything in the room began to whirl around. I stumbled toward the clothes tree, picked up my hat and stick, and rushed out of the room.

"She is neither bald nor blind, why should he get angry?" I heard Chao Ta-niang say.

"You have no idea how queer this shao-yeh of ours is! Everything we think is right he says it is wrong and everything we think is wrong he says it is right."

I walked on as in a dream, not knowing how long I had been gone or where I was. At last I came to a tree with a rock in front of it; I sat down on the rock and leaned against the tree. My limbs were weary and my brain in feverish ferment. My thoughts were like a confused mass of silk threads with each thread a different and conflicting color. Then they combined themselves into one mass of gray as my heart grew numb and apathetic.

After I had sat there I don't know how long, my brain became less feverish. It appeared that I was on the eastern shore of Egypt with the sands burnished red by the setting sun. Suddenly a horde of savages swooped out from a palm grove on the horizon and pounced on me like hawks. Feeling numb and helpless I had to allow them to tie me up without a struggle. Then I saw Ping-fu riding on a camel and garbed like a tribal chief, and I was glad because I thought he was sure to rescue me. When he turned away and pretended not to see me, I was not surprised, for it seemed to me that I had betrayed him. Then a queenly woman appeared and rode with Ping-fu side by side. I felt outraged and berated Ping-fu for betraying Yuchun. "But how could I betray Yuchun when she is married to you already?" Ping-fu laughed and said, and I had to agree with him. As I wondered what to do in the predicament, I was delivered from the nightmare by a flash of blinding red light.

I opened my eyes and found the setting sun on my eyes. I had dozed off.

I turned my face away from the sun and sat on as before with closed eyes. Presently it appeared that I was back in my childhood home with the house full of guests. My sister came in and nodded to me with a significant smile. Every one else, too, was whispering to one another and it seemed that they were talking about my engagement. I was not much surprised, for I was vaguely conscious of having heard about my approaching engagement to Yuchun. Then I recalled that Yuchun had asked me to carve a doll for her and so taking a knife and a piece of wood I went out to the yard under a tree. Just as I squatted down and was about to begin carving, two little hands were placed over my eyes and some one asked from behind: "Guess who?" I said, "Yuchun!"

I was awakened by a burst of laughter and found Lingchun standing before me when I opened my eyes. I had, as a matter of fact, been sitting under an old willow tree by the Bridge of Immortals where I had agreed to meet Lingchun and give her any letters that might have come from Ping-fu for Yuchun.

4

Shortly after Chao Ta-niang's attempt at matchmaking, I turned over to Chin-erh the task of forwarding Ping-fu's letters and went to Peking in order to escape from the restlessness which had possessed me ever since her visit. I found Peking very much the same as it had always been; there were as before the interminable dust and the filthy foodstalls, and political intrigues which vied with the dust and foodstalls to make Peking what it was. There was, however, another world in that ancient city which was not found elsewhere—the world of colleges and universities.

I had been teaching in one of these institutions for over a year when one day my servant brought in a special delivery letter from Yuchun, which read:

. . . My father is about to marry me off to a Huang Pei-ho, the son of a local war lord. I have not only fought in vain against the proposal but have on the contrary incurred my father's displeasure. I have vowed not to betray Ping-fu or marry the son of the war lord, but since Ping-fu is afar away across the ocean and my brother died long before his time, I have no dear one to stand by me, no one to champion my cause. Moreover, the Huang family is as desirous of the immediate acquisition of a daughter-in-law as my father is of the early marriage of his daughter. In this crisis only you, my elder brother, can understand my difficulties; only you, my elder brother, can rescue me from the impending disaster. I hope, therefore, that you will remember the time when we were to each other like brother and sister and the implicit trust that Ping-fu has placed in you and save a helpless woman from fire and water, and thus secure the gratitude of Ping-fu and myself. My soul will listen for news from you in the chatter of the sparrows and the plaintive songs of the orioles and my eyes shall be fixed on the horizon for returning boats that may carry you to me.

A few days later I was back in my native city in a drizzling rain. Chang-ma was both surprised and delighted to see me. She made me change my rain-drenched clothes and made a fire to dry out the room. Her husband also came in, smiling broadly, his white teeth flashing against his bushy beard. Next Chin-erh made her appearance with our cat in her arms, which jumped down and circled around me, rubbing itself against my legs and purring as if trying to say, "He's come back, he's come back."

Chang-ma and Chin-erh made some of their best dishes while Chang Lao-tou went out for wine. I invited them to sit down with me, which they did after refusing politely for a while. It was after dark when we sat down. The sound of rain outside and the shadows cast by the lamp inside combined to increase our appetite for wine. I told them about my experiences in Peking and they recounted to me things that had happened at home.

"Everything has gone up in price since you went away," Chang Lao-tou said with a sigh. "Everyone who has gone away from the city has prospered, some have become high officials, others have made fortunes and bought land and houses. But with us, only expenditures have gone up."

"He is right," his wife broke in. "There are the Wangs on North Street, the Sus on Long Street and the Shens that live near the Temple. Everyone has come back with a fortune. Then there are the Huangs. They have now a general in the family and have built themselves a foreign-style house as grand as if it had come out of paradise. Only you, shao-yeh,"—she took another sip of wine to give herself courage—"only you have to take money from home. Why don't you . . ."

She stopped at a glance from her husband. I felt embarrassed because of their disappointment in me and bowed my head to avoid their eyes.

After a while, I raised my head and asked Chang-ma: "This General Huang that you spoke of—does he have a son?"

"He has two, one about thirty and another around ten. The younger one is born of a concubine."

"Have you ever seen the older one?"

"No, but I have been told that he went to Peking to school several times, but had to withdraw because he could not keep up with his studies. He wanted to enter the army, but his grandmother would not let him. He is staying home and doing nothing at present."

"I don't suppose he is married?"

"He was, but his wife died not long ago. I am told that he is going to get another wife soon."

There was a silence, then I said to Chang Lao-tou, "Is the house in our orchard on West Hill still habitable?"

"You can still live in it, but it is in very bad shape."

"It will do. I shall move in in a few days. Tell Har to clean up the rooms in the northwest corner and say that I shall be moving in soon."

"Will you be taking some things along?"

"Yes, I will, and I want to have the books on the shelves by the south window moved over."

"Do you plan to stay there long?" Chang-ma asked with wide-open eyes.

"I want to spend a year in learning to farm," I answered with a laugh.

"Farming?" Chang-ma repeated with a shake of the head. "My Lord Heaven, what an idea! Do you mean to tell me that that's what you had been learning during the years you were abroad?"

"I wish I had."

After a long silence, Chang-ma said with a heavy sigh, "Who'd think that you would come to indulge in such whims? From the late master and mistress to ourselves and all the relatives, can you think of one who has not been hoping that you would make a name for yourself and do great things? Do you mean to tell me that you would wear coarse clothing and eat coarse food and spend your days with country louts?" Here she glanced at her husband for support and on being assured by his nod, she continued, "Moreover, it is high time that you took a young mistress. You can't remain a bachelor all your life. The house will be a merrier one with a few children and the late master and mistress will be happier in the other world."

My head was bowed and I said nothing.

"Shao-yeh, is there anything troubling you?" she asked, but still I hung my head and said nothing.

"Is it some secret sorrow that you can't confide to any one?" she continued. "If that is the case, would you not be all the sadder staying alone in the orchard?"

"Don't ask him any more questions. Can't you see that you are distressing him?" This was Chin-erh's voice. There was an indescribable sadness in the air and all was still except for the dismal sound of the intermittent drizzle outside the window.

5

On the second day of my return the sky was clear after the rain, the sun filled the entire courtyard, and there was not a speck of dust in the air. I went out after breakfast and as I walked on and thought matters over, my heart became agitated and ill at ease, as though I were on my way to the guillotine. Presently I came to a two-story house, a monstrous thing that was neither Chinese nor Western, and I told myself that this must be Chang-ma's idea of paradise. I took a few steps forward but suddenly my legs stopped of themselves as if a huge rock had fallen from my heart and pinned them down. I took out my cigarette case and lit a cigarette and walked around a few times before I summoned up enough courage to walk up and send in my card.

I was ushered into the guest hall and sat down in a straight chair too large to lean upon anywhere. Tea was brought and as I drank my tea I looked around the room and noticed that the scrolls were all written by governors and war lords. After waiting a long while, a sickly and slender man dressed in the latest fashion came in, preceded by a servant and a strong odor of perfume and soap. He bowed to me, uttering some clichés in greeting. I stood up and asked him if he were Mr. Huang Pei-ho. He twitched his eyes and said "yes" with a smile which exposed some gold teeth. "He looks more like a musician of some theatrical troupe than the son of a general," I said to myself.

"Have you just come back from Peking?" he asked, after some meaningless polite remarks.

"Yes, I came back yesterday."

I noticed his gold rings as he picked his finger nails. Then he asked me, "Do you go to the theater much?"

"I have seen a few plays."

"Hsü Pi-yun is the most promising of the younger generation of actors."

"I have come to make a request of you," I interrupted.

"He sings beautifully in the court scene in the *Yü T'ang Ch'un,*" he said enthusiastically. "His transitional flourishes are simply marvelous, with so many variations and surprises. There is no one like him. Have you seen his . . ."

"I have come to make a request of you," I repeated.

"What did you say?" he said, twitching his eyes.

"I have a request to make of you."

"What is it?"

After some faltering attempts, I managed to say, "Did your family go to the Chous on Flower Market Street with a marriage proposal?"

"That's right, that's right," he said, smiling so broadly that all his gold teeth showed. "I first saw Miss Chou on the beach last year. Ah, there is no one like her. She is ten times prettier than Chin Hsueh-fang, the actress. By coincidence my wife died last month. Mr. Chou is delighted with the proposal, and we expect to bind the engagement soon."

For a moment everything went black before my eyes. Then recovering myself, I said, "This match cannot be made!"

"Cannot be made?" he repeated in astonishment.

"Do you know Tu Ping-fu?"

"No," he answered.

"Miss Chou knows him."

"Miss Chou knows him?" he repeated, more astonished than ever.

"She knows him well. They are very good friends and have been engaged for some time."

He stared at me for a long time and then asked, "Why is it then that her father accepted our proposal?"

"Because he would not consent to their engagement."

He was relieved on hearing this and said with a smile, "That's all right then."

"But Miss Chou has vowed to marry Tu Ping-fu. I have come to ask you to respect her wishes."

His color changed. "I don't understand you. I don't see what others have that I don't. Her father is agreeable to this match and has expressed his readiness to bind the engagement any time that we choose. It is not that I have been trying to force myself on them . . ."

"It is not that," I explained. "I think we should help Tu Ping-fu and Miss Chou to consummate their wishes since they are old friends."

"Help them in their carryings-on?" he sneered.

The remark cut me like a knife, but as I was about to make a retort, he asked me quietly, "Where is this man Tu now?"

"He is in **France.**"

"How do you know that Miss Chou would rather marry this man Tu than myself?" he asked with a sly look in his eyes.

"Miss Chou wrote and told me," I answered without a thought.

"So she wrote and told you!" he said with an ugly laugh. "So she goes so far as to tell you these things! Who knows what sort of carryings-on there are between you two? I knew all along that you can't trust these modern women. I am going to look into this after I have married her. I am going to shut her up in the house and see if she can go on . . ."

Sparks danced before my eyes. I no longer heard what he said but only saw his sneer and his gold teeth glittering before me. I stood up and dashed the tea in my cup in his face. "Get him, get him!" I heard him shout as I put on my hat and got my stick, but the two servants that had been standing in front of the guest hall stood aside for me when they saw me rush out like a mad dog.

Somehow I managed to stumble home. In the yard I heard some one say, "Have you come back, shao-yeh? How flushed your face is!" It was probably Chang-ma's voice. I stumbled into my room and slumped unconscious on the bed.

6

I sent a letter to Yuchun through her sister Lingchun, who came to see me during my convalescence, and told her the result of my visit to Huang Pei-ho. After my recovery, I moved to our summer place in the orchard on West Hill.

One morning Har, the caretaker, told me that the plums, crab apples, peaches, and pears were ready for the market and consulted me about hiring pickers. He went to the neighboring villages and hired droves of men and women, old and young, who filled the orchard like crowds at a fair. The children perched themselves in the trees and dropped the fruits to the older persons, who held up the flaps of their coats to catch them, while young men and women stood on benches and reached among the branches as far as they could. They talked and laughed and teased while they worked. To the green of the trees and the red of the fruits were added the many hues of their garments, and the chattering of the birds gave place to that of human voices.

Here among the branches peeped the smiling face of a child, there among the green leaves flashed the white wrist of a young woman.

"Hsiao Tsui is eating up all the crab apples," someone said here. "Hsiao Hung is pocketing all the plums," another said there.

"My sleeve is caught on a branch," one voice said here.

"I got a prick on my palm," another said there.

Here an old man rubbed his bald head, complaining that a pear had dropped on him.

There a woman nursed her foot, complaining that someone had stepped on it.

They busied themselves among the trees until the sun was low in the west, when they all trouped to the well to wash their hands. One complained that someone had spilled water on her trousers, another that her new shoes had got soiled. One took another to task for dallying too long over her ablutions, saying that you couldn't change ox horn into ivory by washing; the other retorted by saying that you couldn't expect to get horse manure from an ass's rear. Afterwards they all sat in a circle under the shade of a tree and chatted as they munched their favorite fruits. I joined them and listened to them discussing the good points of their neighbors to the east and the shortcomings of their neighbors to the west, or remarking about the bigness of the bowls of their neighbors to the south and the smallness of the dishes of their neighbors to the north.

"Did you know that we have a miracle man in the Southern Village?" said Auntie Yu, taking a large bite of a peach. "Not one that works cures and communes with the gods but a miracle man with a bushel measure." Some one asked, "What do you mean by a miracle man with a bushel measure?" Auntie Yu continued, "One day while this man went to the fair, his wife entertained her lover. He returned home unexpectedly early and there was no place for her to hide her lover. So she ran out to meet him and took the bushel measure he was carrying and put it over his head, saying, 'Guess what I have cooked for dinner.' Her lover sneaked out while her husband considered and said, 'Rice and eggplants!' Thereupon she uncovered his head, saying, 'You are exactly right. You are truly a miracle man!' Now how many of you men here are miracle men?"

They all laughed and said, "Uncle Yu is the only miracle man among us."

"Poo, you conscienceless wretches! You shouldn't make fun of your old mother who has tried to entertain you." Auntie Yu stretched out her legs as she said this and stuck them squarely into Hsiao Tsui's lap, making her drop a half eaten crab apple.

"Look, everybody!" Hsiao Tsui cried. "She is trying to be coy, with big feet like hers."

"Your mother's wind!" Auntie Yu said. "Your grandmother's feet are even bigger than mine."

"Don't try to provoke Auntie Yu," Hsiao Hung warned. "Even Uncle Yu is afraid of her."

Everyone looked at Uncle Yu but he went on smoking with a broad smile and said nothing. Auntie Yu, however, was embarrassed and protested, "Hsiao Hung, you slave girl who loves to chew your tongue, how do you know that your Uncle Yu is afraid of me?"

Hsiao Hung laughed and answered, "Who doesn't know that Uncle Yu is henpecked?"

Auntie Yu got up to grab Hsiao Hung, saying, "You little whore with a sore on your tongue, see if your old mother doesn't break your unmuzzled dog snout!"

Hsiao Hung was too quick for her and she turned her ire upon her husband, saying, "You spiritless male that a thousand jabs with an awl cannot draw any blood from! You have been made a fool of and yet you squat there with your tail between your legs and would not let out a single breath!"

As before, Uncle Yu went on smoking with a broad smile and said nothing.

Some one said, "He is trying to be a miracle man!"

"What did you say?" Auntie Yu said in an angry tone.

"I said that I was a miracle man," the man said, sticking out his tongue in mock fear.

"That's better," Auntie Yu said, returning to her seat.

Then old Mrs. Hsieh began: "Let us forget miracle men for a moment and talk about something else. Does any of you know Miss Chou on Flower Market Street?"

Some one answered, "I saw her once. She is very beautiful."

"She is beautiful all right but not very maidenly," old Mrs. Hsieh said. "My relative Mrs. Su works in the Chou family and knows all about them. She came to see me the other day and told me that this young lady is gentle and obedient in everything except when it comes to the subject of her marriage. Two years ago she and her father had quite a time because of a man by the name of Tu. Recently the Huang family made a proposal. Her father was very pleased with it, but she would not consent. The Huangs got provoked and circulated the report that the young lady is far from blameless and that she goes around with men who are nothing to her. When these rumors reached her father, he questioned her about them. The young lady was greatly humiliated and cried for several days. They say that she may commit suicide."

She spoke with unconcern but I who listened became greatly agitated. My blood left its regular course, leaving too much in my head, which made it feel swollen, and too little in my body, which made it cold. Stiffly I stood up, hardly knowing where I was or who the people around me were and feeling as light as a man made of paper. I walked out of the orchard, went down the slope of the hill and straight to the edge of the sea and sat down on a rock. The sky was empty, the sea was empty, the hillside was empty— everything was empty, dead and insentient.

7

Motionless I sat on the rock I knew not how long. Overhead shone the waxing moon and across the sky slowly coursed a few patches of clouds, light as gauze and white as snow. The pale blue firmament seemed to be permeated with infinite peace and stillness.

But presently black clouds rose from the sea. Light waves began to form and, blown by the wind, they beat against the rocks and poured into the caves with a mighty, desolating sound.

I had almost forgotten about Yuchun since I came out of the orchard earlier in the evening, but now the sound of the waves recalled me to myself, and what old Mrs. Hsieh had said about Yuchun recurred to my mind word by word. "Yuchun, Yuchun, I am the cause of your suffering!" I said reproachfully to myself and wished I had enough courage to dash myself to pieces against the rocks. I told myself that since I was responsible for Yuchun's distress, I must try to rescue her from it. Could I make use of old Mrs. Hsieh's relative who was a servant in Yuchun's house? Would Yuchun accept my offer to help? Suddenly it occurred to me that I might go to the Chous and propose for myself so as to reassure the old man that his daughter was still sought after. When Ping-fu returned from France, I could "return the jade to the State of Chao." It was necessary to see Yuchun first and explain my plan to her.

The waves rose higher. The fishing boats were returning to shore one by one.

It was one past midnight when I went back to my room. As I sat in a chair and thought of the melodramatic possibilities of my plan I could not help laughing when I imagined Ping-fu's distress on finding Yuchun and myself engaged and his relief when the truth was revealed to him. Then quite suddenly my thoughts were interrupted by a violent knocking at the orchard gate.

When I opened the gate I was shocked to see under the moonlight two men carrying a drenched body. They asked for my assistance and I had them bring the body inside. As we walked toward my room the men told me that they were approaching the shore in their fishing boats when suddenly they heard the sound of weeping, that they went toward the spot where the sound came from but that before they could reach it they heard the sound of some one jumping into the water. They went quickly to the rescue but had some difficulty in locating the drowning figure, which turned out, when they succeeded in dragging it up from the water, to be a woman. They had come to my place because it was nearest to the scene of drowning.

A further shock awaited me after the men had carried the body into my room and placed it on the bed, for I discovered by the lamplight that it was Yuchun herself, her face pale and her dripping hair hanging down her shoulders.

By this time Har and his wife had awakened and come into my room. I had Har-ma turn Yuchun's body over on her face and apply to her Shaefer's method of artificial respiration under my direction. Gradually the water emptied out through her mouth and after about half an hour I was relieved to hear Yuchun utter a low moan.

I told Har-ma to make a fire and dry Yuchun's clothes and that Yuchun was to have my room while I would spend the night sitting up in a chair in the outer room, which had served as my study.

The two fishermen and I withdrew to the outer room, where over some wine I told them about Yuchun and secured their promise not to divulge the latest incident to any one. After they left I went inside and found Yuchun sleeping comfortably with Har-ma sitting by her side. "Is this the Miss Chou that they were talking about?" she asked. I nodded and asked her to take good care of Yuchun and keep her presence a secret.

Back in the other room I sat in a chair and pondered over what had happened. What had precipitated Yuchun's desperation? Why instead of jumping into the sea from the north shore, which was nearer to her house, had she come to the west shore, which was several miles away? I could not find a satisfactory answer to these questions.

8

The birds woke me up early the following morning. I stood up, straightened my rumpled clothes and called Har-ma to me to ask her about Yuchun. She said that Yuchun had slept well through the night and that she was still asleep. I went out for a short walk, but Yuchun was still sleeping when I came back. I took my fishing rod and went out again to while away the time. On my return Har-ma told me that Yuchun was up and was waiting to see me.

Yuchun was sitting in an easy chair when I went into her room. She was outwardly calm, but she could not entirely conceal her anxiety and embarrassment.

"Do you feel all right now?" I asked her.

"I am all right except that I am still a little dazed," she answered weakly.

"Would you like to have something to eat?"

"No, I do not have the slightest desire for food."

I wanted to ask her about yesterday but hesitated for fear of embarrassing her. Reading my thoughts, she brought the subject up herself. "How does it happen that I am here?" she asked, her face coloring a little.

"Two fishermen rescued you and brought you here."

After a brief pause she asked, "Is your house the only one around here?"

"Yes, the others are all nearly a mile away."

"Do many persons know what has happened?"

"Only the Har couple and their son, besides the fishermen."

"Has any one told my family or spread the news generally?" she asked with anxiety.

"No, I have asked them not to spread it. As to your family, I wanted to consult you first."

She bowed her head in silence and I continued, "Perhaps you will live here for a while. I can move back to the city and make in-quiries about how things are at your house."

She bowed her head in silence as before. After a long while, she raised her head and asked me with an embarrassed air, "Do you know why I came out here yesterday?"

"I was just going to ask you."

She sighed and said in a very weak voice, "The Huangs have circulated some evil rumors about me. Without stopping to ascer-tain whether they are true, my father reprimanded me severely and said many things to me which I cannot with dignity endure." No longer able to hold back her tears, she quickly turned her head and looked at a picture on the wall.

"I thought to myself that there were only two ways open to me, one was to end my life and the other was to run away from home and seek a new life. I decided upon the latter course because I could not bear to leave Lingchun and Ping-fu. But a woman has no freedom of movement in China. Where could I escape to?" Here she had to stop, overcome with sorrow.

"Finally I thought I would come here first, since you are a friend of Ping-fu, and then think of fleeing farther." She looked at me as she said this; I hastily bowed my head.

"Last night at eleven o'clock I left our house by the garden gate. I had visited this orchard several times when I was around twelve or thirteen and vaguely remembered the way. When I came in sight of your house, however, I stopped and wondered at the wisdom of my decision, for would it not be confirming the suspicions of my father and the Huangs when they learned that I had come to you? Moreover, it was not only myself that I had to think of; I would be involving—you. Therefore, I thought that it was better if I ended it all. I started to walk toward the sea. Suddenly I saw in the dim light a man walking toward the orchard. Knowing that it was probably you, I took a few steps in your direction. But again I hesitated and as I did so I saw you enter the orchard gate and close it behind you. I did not have the courage to knock, though several times I was on the point of doing so. I sat on the ground and cried until I was faint with weariness. Then I walked to the edge of the sea, climbed on a rock and jumped."

I could not think of anything to say to comfort her. I got up and turned around a few times in the room and then sat down again.

"I think you ought to try to get to Peking," I said after a long silence.

She sighed and said, "There is no place for women in Chinese society except to remain in the house and be slaves. That's the only occupation for women in China."

"Then how about going to France to look for Ping-fu and study there also?" I said, brightening.

"But that will take a great deal of money," she said slowly.

"That can be managed, so long as you are willing to go."

After a brief silence she said, "I understand that since your father died your family fortune has declined."

"I am willing to let it decline further," I said with a laugh. "It is easy to live either as a rich man or as a poor man but difficult to be neither rich nor poor."

At this she laughed and said nothing.

"I don't suppose Ping-fu will be coming back now," I asked.

"No, for I have not told him everything though I have written to him. I have urged him to stay out his three years before coming back."

"I shall move back to the city today and send Chin-erh to look after you. I shall come to see you often myself."

She smiled but said nothing.

"Is there anything that I can bring you?" I asked. She shook her head. As I left her, she asked me to let Lingchun know where she was. "I am afraid that she is crying herself sick," she said, turning away her head and covering up her eyes with her handkerchief.

9

"Do you know that Miss Chou has jumped into the sea?" Chang-ma asked me anxiously as soon as I entered my house in the city.

"How do you happen to know?" I asked.

"The Chous were looking for her all over the city this morning, saying that she had disappeared from the house. Later in the day they found her fur cape in the sea and concluded that she must have drowned herself."

I was overjoyed on hearing this and said, "So her cape has drifted from the west harbor to the north harbor! That's fine."

Chang-ma was bewildered by my words, but I soon explained things to her and set her mind at ease. Then I took Chin-erh and Lingchun to the orchard and told Yuchun of the fortunate circumstance.

After this I took Lingchun to see Yuchun almost every day. We strolled around in the orchard and roamed the hillsides or played at fishing. On the seventh day of the seventh month I took Yuchun and her sister to a near-by island to see the ancient ceremony of "Begging for Skill" which was still observed among the young girls in that isolated community.

In the meantime I had sold a piece of land to a real estate shark for $2,400, which would enable Yuchun to go to France, but had not been able to collect because the man had loaned out the money on interest. Though I was annoyed at the delay, I could not help being glad of it because it gave me a chance to be with Yuchun longer than I had expected.

It was the fifteenth of the eighth month, two years after Ping-fu went abroad. As Yuchun, Lingchun, and I were chatting in the shade under the trees, we suddenly saw a young man striding into the orchard, and I heard Yuchun cry, "Ping-fu, Ping-fu! Ping-fu has come back!" before I could recognize him. She ran to him with outstretched arms and saying, "Ping-fu, I did not dream that you would be back so soon!" But Ping-fu turned away from her with anger in his face. Yuchun dropped her arms and turned pale. "Why are you so angry?" she asked.

For a long while Ping-fu did not answer. Yuchun said, sighing, "I did not dream that you would be back so soon, but even less did I expect to see you come back like this."

"What else did you expect?" Ping-fu said angrily. "Your relationship with Lin I-tsun is known all over the city; only your family is in the dark. I did not believe it at first when they told me about it in my family, but what else can I believe when every one says the same thing?"

I felt numb all over as if I had received an electric shock. Yuchun, too, was in a state of stupefaction, staring at the ground as if unable to decide whether it was true or only a bad dream. For a moment Ping-fu seemed to regret his harsh words and took a step in Yuchun's direction, but he hesitated and then turned and stalked off in the direction of the gate.

I followed him, hoping to explain things to him. He was standing in the setting sun not far from the orchard, but as I approached him he walked away and left me standing alone in the wild grass. Around me the hills towered above haughtily as if contemptuous of my distress and the sea sparkled and winked as if mocking my plight.

Back in the orchard I found Yuchun standing at the same spot where I had left her and staring at the ground like one in a trance, with Lingchun holding her hand looking helplessly into her face. "It is my fault, Yuchun," I went to her and said. "I should have been more careful." She stood motionless as before. It was not until I repeated what I said that she sighed, tears flowing from her eyes. She went back to her room with Lingchun while I stood with bowed head in the orchard, knowing that she wanted to be alone.

Presently Lingchun ran out weeping and said that Yuchun had fallen sick. I hastened into her room with Lingchun and found her lying in bed in a semiconscious condition, her cheeks flushed the color of bright rouge and her eyes closed. It was necessary to send for a physician but it had to be some one that we could take into our confidence. I managed to persuade Lingchun to let me take her home. I found a former schoolmate of mine who had studied medicine and returned with him to the orchard the same evening, after confiding to him about Yuchun.

Yuchun's condition had not become worse when we entered her room. After examining her, my friend said that it was only shock and that all she needed was quiet and rest. He left some medicine, directing that it should be taken every hour. I stayed in the orchard that night to watch over Yuchun since I was afraid that Har-ma, who was getting on in years, might not be a very competent nurse.

By the fifth watch Yuchun had taken three doses of medicine and was feeling much better. Suddenly she opened her eyes and asked me where Lingchun was. She closed her eyes again without comment when I told her that I had taken Lingchun home. After a while she shouted in her sleep, "I-tsun, help! help!" She had awakened when I hastened to her bedside. She stared at me for a moment, as if not sure whether she was still dreaming, then she became embarrassed and turned over in bed, pretending she was asleep.

Towards dawn Yuchun had improved to such an extent it became unnecessary to give her medicine every hour. I had Har-ma put out all the lamps and lower the screens over all the windows so that Yuchun could sleep in the darkness. We then withdrew to the outer room and dozed off in our chairs.

Yuchun was still sound asleep when Lingchun came near the noon hour. Not wishing to have her disturb her sister I went out with her to hunt for crickets along the hillside.

When we returned, Yuchun had awakened and was sitting up in bed, the flush in her cheeks had practically gone. Lingchun jumped up on her bed and hugging her with her arms around her neck, she said, "Chieh-chieh, I dreamed all last night. In one of my dreams you and Mr. Lin and I were walking on the hillside when a robber appeared and killed Mr. Lin. Then you cried."

"How extraordinary that you should also . . ." Yuchun started to say, but she began her sentence over again with a blush, "How extraordinary that you should have such a dream!" Then turning to me she said, "I-tsun, did I say anything crazy in my unconscious state last night?"

I replied, "What one says in one's dream or unconsciousness is always true. One says crazy things not so much because of loss of consciousness as because of freedom from its inhibitions."

Yuchun said laughing, "Would you call it crazy if I were to go to live on the island and teach the island girls reading and drawing?"

"I would call it dreaming rather than being crazy, for that's one of the things that I have dreamed about."

"Do you think that I am qualified to teach them?"

"I can think of no one who is better qualified," I said, recalling her way with the island girls on our previous excursions. "The money set aside for you to study abroad is still intact. You can use it to go abroad or to start a school as you like. I can raise more if you need it."

"It would be wonderful to go to Europe to study, but I have no one to go with me and I cannot leave Lingchun. I shall, therefore, go to the island. I am no longer afraid of what my family may say or do; I want to take my place openly in society."

"What kind of equipment will you need? I shall start getting the things tomorrow."

"I need only a large hall with paintings on the walls, a conference table in the middle of the room, book cases along the walls and desks by the windows. There should be a verandah from which to hang bird cages and an open plot of ground in front to plant flowers, for besides teaching them to read and paint, I shall want them to cultivate flowers and keep birds. After supper we shall tell stories and read poetry. There will also be games."

10

A few days later Yuchun had completely recovered. At her suggestion we set out to find a site for her school. She took along her diary, in which she had drawn up plans for the school house and her ideas for the school. We arrived on the island in high spirits. She selected a plot of ground on the southern slope of a hill facing the sea. When she looked for her diary to show me the plans which she had drawn up, she was distressed to find that she had lost it somewhere. "There are a great many things in my diary that I would not want any one to read," she said. "What am I going to do?" I reassured her that it was probably left in the boat or in the orchard.

The sun was just over the hills when we returned to the orchard. There was a man strolling under the trees and he came toward us as we entered. It was no other than Tu Ping-fu. As he drew near her, Yuchun stopped, but she bowed her head and said nothing. "It was my mistake," Ping-fu said apologetically. "I have come here several times since that unfortunate day, but I did not come in. Today I happened to find your diary and after reading it I realized how wrong I had been to believe the rumors about you. I am very ashamed of myself for having suspected you and I-tsun."

For a while Yuchun continued to be silent, then suddenly turning to Ping-fu, she said: "I said in my diary that I would never marry that man Huang because he loved only my flesh while you loved my soul, and that because of this I would rather die waiting for you than to marry that man Huang and live. But in reality you also love my flesh and not my soul!

"I-tsun has loved you like a brother and loved me like a sister, but you have abused him. Because of you I have abandoned my family, suffered shame and humiliation; because of you I have tried to kill myself and have involved I-tsun. You have treated me exactly as an old fashioned family would have, and your suspicions have been more unjust than any that could have come from the most reactionary community.

"The fact that you have suspected my integrity shows that you have no integrity yourself. Until now I have submitted to the evil institutions of society because of my love for you but from now on I shall fight these institutions because I am opposed to you. I am opposed to you because of the hypocrisy of your heart and I shall

fight the evil institutions because their false morality is responsible
for producing hypocrites like you.

"Why don't you go away? You are soiling the trees in the garden,
the grass, and the birds and flowers. I had disregarded everything
because of my true love, but you have cherished suspicion and
jealousy because your love for me was false. Why don't you go
away from here?"

After she finished speaking Yuchun went back to her room.
Ping-fu stood with his eyes on the ground for a while and then
turned and went away. In her room I found Yuchun weeping with
her head between her hands. I withdrew quietly and went back to
my house in the city in a melancholic mood.

I went several times to the island to talk with the inhabitants
about the school. They were all delighted with the prospect and
helped me in every way they could. As it would take a few months
to build the schoolhouse, we decided not to wait until it was com-
pleted but to start school as soon as possible by making use of
the temple of the Goddess of the Sea. It was estimated that it would
require about three weeks to get the temple in readiness.

One day I found the inhabitants of the island in a state of tur-
moil. Upon making enquiries I was told that the night before the
island had been terrorized by a gang of bandits and that they had
not only robbed and kidnapped men but had also committed rape.
I returned to the city in a very depressed mood.

Just as I was about to reach home I encountered Yu Keng-sheng,
a former schoolmate. He told me that his sister was going to
France to study and he was looking for me to give her a few letters
of introduction to my friends in France. I asked him if his sister
had a companion of her own sex for the journey, and he said that
she did not and that he was going to go with her as far as Shanghai.
I then asked him when they were leaving for Shanghai and he
replied on the fifteenth of the ninth month. "Come on the evening
of the fourteenth for the letters," I said to him. "I may have a
request to make of you."

Whenever Yuchun asked me how things were going on the
island, I told her that everything was going well, saying nothing

about the bandits. But when she asked me to take her to the island I always put her off on some pretext.

One day she asked me when she could move to the island and start teaching. I told her that she could go on the fifteenth of the ninth month, at nine in the morning, and asked her to be sure to get everything ready the day before so that we could make an early start.

At the appointed time that morning I went to the orchard with Lingchun. After putting the luggage on the boat we sailed in the direction of the north harbor.

"Why are we heading for the north harbor?" Yuchun asked.

"So that you can take a boat to Shanghai and from Shanghai take a boat for France."

"France?" she said in astonishment.

"Didn't you want to go to France?"

"I do, but it can't be done."

"It can be done," I said, taking out a package of letters and handing it to her. "I have told your father everything and he has relented and given his permission for you to go abroad to study. This is his letter, which I received only yesterday. These are letters of introduction for your use in France. In this envelop you will find a check for two thousand and another four hundred dollars in bills. Here is a letter to your stepmother I have drafted for you, informing her that you are taking Lingchun with you. If you think it is all right, you can sign it and I'll mail it for you. As to your father, be sure to write him from Shanghai. For a traveling companion, you will have Yu Keng-sheng's sister. The island is out of the question now because bandits have appeared there."

After staring at me in bewilderment for a long while, Yuchun turned to the letters that I had given her. When she finished reading them, she took my hands and said simply, "I-tsun!" There were tears in her eyes. Lingchun came over to me and put her arms around my neck, saying, "Don't you cry now, Mr. Lin. Let us all go to France."

Presently our little boat drew alongside the steamer. I helped

Yuchun and Lingchun aboard and introduced them to Yu Keng-sheng and his sister. I stayed with them until the whistle blew. I had barely walked down to my own boat when the steamer sailed off, but for a long time I was able to see Yuchun standing at the rail and Lingchun waving her handkerchief at me.

Alone in my boat, I drifted right and left, not knowing where to go. When I raised my eyes and surveyed the immensity of sea and sky around me, all I could see was a wild goose that had strayed from its flock flying among the lonely clouds.

Glossary

Of Chinese words and honorifics of frequent occurrence, together with a few notes on points that may perplex the Western reader. Most of the entries are found in this volume, but a few occur only in *Traditional Chinese Tales*.

Ah: In south and central China, prefixed to personal and pseudo-personal names when these are of only one syllable, because of the Chinese tendency for disyllabic names and phrases: e.g., Ah Q, Ah Sing. For corresponding prefix used in northern China, *see* Lao.

Chi: Seven, seventh. *See* Enumeration.

Chieh-chieh: Elder sister, without reference to the order of her birth in the family. If one elder sister is to be distinguished from another, a numeral (*see* Enumeration) or the distinctive part of the name (*see* Name) is prefixed to one of the syllables; e.g., San-chieh (elder sister three), Ying-chieh (elder sister Ying).

Chiu: Nine, ninth. *See* Enumeration.

Da or ta: *See* Ta.

Didi: Younger brother. When distinguishing prefix is added, only one syllable is retained. *See* Chieh-chieh.

Enumeration: In the family circle and among friends of the family, personal names are rarely used, except when addressing servants and other "inferiors," that is, sons and daughters, nieces and nephews, and others in the generation or generations below oneself. Instead, one is referred to as One, Two, Three, etc., according to whether one is first, second, or third grandson or granddaughter of the family. The third grandson would be San-di (third younger brother) to those of his generation older than he and San-ko (third older brother) to those younger, San-shu (Uncle Three) to those in the generation below and San-chih (Nephew Three) to those in the generation above. The numerals are also prefixed to various honorifics, such as Yeh, Lao-yeh, Taitai, etc. When it is necessary (as in the clan village) to distinguish one series of grandsons and granddaughters from another, one may prefix the distinguishing part of the name to the relationship word, either with or without the enumerative. However, in the case of one's "superiors," one has to use some other method of distinction, since their names are more or less taboo. One has to say, for instance, Uncle Two of such and such a street or of such and such a house, each separate household being distinguished by a "hall name," usually consisting of two high-sounding words prefixed to the character *t'ang* (meaning Hall; it is the same word as *tong,* made notorious by the "tong wars" of the China-towns.)

Erh: Two, second. *See* Enumeration.

Foreign devil: *Yang kuei tzu.* It should be noted that the word *kuei* is often used in the sense of clever, ingenious, or cunning, besides its primitive meanings of ghost, spirit, and devil. Foreigners were nicknamed "devils" not because they were thought to be satanic but because they were regarded as extremely clever in money matters (note Tung Pao's complaint against them in "Spring Silkworms") and because of their mechanical ingenuity.

Foreign devils once removed: *Erh mao tzu,* literally the second hairy one, *mao tzu* or *ta mao tzu* being nicknames for the "devils" themselves. A term that originated during the Boxer uprising and was applied to Chinese converts to Christianity and to foreign ways in general.

Hsiao-chieh: A young lady; honorific for an unmarried young mistress.

K'ang: Raised platform or bed built of bricks, prevalent in North China.

Kaoliang: A powerful, colorless spirit distilled from a grain by the same name. Also known as *shao chiu* (fiery or burning liquor), pronounced *shio dzou* in Cantonese.

Koko: Elder brother. When a distinguishing prefix is added, only one syllable is retained. *See* Chieh-chieh.

Lao: Literally, old. In northern China prefixed to personal and pseudo-personal names of one syllable. As prefix it suggests (as Ah does) familiarity, but as suffix it indicates respect.

Lao-yeh: Literally "old father." Honorific applied to lesser mandarins and to the master of the house. It is equivalent to "Your Honor."

Li: Measure of distance about one third of a mile (which the Chinese generally call an "English li.")

Liu: Six, sixth. *See* Enumeration.

Ma: Corresponds to English word "ma", and hence "mother" in most dialects. As a suffix to names, however, it generally indicates a servant or a woman low in the social scale.

Meimei: Younger sister. When a distinguishing prefix is added, only one syllable is retained. *See* Chieh-chieh.

Mother's or Ma ti: In its complete form it is unprintable in Chinese as its translation would be in English. Its use in the clipped and impersonal form is no occasion for a fight, but one should be careful not to add the second person genitive before "mother's," or worse yet, add a verb before that. For a discussion of this "national oath," see Lusin's essay "Mother's——" in Edgar Snow's *Living China*.

Names: Too complicated to go into in detail here but the following points will be helpful: 1. Family names are generally in one syllable. Exceptions that may be encountered occasionally are Ou-yang, Ssu-ma, Shang-kuan, Ssu-tu (often spelled Seto) and Tung-fang. 2. Personal names are generally in two syllables, the first indicating the generation of the bearer, and hence shared by all his brothers and cousins of the same generation on his father's side (*see* Relationship). Only the second part of the name is, therefore, distinctive, though it is not uncommon to find the reverse true. E.g., the brothers in "The Puppet Dead" are Chueh-hsin, Chueh-min, and Chueh-hui. Girls generally have a different generation name. For example, the cousins in the same story are Shu-hua, Shu-ying, etc. As a rule only the distinctive part of the name are prefixed to such relationship words as Chieh, Mei etc. and to honorifics. 3. Family names come before personal names, but when writing their names in transliteration, Chinese often reverse the order to avoid confusion. But then Westerners familiar with the Chinese custom of family name first are likely to "mister" him by his personal name. The safe rule to follow is to assume that the hyphenated syllables represent the personal name. When the personal name consists of only one syllable or when it is not hyphenated, there is no way of telling which is which, unless one happens to know the person. 4. One has usually several personal names, the number being generally in direct ratio to one's position (or pretention). As a rule a man has a minimum of two names, a milk or infant name and an adult name, though extremely humble persons may (as Ah Q) have only the former. The adult name generally coincides with the typical personal name discussed under 2, though one may in addition take a school name. From the distinguishing word in the adult or school name one derives his *tzu* (which may therefore be translated as "derived name"). Then one may assume a *hao,* a name suggestive of qualities he pretends to or attributes to himself. The *tzu* and *hao* may be described as "preferred names," for it is by one or the other of these two names that a Chinese prefers to be addressed by his own friends and with which he signs himself, except in official documents. Except for the *tzu* and *hao,* all other names are taboo in varying degrees. Hence, in the family circle and among family friends, one is generally designated by a number. *See* Enumeration.

Niang: Equivalent to Ma; honorific suffix for women.

Numerals: The numerals from 1 to 10 are yi (i), erh, san, ssu, wu, liu, chi, pa, chiu, shih; from 11 on they are shih-yi, shih-erh etc. Numerical designations above twenty are, of course, rare.

Relationship: In reckoning relationships the Chinese system makes reference to the generation that one occupies in the genealogical tree rather than to the degree of consanguinity. That is, all the lineal descendants of a common ancestor of any given generation (though it may be as far down the line as the fourteenth or even the seventieth generation) call one another brothers and sisters. Anyone in the generation above is an uncle, and anyone in the generation below a nephew. In villages where the same "clan" has lived for generations it is not uncommon to find a venerable man with a white beard call a child great-uncle or great-aunt, or even great great-uncle or aunt. In the same manner one traces his relations on his mother's side and thus acquires an additional host of brothers and sisters, etc. There are qualifying words to indicate what kind of brother or sister, and aunt or uncle, a particular person is, but he is brother or sister nevertheless and is generally thus addressed in direct speech without qualification.

San: Three, third. *See* Enumeration.

Saosao: Elder sister-in-law. When a distinguishing prefix is added, only one syllable is retained. *See* Chieh-chieh. Sometimes suffixed to the family name of younger maid servants.

Shao-nainai: Shao-yeh's wife.

Shao-yeh: Young master of the house.

Shih: Ten, tenth. *See* Enumeration.

Ssu: Four, fourth.

Ta or da: Literally great; used in the sense of first.

Taitai: Lao-yeh's wife, or the mistress of the house.

Wowotou or wotou: The staple article of food in northern China, made in the form of a hollow cone from a mixture of soy and millet (either the yellow or red variety, the latter being known as kaoliang) flours or sometimes of corn meal. It is unseasoned and unleavened and, like Chinese bread, is steamed and not baked.

Wu: Five, fifth. *See* Enumeration.

Yahuan: Same as Yatou.

Yamen: Combination office and resiuence of a mandarin; no longer used in official documents.

Yatou: A bondmaid or slave girl, generally married off around twenty, with a dowry if the master is generous and rich or for profit if he is otherwise.

Yeh: Literally "father," but usually encountered as an honorific suffix in such combinations as Lao-yeh and Shao-yeh. It is also frequently suffixed to enumeratives and family names.

Yi: One, used only in 11, 21, etc. An aunt on one's mother's side. When prefixed to Taitai, a concubine is indicated.

Bibliographical Note

There are three volumes of contemporary Chinese stories available in English: Edgar Snow, *Living China,* London & New York, 1936; Kyn Yn Yu, *The Tragedy of Ah Qui,* New York, 1931 (translated from the French); Lusin, *Ah Q & Others,* New York, 1941. None of the stories in the three volumes mentioned are duplicated in the present anthology. Readers should also consult the *T'ien Hsia Monthly,* which contains many translations of contemporary stories not found anywhere else.

Notes on the Authors

Chang T'ien-yi

Chang T'ien-yi is the youngest of the writers in this anthology and the most advanced in technique. There is no more striking contrast to the leisurely narrative of traditional Chinese fiction than his direct, dramatic openings, his almost exclusive use of dialogue, and his short, clipped paragraphs. His characters—beggars, thieves, opportunists and petty tyrants of the revolutions and civil wars, workers, peasants, and soldiers—talk (and swear) their parts as they do in real life, instead of delivering little homilies or making obvious remarks as characters do in traditional tales.

However, he has a weakness for reiterating revolting details that are of no particular significance in the development of his themes. In "Reunion," for instance, Da Gen's running nose is referred to in no less than sixteen paragraphs, sometimes more than once in a paragraph. In "The Inside Story" Lao Ming's narrative is punctuated with a toothpick, while in "Smile!" Chiang San is forever belching. Then he is fond of repeating certain mannerisms not only from story to story but in the same story as well, and of indulging in such preposterous extravagances as Tiao Chin-sheng's confession in "The Inside Story." Because of these weaknesses and mannerisms and because of his almost exclusive use of unsavory themes, he makes rather depressing reading. (It is for this reason that I have divided his stories into two groups.) But to readers surfeited with the sweet and devitalized generalities of traditional Chinese fiction, he also makes refreshing reading. Hence his great popularity among students and intellectuals.

Chang was born in 1907, according to an autobiographical sketch printed in Snow's *Living China*. Between 1931 (when the first collection of his short stories appeared) and 1937, he published at least fourteen volumes of fiction, including three novels and one juvenile.

Lao Hsiang

Lao Hsiang is the pen name of Wang Hsiang-ch'en, a writer best known for his humorous essays. He was born and brought up in the country and is thoroughly familiar with conditions in the rural districts in the interior. For several years he was identified with the rural education experiment at Tinghsien and it was during this period that he wrote "A Country Boy Withdraws from School." For another version of this story, and an example of the author's essays, see Lin Yutang, *A Nun of Taishan.*

Lao She

Lao She is the pen name of Shu Ch'ing-ch'un, born around the turn of the century. He has studied in England and is Clement Egerton's collaborator in a translation of the novel *Chin P'ing Mei* (in English, *The Golden Lotus*). He is regarded as a humorist and is particularly successful at transcribing faithfully the vernacular of his native Peking. He began his literary career as a novelist, but I am inclined to think that his type of humor does not stand up well under the hard usage of that medium and that he will be remembered for his short stories rather than his novels, with the exception, perhaps, of *Cat Country,* a satire written in a serious vein against China's civil wars, her helplessness in the face of foreign aggression, and her opium dream of the past.

Pa Chin

Pa Chin's real name is Li Fei-kan. As far as may be inferred from his autobiographical pieces, he was born in 1905 (not 1896 as given by Snow) into a wealthy family of retired officials in Szechwan. His background seems to have been very much like the one described in *The Torrent of Life,* a novel in four parts of which three have appeared. Though he professes no special creed and has no political affiliations, there is no question of his fierce love for freedom and his equally fierce hatred of all forms of oppression and hypocrisy. Before his first book appeared (*La Pereo,* 1929;

most of his early stories carried both Chinese and Esperanto titles)
he had translated most of Kropotkin and several other books on
anarchism. He calls Emma Goldman his godmother and dedicated
his translation of *On the Scaffold* "to the sacred memory of my
beloved comrade and teacher, Bartolemeo Vanzetti and his brave
comrade Nicola Sacco." He is intensely emotional. Hardly a single
book of his (there are over twenty volumes of stories and novels,
besides about an equal number of translations and essays) was
written, according to his own confession, without tears in his eyes,
and sorrow and hatred and indignation in his heart. To more
sophisticated American readers Pa Chin will seem childishly melodramatic, but he does not appear so to his Chinese readers because
they share fully his views and sympathies.

Even on his present record (he is not yet forty) Pa Chin will
be remembered as the first great novelist produced by the Literary
Revolution. It is not too much to rank his *Torrent of Life* next to
The Dream of the Red Chamber, which the Chinese consider their
greatest novel. It is the most effective and best documented indict-
ment of the old Chinese family system that has yet appeared, and
it has the virtue of unity and well-integrated situations, not often
found in Chinese novels of its length. Unfortunately, he is difficult
to translate. I was profoundly moved when I read *The Torrent of
Life,* but after rendering passages from it into English, I find them
disappointing. Could it be because English is too red-blooded a
language for tearfulness?

"The Puppet Dead" is an adaptation of Chapters 36 and 37 of
The Family, the opening volume of *The Torrent of Life.* Though
I have made abridgments here and there, I have taken care not to
alter the character and style of the original. I have not tried to tone
down the exaggerated emotionalism evident on every page, nor
have I tried to eliminate such generalized statements as "A wave
of emotion engulfed everyone in the room."

Shen Ts'ung-wen

Shen Ts'ung-wen was born in 1904 in the Fenghuang district in
Hunan. So far as I know, he is the only modern Chinese writer
of the new school who does not know any foreign language and
yet he has developed a decidedly "Europeanized" style, probably

from reading and rereading a copy of the Bible in Chinese that happened to fall into his hands. He has had no formal education beyond primary school. At fourteen or fifteen he joined one of the regional armies and a good third of his stories are reminiscent sketches of his soldier life. Having been born and brought up in a region where the aboriginal Miao tribes were still very much in evidence (his grandmother was a Miao), he also frequently draws upon this background for material. His nostalgia for this personal past gives many of his stories a quality that may be described as idyllic, though they deal with material which in the hands of a writer like Chang T'ien-yi would have resulted only in sordidness. Another good third of his stories are drawn from the student-intellectual class in which he moved after he quit the army. Among his longer works is *Alice in China,* in two volumes, which began as a satire but soon lapsed into a sort of journal of the author's own woes and complaints. During his most active years he was always under the necessity of writing to keep the pot boiling; as a result most of his books suffer from haste and padding.

Feng Wen-ping

Feng Wen-ping was born in 1902 in Hupeh. He is better known by his pen name Fei-ming (Name abolished). Most of his so-called stories are in reality sketches of childhood life, written with a studied simplicity and lightness of touch that often leaves the reader wondering what the author is driving at. I have included the present story largely because it brings out poignantly the tragedy of neglected childhood. Restrained and circumspect as it is, I have not been able to find anything more forthright among the author's writings.

Ling Shu-hua

Though she has published only a few slight volumes of stories, Miss Ling is highly esteemed by discriminating readers for her meticulous craftsmanship and her objective and dispassionate sketches of Chinese women, of which "The Helpmate" is a good example. She is the wife of the well-known scholar Professor Chen T'ung-po.

Mao Dun

Mao Dun was born in 1896, not 1902 as given by Snow. His real name is Shen Yen-ping. He is one of the most active and best-known figures in contemporary Chinese literature. It was under his editorship that the *Short Story Magazine* became in the early twenties one of the most influential literary journals. He participated in the Northern Expedition (which culminated in the establishment of the present Kuomintang government) but retired from political life to devote himself to writing after the triumph of the conservative elements within the Kuomintang.

Upon the publication of his trilogy *Eclipse* (1927-28) he was immediately hailed as China's leading novelist, and the appearance of *The Rainbow* (1929) and *Midnight* (1933) further enhanced his reputation. *Eclipse* deals with events of the 1926-27 revolution from the point of view of a group of students who took part in it and remains the best thing of its kind. (A rough summary of the first part of the novel will be found in Kyn's anthology, where the author's name is given as Mao Teng.) *The Rainbow* traces the evolution of a young woman revolutionary, while *Twilight* is the story of Shanghai big business. In his short stories, too, Mao Dun often addresses himself to timely subjects, as in "Spring Silkworms" and its sequel "Autumn Harvest."

Being a keen student of Western literature, he is familiar with its methods and devices. Unfortunately he has made use only of such obvious tricks as the flash-back and nightmarish glimpses into the future which the movies have exploited *ad nauseam*.

Yeh Shao-chün

Yeh Shao-chün is different from most contemporary Chinese writers in that he was never Bohemian. He was married early and assumed family responsibilities at an age when other literary young men were trying their best to play the Bohemian. He is, therefore, familiar with the life and problems of the average lower-middle-class family which he describes with tenderness and gentle irony. He is seldom indignant or bitter; he is never contemptuous of his characters nor does he condemn them wholesale. He is a careful and meticulous writer and has devoted himself consistently to the task of creating a new literature, though he has never been vociferous in championing or denouncing this or that literary fashion.

Yeh was born in 1893 or 1894. For many years he was editor of the *Ladies Journal,* mentioned in "Mrs. Li's Hair." He is also the author of *Ni Huan-chih,* a novel based on his own experience as a teacher in a primary school.

Lusin

Lusin or Lu Hsun is the pen name of Chou Shu-jen (1881-1936). I have already published the most important of his stories in *Ah Q & Others.* For biographical data and Lusin's place in modern Chinese literature, see my introduction to *Ah Q.*

Yang Chen-sheng

Yang Chen-sheng was born in 1890 in eastern Shantung, the scene of *Yuchun.* Though primarily an educator, his name has been associated with modern Chinese fiction, because at the time of its appearance in 1924 *Yuchun* was the longest piece of new fiction that had yet been attempted and was therefore greeted as the first "novel" written under the inspiration of the Literary Revolution. Compared with the novels of Mao Dun and Pa Chin, however, *Yuchun* is only a long story or at most a novelette. It is only about 25,000 words long in the original and will probably take no more than that many words to translate into English. In the present abridged version I have omitted altogether some sections that have nothing to do with the main story and have summarized some of the more than ordinarily perfunctory descriptions and dialogues.

In language and technique *Yuchun* is a mixture of the old and new, and I have included it here, in spite of its obvious faults, to mark the transition between the two schools. The story is also interesting in itself as a kind of unconscious burlesque of a mode of behavior typified by Lin I-tsun, a man so anxious to appear "correct" that he gives up the girl he loves after she is free just to prove that he had not coveted her when she was still his friend's fiancee!